Education in
national development

Education in national development

Edited by

DON ADAMS

School of Education
University of Pittsburgh

DAVID McKAY COMPANY, INC.
NEW YORK

First Published in the United States 1971
by David McKay Company Inc.
750 Third Avenue, New York, N.Y. 10017

Printed in Great Britain

Contents

one

Introduction

DON ADAMS

Insight into the contribution of education to national development is frustrated by a number of obstacles, not the least of which is the fuzziness of the notion of development and our level of ignorance about the functioning of an educational system. Since, in subsequent chapters, the social and economic context of discussions is made clear, it is not necessary to discuss here the nuances of the concept of development. Some consideration of the deceptively complex process which is called education may, however, be useful.

For example, most discussions of education[1] appear to suggest that (1) educational systems are easily influenced and altered and (2) education is a homogeneous process whose characteristics are well known. While it is true that educational systems are moulded extensively by the greater society and culture, it should be equally clear that educational systems may either resist or influence outside efforts at organizational or curricular change. Thus, educational change cannot be viewed merely as a set of responses of demographic, social and economic pressures, for such pressures do not necessarily dictate particular organizational arrangements or specific educational curricula. At best such external factors offer firm output targets (e.g. number of skilled persons demanded by certain industries) and guide-lines for inputs (e.g. number of pupils to enter the first year, or grade

1); at worst they generate only statements of intent and do not offer precise data for educational planning.

The inabilities of the educational system to respond satisfactorily to the objectives and targets of educational plans and policies are not well documented. Nevertheless, they are well known. Manpower or other planning targets require specific skills and knowledge of the educational system; this output in turn demands specific capacities and competencies within the system. Programmes, facilities and instruction must be altered to fulfil such targets. While this is all too obvious, not fully appreciated are: the subtlety of some of the external restrictions on the functioning of the educational system, the constraints on planning and policy-making resulting from basic characteristics of the system, the kind and extent of socialization provided within the educational system and the receptivity of the system to innovation and change.

Distinguishing features of education

There may be value, then, before proceeding to the analyses presented in the subsequent chapters, in identifying a number of distinguishing features of the formal educational system. Even within the wide range of cultural diversity, certain tentative generalizations may be suggested:

1 Historically, education has been an institution operated for very limited and inherently conservative ends. To the extent that it performed a homogenizing function, it did so for the new entrants to a tiny élite. By contrast, modern educational systems frequently constitute an attempt to provide vast social and cultural changes and extend the homogenizing function to the masses.

2 Education is marked by a complexity of levels and programmes which obstruct analysis and generalization. Educational systems in industrializing societies are characterized by a growing degree of differentiation and specialization. A long lag is assumed between the initiation and completion of any of the conventional stages of education, thus complicating planning which emphasizes the future. Increasing our understanding of education may be related partly to (a) the identification of

relatively autonomous sub-systems and (*b*) better understanding of educational change and innovation.

3 National educational systems usually reflect a wide distribution and great diversity with respect to age, sex and social and cultural groups, personality types and geographic coverage. Moreover, international and intranational comparisons likewise show great variation in the size of enrolments, staff, plant and extent of financial support.

4 Education is a composite of skills, techniques, non-cognitive and cognitive learnings, many of which have long-range rather than immediate consequences. Many of the activities of educational systems serve mainly to perpetuate the system itself. Moreover, education develops a 'culture' of its own which may reinforce or interfere with the official educational and other objectives.

5 The operation of educational systems has been labour-intensive rather than capital-intensive, i.e. technology has not yet been applied to significantly reduce the needed numbers of teachers and administrators. This condition has restricted its capacity for increased productivity.

6 Whereas much of the socialization and enculturation processes take place outside of the school system, it is equally true that learning as a function of explicit instructional activities is too narrow a view of what happens in schools. However, the influence of extra-school agencies and the inadequacy of measurement technology make it extremely difficult to measure educational outcome or determine the return on a particular educational investment.

7 Major educational policy is rarely influenced directly by the clientele (those 'receiving' education or those paying the costs of schooling). Nor, with a few exceptions, do teachers, individually or through professional organizations, greatly influence national policy. Mass education and other factors have reduced the status of the teacher of the early stages of education and have made him relatively unimportant in control or governance of education.

8 Conflicting views of the functions of education are apparent among the various interested social and professional groups. Modern teachers and professional educators tend to view schooling as the preparation for lifelong learning. Students and

parents frequently view it as the preservation or enhancement of status.

These characteristics impinge upon and constrain both the analysis of education in economic or social change and the planning of education for the goals of development.

Characteristics of descriptions of education in developing societies

Our inability to analyse the process of development in any refined way and our practice of treating only the external manifestations of education have given rise to two unfortunate characteristics in much of the literature on education and development. First, there are those articles, books, reports and recipes which are largely impressionistic and worry little about using conceptual apparatus to focus analysis and even less about qualifying interpretations or recommendations. This is dangerous literature in the hands of the gullible, because there is no easy way to identify the over-simplifications and over-generalizations. Yet the discriminating reader may find in these materials some of the most profound insights and most practical policy suggestions.

On the other hand lies a growing body of literature, generated largely from the social sciences, which describes education and development in highly aggregated or abstract terms.[2] Here levels of national development are measured and compared by single or composite quantitative indices, which usually consider only very limited structural characteristics of the society or a few of the consumption habits of portions of the population. Such aggregated measures are then juxtaposed or related statistically to obtainable indicators of educational progress. The utility of such efforts, either in terms of theory-building or merely in furthering explanation of particular educational phenomena, has been limited.

Nor have the non-quantitative conceptual and model-building attempts of the social sciences this far been of much help to educational analysts and planners in developing nations. Ideal typologies of (1) traditional v. modern societies, (2) folk v. urban societies, (3) ascriptively normed v. universally normed populations, (4) simple v. complex social structures and the like, represent concepts common in the literature of the social sciences recently employed to describe development. Rationality models, neo-versions of the Protestant–ethic argument, historical–psychological interpretations of 'innovative personalities' and so forth, also abound as explanations of development as behavioural scientists reach into their bag of lore and attempt to force available notions on a newly examined process. The aggressive but ineffectual efforts along these lines almost suggest that Western scholars may never quite forgive the developing societies for not easily complying with their preconceptions.

For those who seek operational insights into the process of development the results of these attempts have been a growing suspicion that (1) concepts which may have had explanatory power in Western social history are less than satisfactory in explaining social changes in developing societies; (2) the heterogeneity of the less developed world confounds generalization and prescription.

While many of the impressionistic descriptions have focused directly on education, the more abstract and academic approaches have tended to treat education by deduction or extrapolation. The former type of literature probably overemphasizes the significance of such aspects of the educational process as curriculum and teaching methods as the crucial factors in better relating education to development needs. Educational reform is seen as pedagogical reform, and prescriptions centre on improved teacher education, curriculum revision, use of educational technology and so forth.

By contrast, the models and schemes offered by social scientists give but rare attention to practice and technique in education. Rather, the focus tends to be on education as a skill-producing process, as a recruitment and selection agency for the élite or as an institution which supplements the family in the socialization and enculturation processes.

Some initial insights

Although the accumulated knowledge is frustratingly inadequate, experience and research have taught us something about the problems and possibilities of education in developing societies. Perhaps many of the insights acquired might be viewed as negative learning because a number of techniques, ideas and programmes have failed to live up to expectations. For example, little support is currently given to a number of suppositions and generalizations rather commonplace in earlier literature. The following are but a few of the several possible examples:

1 Policies of general and unselective expansion of schooling adequately support economic and social goals

These have proved unsatisfactory for either the fulfilment of manpower needs or for equalizing participation rates in schooling for different social groups. While the mix of occupational skills needed in a developing economy is a matter of controversy, it is increasingly assumed that the variety of required skills suggests explicit priorities for certain kinds of schooling. On the other hand, growth in enrolments generally has not benefited all social classes equally and schools do not always provide a door to the greater society.[3]

2 Pedagogical arguments have resulted in successful policies for reduction of wastage and drop-outs

Even though wastage is considered by educational administrators in many of the less developed nations to be one of the most pressing problems, the arguments supporting solutions to these problems have largely proved to be hollow. Several social scientists have pointed out that wastage is a typical accompaniment of rapidly expanding enrolments and periods of rapid social change. In effect, a high proportion of drop-outs reflects that the family, community, economy and value systems are not developing in harmony with the educational system.

A corollary of this fallacy might be the often expressed view that academic instruction promotes 'white-collar' attitudes. Like the pedagogical prescriptions for wastage, this conclusion is suspect for similar reasons. For example, a study by Mark Blaug and associates on the causes of educational unemployment in India (presumably a classic case of literature and academic schooling creating educated unemployed) suggests: (1) large numbers of educated unemployed exist, but, compared with commercial rates of interest, all higher education is a good individual investment; (2) many university students wish to enter technical and engineering pursuits; but (3) technical courses are just not open to large numbers of students, due to lack of facilities or other restrictions.[4]

3 A shortage of industrial, commercial and agricultural skills requires vocationalization of primary and secondary education

The role of vocational schools in developing nations remains controversial and unresolved. While the feasibility and viability of providing formal vocational instruction undoubtedly depend on a number of cost, incentive and prestige factors, a rule of the thumb would suggest that it is better to make 'factories into schools' rather than 'schools into factories'. Success stories in vocational education in the less developed nations, such as SENATI (National Apprenticeship Service for Industrial Work) in Latin America, suggest: (1) vocational training should be preceded by a careful examination of the supply and demand of particular skills; (2) where feasible, a significant financial and technical contribution to training programmes should be made by the employer; (3) the creation of appealing rewards is necessary for those being upgraded.

Arguing in this manner does not necessarily commit one to the traditional sequential pattern of schooling, then work; at times, of course, these activities may well be concurrent. Unwarranted, also, may be the conclusion that the wide variety of skills typically needed in the less developed nations must be acquired in as informal a manner as they were historically, say, in the United States.

4 Educational planning, particularly a manpower approach to the setting of educational targets, provides a precise guide for maximizing the contribution of education to a developing economy

The halo surrounding manpower forecasts has become a bit tarnished and perhaps the faith in the predictions of economists and educational planners in general has been shaken. Data inaccuracies, inability to anticipate shifts in occupational structure and questions of appropriate occupation–education relationships have all frustrated accurate identification of manpower needs. Indeed, the formation of educational plans has at times been an escape from reality. Planning in the sense of allocation of educational resources to satisfy national needs may only gloss over vast ignorance about the possible degree of manipulation of the school system and the seemingly impenetrable obstructions to improved measurement of educational input. The mere fact that some nations have been able to develop relatively effective school systems without elaborate planning exercises appears to have been overlooked (one might almost conclude resented) by the more ardent advocates of educational planning.

Nevertheless, a planning atmosphere with its focus on the future, its requisite attention to education as one of several interacting social systems, and its interdisciplinary perspective and analyses make the planning context useful both in studying education and in promoting educational change. Moreover, even though the early promises of educational planning techniques have been unfulfilled, a certain restrained optimism for the future is justified. New levels of proficiencies are being developed in manpower analyses; simulation models are proving to be of value in forecasting student flows within the educational system; initial efforts in micro-educational planning, through the use of cost-effectiveness and other models, are promising and may in the future prove to be powerful tools in evaluating educational policies and programmes.

Focus and coverage of subsequent chapters

In this book an attempt is made to proceed between the more impressionistic descriptions of education in developing societies and the often forced generalizations which flow from social-science abstractions. The questions with which the authors are concerned may perhaps be viewed as being of a higher or more general order than those usually discussed by impressionists, but representing a lower or more concrete order than those frequently considered by the social scientists. Most of the authors, because of their training, lean on the language and tools of the social sciences. All, however, are experienced with and interested in operational and policy matters. To be more explicit, the following are some of the more important questions to which attention is given in subsequent chapters:

What is the relationship between educational expansion and the equalization of educational opportunity?

What conditions restrict the achievement of equality or opportunity—particularly in terms of school access and school success?

What is the potential role of education with respect to national integration in societies with sharp ethnic or religious diversity?

To what extent do adjustments in curriculum, organization, etc., within the educational system lessen inequities in access to and success in schooling derived from political and cultural considerations?

What are the assumptions underlying the analogy of education as a production process?

In addition to the size of enrolments and other common quantitative indicators, what may be considered indices of educational progress?

What are some of the 'proxies' or alternatives to traditional educational patterns for various economic and social ends?

What are the implications for educational structure and programme of a paucity of industrial, commercial and agricultural skills in a society?

What incentives or policies might deter the 'brain drain' from the less developed to the more developed nations?

What is the magnitude of losses in human resources resulting from foreign student non-return?

In what ways do fertility rates and attitudes towards family planning appear to be affected by educational level?

To summarize, it might be said that the primary concerns of the subsequent chapters are with questions of equity, efficiency and effectiveness. In Chapter Two Philip Foster addresses himself primarily to the fundamental question, 'Who goes to school?' Professor Foster goes much beyond the oft-found and tiresome documentation of international evidence that 'rich kids get more schooling than poor kids'. He analyses the variations in aspirations, constraints and conflicts in access to education and suggests a number of implications for educational policy.

In Chapters Three and Four John Vaizey and Daniel Rogers focus on the somewhat slippery concepts of productivity and efficiency. Professor Vaizey emphasizes the problems in giving operational meaning to the idea of productivity. He further identifies the dangers of application of the concept to the educational process. Professor Rogers, in effect, carries on where Professor Vaizey leaves off by focusing particularly on the decisions and policies which may, under given conditions, increase the efficiency of educational systems.

Chapter Five, on 'Educational Technology', by Robert Cox, treats a topic currently receiving a large amount of attention by the less developed nations and the various 'donor' agencies. However, Professor Cox is concerned not only with possibilities in the use of modern media for instruction, but also with the criteria which must be applied in determining the feasibility of or evaluating the results of any of the applications of educational technology.

In Chapter Six Everett Reimer addresses himself both to questions of efficiency and questions of effectiveness. Professor Reimer expresses frustration with existing patterns of education, which he argues are not coming close to providing a reasonable quality of education for the majority of the populations in the less developed nations. He then offers a partial strategy for further evaluating the present educational situation as a basis of understanding feasible alternatives.

Chapter Seven and Chapter Eight, by Manuel Zymelman and Robert Bjork and, to some extent, Chapter Nine, by Robert Myers, are more concerned with educational output. Professor Zymelman examines the nature and changing conditions of stresses and strains between educational systems, the labour force and productivity in the process of economic development. Professor Bjork is primarily interested in the pressing problem of rapid population growth and, more particularly, in education as an influence on population change.

Professor Myers analyses a problem related to questions of input, efficiency and output in education—with some emphasis on the latter. Brain-drain or the non-return of students from less developed nations who study abroad is of momentous importance to many under-developed and developed nations. The problems associated with this phenomenon have been widely publicized, but very rarely analysed in any serious way. Myers attempts to provide just such an analysis.

Chapters Ten and Eleven are not directly concerned with operational analysis or prescription. In these final two chapters, Lawrence Thomas and Hector Correa propose different approaches to the conceptualization and explanation of problems of educational development. Professor Thomas posits that there are identifiable styles of education to be found in developing societies, and only through examination of these styles is it possible to understand qualitative educational variations and thereby acquire a basis for new educational policies. Professor Thomas further sketches the nature of the research necessary to verify his 'types of schooling' and to link these with social and economic characteristics of development.

Professor Correa, like Professor Thomas, is also concerned with conceptual matters, but focuses, not on qualitative distinctions in schooling but directly on the decision-making process. He offers some applications of mathematical and non-mathematical models for decision-making, using as illustrations common choices facing educational administrators and planners in developing nations. The primary purpose of Professor Correa, however, is not to offer lessons in abstract model-building, but rather to force decision-makers to sharpen their questions as a means of acquiring further insight into persistent development problems.

Notes

1 For useful bibliographies which cover references to the literature on education and development as well as on educational planning see: (1) Webster, Maureen, et al., 'Educational Planning and Policy: An International Bibliography', Syracuse, New York: Educational Policy Research Center, June 1969, Mimeo., (2) Blaug, Mark, Economics of Education: A Selected Bibliography, London: Pergamon Press, 1966, and (3) Review of Educational Research, xxxviii, June 1968.

2 For a bibliography on the sociocultural aspects of development see Brode, John, The Process of Modernization, Cambridge: Harvard University Press, 1969.

3 Ivan Illich has suggested that, in order to foster equality in education, school systems as we now find them must be eliminated: 'This is the

B

time of crisis in the institution of the school, a crisis which may mark the end of the "age of schooling" in the Western world.' Illich, speaking at a university commencement in Puerto Rico, further argued that the school is now identified with education as 'the church once was with religion' and 'that it will soon be evident that the school is as marginal to education as the witch-doctor is to public health'. *New York Review of Books*, 9 October, 1969, A. Whitney Ellsworth, 12–15.

4 Blaug, M., Layard, P. R. G., and Woodhall, M., *The Causes of Educated Unemployment: The Indian Case*, London: Allen Lane, The Penguin Press, 1969.

two

Access to schooling

PHILIP FOSTER

In many less developed nations (particularly those that have recently emerged from a period of colonial overrule) attempts to achieve a greater measure of social and economic equality of opportunity are often perceived as an intrinsic part of the whole process of modernization.[1] While recognizing that a formidable gap often exists between egalitarian ideology and harsh reality in the new states, we must also realize that a similar commitment to egalitarian principles was not characteristic of most Western nations in the earlier stages of their development. From this perspective, the task of modernizing élites in most contemporary developing areas is a formidable one. For not only are they obliged to press for economic growth, but also they must do so within constraints imposed by notions of mass welfare and social equality. In the short run, at least, development strategies predicated on notions of social equity may well clash with those designed to achieve maximal economic growth and the most efficient allocation of limited resources.

Nowhere is the tension between egalitarian objectives and aspirations for economic advance more evident than in the field of educational planning, and several factors have conspired to make educational provision, both in terms of gross enrolments and differential access to schooling, one of the key political issues in the new states. The élites in many of these areas have embarked on ambitious programmes of educational expansion in the hope that the provision of more schools would in itself constitute the 'royal road' to economic development. To be sure, in recent years much evidence has suggested that expansion in educational facilities is by no means a sufficient condition for growth and it is now evident that the interrelationship between economic and educational development is far more complex than was at first supposed. None the less, governments continue to pour resources into education in the expectation of an ultimate economic pay-off to their investment.

Further, from the viewpoint of the clientele of the schools, there can be little doubt that education is perceived as the key factor determining occupational placement and opportunities for social mobility. In developed nations there is still some measure of controversy over the closeness of fit that exists between educational and occupational status, and some ambiguity surrounds the role played by schooling *per se* in facilitating the upward mobility of the individual. A fair summary of existing evidence would suggest that, although level of formal education may be the most important single factor associated with upward social mobility, its effect is less than the cumulative impact of other variables, including, among others, paternal status, measured IQ, and even sheer personal drive and persistence.[2] Moreover, in structural terms a developed and rapidly expanding economy may also provide a variety of ancillary opportunities for mobility that are not entirely dependent upon the possession of a high level of formal schooling.

By contrast, it is likely that in many developing nations education plays a far more critical role in processes of individual group mobility and it is often decisive in determining access to many élite roles. In former colonial territories, in particular, the relatively small size of the modern sector of the economy and the fact that the bulk of occupational opportunities in that sector are controlled by public agencies tend to place a premium on the possession of educational qualifications. Moreover, the combination of limited opportunities for paid-wage or salaried employment combined with a rapid expansion in the size of the outputs of the educational system tends to rapidly raise the minimal educational qualifications associated with a given occupational level. This situation tends in turn to generate new public demand for access to secondary and higher education;

as the occupational currency of a primary school education declines, public pressure for parity of access to superior educational opportunities continues to mount.

It is not surprising, therefore, that the problem of 'who gets educated' should be such a salient issue in the new states. Limited resources and rapidly expanding child populations make even universal primary schooling a remote possibility in some areas, while it would be Utopian to suppose that secondary and higher education will be accessible to more than a small minority in the foreseeable future. Access to schooling becomes, therefore, a focus for individual and group conflict, whether it is perceived in terms of a rise in personal rank and monetary rewards or whether it is seen as an instrument through which diverse ethnic or social groupings can achieve an enhancement of their *collective* status in the emerging social structures of the new states.

The historical background

Present controversies over access to education must largely be understood in the context of the early spread of schooling in developing nations, for it is apparent that patterns of educational inequality are remarkably stable over time. Frequently, existing differentials can be traced back to the period of the earliest establishment of metropolitan-type schools in colonial territories or the importation of Western systems of education into independent states whose élites were anxious to modernize along Western lines.

The fact, therefore, that the schools of most developing areas are 'transferred institutions' is of considerable significance. Within their societies of origin most educational systems functioned in such a manner as to largely maintain existing status differentials and to perpetuate the life styles deemed appropriate to distinctive social strata. Indeed, the complex structure of most European systems of schooling was largely predicated on the assumption that in terms of quantity and curricular content, the schools should reflect the characteristics of existing systems of social differentiation. This is not to suggest that individuals of lower-class origin did not gain access to 'middle-class' institutions, and there has perhaps been a tendency to underestimate the permeability of the educational system to new types of clientele. None the less, the amount of educational mobility that occurred was limited, and it can be suggested that a modicum of controlled access by individuals from the 'lower orders' to selective secondary and higher institutions was essentially functional to the maintenance of the overall system of stratification.

The situation that emerged in those nations that imported Western schools was, however, very different, for it could hardly be expected that educational structures developed in the context of Western-type systems of social stratification would continue to exercise a 'status-maintenance' function in societies whose indigenous systems of social differentiation were radically different. In other words, the relationships between schooling and 'social class' that existed in European nations could not obtain in most non-Western areas; access to formal education tended, in the first instance, to be determined by a range of other variables, most of which were exogenous to the educational system itself.

Examples of the shift in patterns of educational recruitment are forthcoming from a number of colonial territories. Although the amount of schooling available to local populations was very limited in most colonies, few colonial administrations really made systematic attempts to regulate access to schooling in the interests of particular geographical or social minorities. This was evident in most British dependencies, where major responsibility for educational development was developed upon mission agencies subject to general government supervision and grants-in-aid to those schools meeting minimal standards. This *laissez-faire* approach to educational provision militated against direct effective control of the schools, and in most regions a small number of government institutions existed amidst a proliferation of both aided and non-aided mission or proprietary schools whose recruitment policies were hardly subject to supervision by the central administration. To be sure, French authorities attempted to establish more centralized patterns of control in some territories. For example, a series of educational ordinances laying down the projected pattern of development for the components of the French West African Federation provided for the creation of distinct types of schools for rural and urban populations.[3] Moreover, the quantitative expansion of the educational system was more strictly regulated by government, with greater efforts being expended in the provision of schooling in such territories as Senegal and Dahomey. These areas were to be regarded as principal suppliers of low- and middle-level manpower for the whole federation, while the educational development of such territories as the Ivory Coast was regarded as a less pressing matter.

It can hardly be contended, however, that such attempts at centralized planning were particularly effective, and in most colonial territories access to schooling was controlled more by the parsimony of colonial regimes and the limitations of mission resources than it was by any systematic planning.

The failure of colonial policies was also manifest in the sporadic efforts to control the social characteristics of pupils in the schools. Most regimes were anxious to attach traditional élites to the colonial interest, and attempts were made to recruit the offspring of traditional rulers and local 'notables' into special institutions. Western education, it was argued, would create a class of traditionally legitimate rulers who, at the same time, would become effective intermediaries between the administration and the masses. Such policies rarely met with success. In Africa various schools for the sons of chiefs in British territories or the *Ecole des Otages* in Senegal were rarely effective in recruiting from local traditional élites. Moslem rulers usually strongly resisted sending their children to schools, while in other areas, where chieftaincy was associated with specific ritual functions, attendance was considered a bar to selection for traditional office. It seems likely, indeed, that the early pupils were most often slaves, the children of African traders or individuals who were otherwise peripheral to the traditional structure and ineligible for positions of traditional authority. Similarly, in British India, nineteenth-century policies of educational 'downward filtration' that emphasized the recruitment to the schools of representatives of the secular Indian ruling groups, such as the landed Hindu castes or the Mogul aristocracy, were generally a failure. The groups that pressed for Western education were usually the literary castes, such as Brahmans and Kayasths, or traders, including the Marwaris and Banyas.[4] Moreover, there was a predominance of recruitment from lower- and middle-income groups rather than from the more wealthy strata.[5] Most strikingly, the relative failure of British policies aimed at attracting Moslems to Western schools became ultimately a major contributory cause to the 1948 partition of India and Pakistan; favourable treatment of the Moslem minority did not lead to parity of educational provision between them and the Hindus, whose educational lead enabled them to increasingly dominate the emerging modern occupational and administrative structure throughout the colonial period.

Thus the corollary of educational expansion in many colonial territories was often the emergence of incipient 'social strata' whose status was not dependent upon traditional criteria, but rather upon the possession of formal education that alone enabled them to obtain access to the new occupational opportunities created by colonial overrule. These minorities were occasionally led into overt conflict with more traditionally oriented élites, and unquestionably experience in Western-type schools was itself a major factor in their espousal of nationalist ideologies. More significant from the viewpoint of the present paper is the fact that colonial regimes often did not clearly anticipate this kind of outcome, nor were they conspicuously successful in consciously regulating educational access in the light of general policy considerations.

The dynamics of educational growth in the colonial period must therefore be sought in an examination of the interplay of factors other than government policy. Where Western schooling is viewed more in terms of instrumental, economic and status benefits we have suggested that traditional élites are less likely to send their children to school than the families of less 'privileged' segments of the population. Sufficient historical data do not as yet exist to adequately test this proposition in comparative perspective, and it is doubtless a considerable oversimplification, but it is evident that in many areas the educational system played a significant role in the progressive erosion of traditional status differentials and the emergence of new, educationally privileged minorities.

Further, many of the new nations are as yet little more than congeries of diverse ethnic groups that have been brought together through the fortuitous results of colonial overrule. This situation is typical in sub-Saharan Africa, where most states present a bewildering pattern of ethnic fragmentation. It has been suggested that, other things being equal, the traditional socio-cultural organization of certain ethnic groups has made them particularly receptive to Western norms and values and to the assimilation of schooling. Typically, the Ibo and Ewe of the West African littoral and the Kikuyu of Kenya have been described in these terms. It has been hypothesized that the social structures and cultures of these peoples have emphasized norms of individual achievement and the enhancement of traditional status through personal effort. These traditional orientations led in turn to a greater initial appreciation of the instrumental advantages of schooling that resulted in high levels of public demand for education. Moreover, in the case of these three peoples the desire for schooling was probably enhanced by the marked pressure on limited land resources created by rapidly expanding populations, and hence the need to seek alternative occupational outlets.

Such efforts to explain variations in educational demand and access in terms, for example, of different levels of achievement motivation generated by distinct types of traditional social structure and culture are plausible. Indeed, recent empirical evidence supports this kind of hypothesis in the case of the Ibo.[6] Explanations based, however, on this approach cannot account for variations in educational demand and access as between groups whose traditional social structure was relatively homogeneous. Here we are obliged to seek for the roots of educational inequality among diverse populations in terms of more pedestrian types of explanation.

Clearly, the straightforward geographical proximity of certain peoples to the initial centres of European penetration was of crucial importance. Early census data, and colonial publications, indicate the marked disparities between levels of education along the West African coastal region and those prevailing in the hinterland. Similarly, in East Africa the educational provision for Africans tended to be closely associated with the major zones of European settlement and influence.[7] Likewise, in India the diffusion of schooling was usually highest in the urban coastal trading centres. However, the crucial factor generating a demand for education was not merely the presence of a European minority *per se*, but rather the concomitant development of monetary economy that resulted from their presence. The emergence of exchange activities and the consequent creation of a more complex occupational structure in most cases was an essential *pre-condition* for educational development. In other words, public pressure for schooling did not develop until the requirements of a nascent modern economic structure made a few years of schooling functional in essentially economic terms.

The growing urban centres were, of course, the areas in which education advanced most rapidly, and these became the nodal centres of development from which schooling diffused slowly outward into the rural hinterlands. In these latter areas, moreover, educational expansion was again a response to a progressive shift from subsistence to exchange activities; the development of cash-crop farming in many regions provided an incentive for the acquisition of Western schooling and generated the wherewithal to pay for it.

In ecological terms, the quantitative diffusion of education was thus intimately linked to a series of other indices of economic modernization, including the proportion of the active population engaged in non-agricultural pursuits, the presence of urban centres and the percentage of the rural population engaged in cash-crop farming. In arguing, however, that the pattern of access to schooling was largely a reflection of shifts in the pattern of economic activities we do not wish to ignore the influence of other factors with more specifically local impact. Thus the rapid development of education in Buganda in the late nineteenth and early twentieth centuries can be plausibly interpreted as a response to the religious conversion of a substantial proportion of the Ganda population to Christianity. Here the motive for literacy may well have been initially religious in origin, and a similar explanation might be advanced for the relatively high levels of schooling in parts of southern India, including Kerala. None the less, the influence of unique factors, such as the religious impact of the missions, does not obscure the general association between levels of educational development and structural economic change. In making this point, we have also suggested that although schooling usually provided a powerful stimulus to economic growth, it was not, in the first instance, a necessary precondition. Educational planners might well consider the implications of this observation before mounting large-scale programmes for the expansion of schooling in the most economically laggard areas of a developing nation.

By the end of the colonial period the pattern of educational diffusion was rather similar in most territories, and it tended to be replicated in those developing areas which had never ostensibly known a period of overt colonial control. In vertical terms, sharp differentials existed between urban and rural areas; the latter tended also to be educationally stratified in association with the degree of shift from a primarily subsistence economy. In many territories, moreover, the picture of educational development was complicated by the fact that zones of geographical variation in the amount of schooling among local populations tended to be associated with ethnic differentials. Thus in Africa, classifications of population based on 'tribe' tend to be frequently associated with variations in mean levels of education and occupational profile. This confounding of education, occupational status and ethnic provenance is frequently of political significance, but it is also of considerable importance when we consider the nascent systems of social differentiation that are emerging in many developing areas. In terms of the horizontal dimension, we have suggested that Western education was frequently responsible for the erosion of traditional patterns of authority and status differentiation. The gradual acceptance by indigenous populations of new criteria of social rank and the emergence of new political social and economic élites can be properly regarded as a major consequence of Western schooling.

The contemporary scene

In gross quantitative terms the educational achievements of most developing nations have been impressive over the last twenty years. For example, since 1950 primary school enrolments in most Asian and sub-Saharan territories have typically been doubled or trebled and in several notably laggard regions the increase has been virtually tenfold.[8] Post-primary enrolments have similarly risen rapidly in the last decade, and at present, secondary school expansion is often proceeding at two or three times the primary rate, reflecting a progressive flattening out in the curve of primary school growth. The ratio of primary to secondary enrolments, however, is extremely variable. Over most of tropical Africa secondary enrolments usually constitute about 5 per cent of those in the primary sector, rising to a high in Ghana of approximately 21 per cent. Asian countries present similar profiles, although India and Pakistan, in particular, provide an impressive picture of quantitative (if not always qualitative) development in secondary schooling with enrolments constituting about 30 per cent of those in primary institutions. Finally, it can be expected that over the next two decades many developing areas will experience a dramatic increase in enrolments at the university level as rapidly growing secondary cohorts increasingly demand access to the tertiary sector.

Clearly, nearly all developing areas have experienced a dramatic increase in *gross* educational opportunities. But it does not necessarily follow that there has been any substantial change in the relative pattern of opportunities as between regional or ethnic groupings or socio-economic categories within national populations. A glance at census data frequently indicates, for example, that the range between the most educationally advanced and laggard regions in a country may not diminish during a wave of accelerated primary school development. Thus Ghana represents one of the most educationally advanced nations of sub-Saharan Africa, with an unrivalled pace of growth in primary schooling over the decade 1950–60. Yet over this period the expansion of primary school enrolments was greatest in the most economically developed southern regions of the country. By contrast, although northern figures rose, the increase was smaller than that registered in the south. In other words, in a period of growth the educational gap between lead and laggard areas actually increased. By 1960 enrolment percentages varied from 60 per cent in urban Accra to 12 per cent in the Northern Region. In 1964 these percentages stood at 78 and 25 per cent respectively, showing that the gap was still increasing.[9] Clearly, over the long haul regional disparities *must* diminish as primary enrolments continue to grow, but we wish to stress that certain stages of rapid educational expansion are characterized by increasing relative inequality of opportunity. This situation confounds the short-run efforts of governments to 'democratize' primary education, since, as we have noted, the dynamics of educational demand and growth are greatly influenced by factors exogenous to the educational system itself. Indeed, attempts to artificially step up the pace of educational development in 'backward' areas are rarely successful, and in this regard it is to be noted that interregional variations in primary school enrolment are proportionally greater in Ghana's neighbour, the Ivory Coast, in spite of a rather more centralized pattern of control over the distribution of educational facilities in that territory.[10]

In some respects, problems arising from imparities in access to primary schooling have less salience than those stemming from restrictions on entry to secondary and higher institutions. Whatever long-run contribution to development will be achieved through the extension of widespread primary education and literacy, there is little doubt from the viewpoint of the clientele of the schools that a primary education alone now provides little opportunity for occupational or social mobility in an increasing number of less developed nations. Increasing pressure for entry is therefore placed on secondary and higher institutions which largely control access to upper- and middle-level occupational roles. Since post-primary education is in short supply, studies of recruitment patterns into this sector can provide insights into general mobility processes in these societies and cast light on the characteristics of their potential élites. Studies of secondary rather than university populations are particularly significant in so far as the secondary schools frequently have a dual function of providing terminal education for a proportion of their pupils while routing others to higher institutions. Moreover, it is often the case that access to secondary schooling is more difficult than the passage from secondary to higher education. In other words, secondary schools are particularly strategic links in the educational structure and frequently constitute bottle-necks that are especially restrictive in their effects on the total flow of manpower through the system.

Unfortunately, relatively few investigations of recruitment patterns into selective secondary institutions have been undertaken in the developing areas. Moreover, many of these deal with single institutions and are not based on representative national samples, while the different classifications of student background that have been employed by investigators make cross-national comparisons extremely hazardous. Present evidence makes it impossible, for example, to test the proposition that as between developing nations there is any systematic relationship between student socio-economic background and the level of economic development.

In general terms, all studies indicate a skew in recruitment patterns towards the upper end of the socio-economic scale. In other words, the children of professional and white-collar workers are over-represented in proportion to their distribution in the population as against the offspring of farmers or unskilled workers. Further, there is a distinct bias in favour of urban youth and, where ethnicity is relevant, those groups who obtained early access to schooling are disproportionately represented in the ranks of secondary schools.

Such findings are hardly surprising in view of the considerable literature already available from Western nations concerning the relation between educational access and social or ethnic background. Yet further observations can be made concerning this type of data. Frequently, massive inequality of opportunity may exist in the sense that very often the child of a professional worker may have some thirty times the chance of entering secondary school as the offspring of an unskilled urban labourer, and such differentials are even sharper if parental education rather than occupation is treated as the independent variable. Yet at the same time inequality of opportunity may be associated with a substantial minority or often a majority of secondary school students being drawn from lower socio-economic 'strata' or under-privileged ethnic groups. Whether we use a 'life chances' or an 'absolute distribution' approach in the study of access to education depends largely on the research questions we have posed ourselves. At this juncture it is sufficient to say that the co-existence of gross inequalities of access to advanced schooling with relative 'openness' in absolute profiles of representation can occur in those societies where the socio-economic profile of the population is broad at the base but extremely constricted at the apex.

Further, as we have already noted in the case of primary schooling an increase in the overall provision of secondary education need not be associated in the short run with diminishing inequalities in access. Thus in some Western nations as gross opportunites for selective secondary education have increased, the proportion of pupils of lower-class origin has remained stable or even declined as new places are overwhelmingly taken by middle-class children. The type of longitudinal data required to examine this process in developing nations does not as yet exist. However, cross-national data, if treated with caution, are suggestive. Thus Ghana and the Ivory Coast can be considered very comparable territories with regard to their level of economic development, but they vary greatly in terms of the size of their educational systems. A Ghanaian child has *overall* a far better chance of entering a secondary grammar school than does his Ivory Coast counterpart of entering a comparable *lycée*. Yet the empirical findings suggest that *differentials* in access in terms of ethnic or socio-economic origin are generally greater in Ghana than in the Ivory Coast.[11] In other words, a sheer increase in the size of enrolments is not necessarily associated in any linear fashion with greater relative equality of educational opportunities for socio-economic or ethnic groups. Governments in developing areas have proceeded on the assumption that more schooling leads to greater equality of access—as indeed it ultimately must—but they must be prepared for considerable short-run 'stickiness' in recruitment patterns or even reversals in the process of educational 'democratization'.

Finally, in considering post-primary education two other issues must be noted. First, there is the question of continuance as contrasted with mere entry into secondary school—no mean matter in territories where retardation and drop-out are high and where gaining a secondary school certificate is far more important than having had some kind of post-primary experience. Second, most secondary school systems in developing areas are, like their European prototypes, highly differentiated internally, and no one is under any illusion as to the relative social or occupational worth of, for example, an education in a *lycée* as opposed to study at a *cours complémentaire* or a *centre d'apprentissage*. Typically, in Europe the academic secondary school has provided opportunities for access to élite status and, as we are aware, recruitment into various kinds of secondary school institutions has usually been associated with variations in the social composition of their student bodies.

We may well ask whether this traditional pattern is now being replicated in the new states.

Few data, unfortunately, are available that throw any light concerning the relationship between a student's background and the type of secondary education he enters and how far he progresses. Once again we are obliged to rely on material from Ghana and the Ivory Coast that is of limited comparative utility. The investigation in Ghana was confined to the senior classes of a national sample of secondary grammar schools, and thus could not provide longitudinal data as to student vertical progress in the system. However, when the socio-economic composition of the student body in the most established (and academically successful) schools was compared with that of the newer (and academically weaker) institutions no significant differences were apparent. However, there was an exception in that students in the two most distinguished academic secondary schools in Ghana were much more likely to be drawn from urban households with higher socio-economic origin than pupils in all other institutions.[12] The academic pre-eminence of these two schools has long been recognized, but the greater social 'exclusiveness' of their clientele was not previously demonstrable.

The Ivory Coast investigation provided nationally representative data on students in different types of secondary school (*lycées, cours complémentaires, centres d'apprentissage,* etc.) and also compared students at different stages of secondary education—notably at the end of the first and second cycles of study. Cross-sectional data of this kind are less valuable than longitudinal studies of students, but they do throw some light on social and ethnic differentiation by type of school and level of seniority. Perhaps in striking difference to the situation in some Western education systems, the Ivory Coast material indicated that socio-economic or ethnic origin was only minimally related to the secondary stream a student entered or to how far he progressed in his studies.[13] Indeed, the influence of these factors was progressively attenuated the further one moved upwards into the senior classes. In other words, although a student's social and ethnic provenance had a good deal to do with whether he entered secondary school in the first place, it had less predictive value concerning his future course of study or his general progress upward in the system.

In general, therefore, one is struck by the looseness of relationship between socio-economic or ethnic origin and access to post-primary education in certain developing areas, although such a relationship is everywhere discernible. We have not yet discussed, however, sex differences in the context of inequalities of educational opportunity. The under-representation of women at all educational levels is a far more ubiquitous feature of the educational systems of developing areas than imparities resulting from either ethnic or social origin. The cynic might suggest that the frequent lack of governmental concern—apart from occasional pieties—over female representation in the schools stems frequently from the fact that women—unlike vocal ethnic minorities—do not constitute an effective political constituency. The fact remains that in sub-Saharan Africa girls average only about 35 per cent of primary enrolments, ranging from a low of 19 per cent in Chad to a remarkable high of 62 per cent in Lesotho.[14] The Asian average is somewhat higher, although once again female enrolments almost everywhere lag. The rate of female wastage from the schools is also substantially higher than that for males, and in most African and Asian states girls constitute only about one-quarter of gross post-primary enrolments. Moreover, they tend to be more typically concentrated in the less prestigeful terminal types of secondary institution which often provide a more specifically 'vocational' training.

The reason for the under-representation of females is clear enough; even where specifically religious objections to the education of women are absent, limited familial resources must be expended first on boys whose potential contribution to the family economy is likely to be greater. This results in a very striking relation between the level of female representation and their socio-economic or ethnic origin. Where girls constitute a small minority of enrolments, at whatever level, they are far more likely than boys to be drawn from educated homes with fathers of relatively high occupational status.[15] Secondary school girls and female university students, indeed, constitute very much of a district 'class' and social differences associated with sex only disappear when virtual parity of representation with males is achieved. It is notable, however, that in spite of their relatively higher socio-economic origins, the educational and vocational aspirations of girls are more limited and constricted in range

C

than those of boys, indicating that early patterns of socialization into appropriate sex roles are often far more potent
factors than 'social class' origin in influencing educational and
vocational ambition.[16]

It is to be anticipated that dramatic rises in female enrolment
ratios are not likely to be achieved in many areas until a substantial proportion of the eligible male population is already in
school. It is probably tactically inadvisable, for example, for
any country that still has less than 30 per cent of the eligible
male age cohort in primary school to launch major campaigns
to raise the level of female representation. The same type of
campaign, however, might have considerable impact in those
areas where substantial success has been already achieved in
getting the majority of males into primary schools. This again
is one of the hard choices that educational policy-makers are
obliged to make; powerful arguments can be adduced to support
major investments in schooling for girls at early stages of educational growth, but in terms of short-run perspectives the
long-run 'indirect' returns that might accrue are more difficult
to justify.

The élite-mass gap

So far, we have suggested that, in spite of considerable inequality
in access to education in most developing areas, it is still true
that the schools have not functioned in such a way as to close
the doors of educational and occupational opportunity. Indeed,
what is striking in Africa, in particular, is the substantial proportion of students at secondary schools and higher universities
who are drawn from rural areas and families of lower socio-
economic status; the offspring of 'the élite' (however we may
define this slippery term) are disproportionately over-represented
in selective institutions, but still constitute only a minority of
students. The schools have therefore done a moderately successful job in facilitating mobility, and this in spite of the fact that
entrance requirements to post-primary education are often
geared to demanding academic standards. The corollary is that
numerous members of existing élites are themselves of humble
origin, and formal education more often than not played a
crucial role in their earlier upward mobility. This openness in

access to élite roles, however, is not associated with high aggregate rates of upward mobility in these societies. Frequently opportunities at the top and middle levels of the occupational structure expand but slowly, and relatively few individuals at the base achieve upward mobility though the careers of those that do often provide striking success stories.

It might be hypothesized, however, that this association of low aggregate rates of mobility with fluidity of access to élite roles is a transitional phenomenon, for observers have drawn attention to a growing 'élite-mass gap' in many developing nations. As development proceeds, objective differentials between segments of a population increase. Inequality between geographical regions, urban and rural districts or occupational strata seems to be an almost inevitable concomitant of early stages of growth. And parallel with this process of objective differentiation it can be suggested that there is a progressive emergence of élite minorities who are differentiated from the mass in terms of their culture and life-style and who become progressively conscious of their own self-interest in opposition to that of the majority of the population. It is undeniable that processes of structural differentiation do lead to the emergence of distinctive élite subcultures, but how far this has yet involved the crystallization of 'class consciousness' is difficult to assess.

Quite obviously, formal education in so far as it is unevenly distributed contributes to the process of structural and cultural differentiation. But substantial problems arise if privileged groups 'capture' the educational system in such a manner as to use it as an instrument for maintaining existing status differentials. In other words, far from being an institutional device for promoting a degree of mobility from the mass, the educational structure largely exists to transmit status to the offspring of existing élites.

There are several historical examples of attempts to control access to education through the enactment of formal regulations debarring certain social groups from specific types of schooling. Alternatively, the children of the élite may be exempted from certain initial examination requirements that give them marked advantages over aspirants from other sections of the population.[17] However, 'rigging' the formal conditions of entry to education are not always necessary to ensure the increased proportional representation of the offspring of higher status groups in post-primary schooling. It is conceivable that, in the face of a burgeoning child population and limited financial resources, checks will have to be placed on the growth of the educational system. So far as secondary and higher education is concerned, absolute numbers of students may continue to increase while the proportion of the relevant age cohorts enrolled may diminish. Undoubtedly, systems of selection based on formal academic performance will tend to favour children of élite households, and such families will normally continue to be large in most developing areas. The process of 'squeezing out' the children of less privileged groups from post-primary education can, therefore, occur where access to schooling is limited, associated with relatively slow rates of economic growth and with an élite that numerically more than replaces itself.

One does not have to be an orthodox Marxist to point to the possibility of more rigid systems of social stratification emerging in many new nations with the schools contributing in no small measure to such a development. It is precisely a recognition of this that has led to Julius Nyerere's charting a new course for the schools in Tanzania.[18] Primary institutions are no longer to be geared to the selection-requirements needs of secondary schools, but are to be related to the needs of local communities; academic systems of selection are to be modified by the employment of broader criteria of merit and the schools are to undertake what amounts to a massive task of political socialization in pursuit of the goal of an egalitarian society. One may question the probable effectiveness of this programme of 'Education for Self-reliance' while at the same time recognizing the very real concerns that have inspired it. For Nyerere implicitly accepts the fact that an educational system geared to the need for economic growth and the efficient production of high-level manpower may subvert basically egalitarian national objectives. The danger that formal education will generate and reinforce massive social cleavages within the Tanzanian population is in Nyerere's opinion a far more tangible threat to the new polity than the risk of a slow-down in the rate of economic growth. His concern with the social consequences of educational inequality brings us back to the problem posed in the opening paragraph of this chapter. Where economic objectives are paramount, a good deal of inequality in access to education must result and benefits are likely to be maximized if resources are concentrated on regions and groups most likely to profit from them. In other words, educational investment on primary education will tend to be concentrated in geographical areas that are already the most modernized, while the development of 'efficient' means for the selection of individuals for further training tends to benefit already favoured minorities within a population. Alternatively, strategies designed to allocate educational resources and opportunities more evenly among a population may spread these resources so thinly that they may make little tangible contribution to economic development.

In practice, of course, governments frequently make pragmatic compromises between different sets of objectives. Where primary education, for example, is still heavily financed by the central government, attempts may be made to devolve the costs of schooling on the local authorities. Inevitably, this means that those wealthier areas more willing to finance primary schools increase their educational lead over less developed regions. These imparities can be mitigated through supplemental financing of laggard districts by the central government, but this does not often occur without opposition from more prosperous groups. Similarly, the social and ethnic profile of the student population that results from existing methods of selection for schooling can be modified by varying standards of entry for different groups or even by employing an implicit or even explicit quota system.[19] These compensatory devices always involve substantial economic costs, but they may frequently be essential if certain groups are not to be completely excluded from selective secondary and higher education. Complete equality of access to schooling is, of course, impossible in the developing areas, and theoretical 'equality of opportunity' often masks gross imparities. Yet men are often prepared to accept such inequalities if they perceive that the doors of educational opportunity are not entirely closed and that some chance exists for their offspring to climb the educational ladder. Therefore expediency alone often requires that the governments of the new states respond to demands for greater equality of access to schooling even if purely economic considerations would suggest an alternative course. In the short run, indeed, the politics of educational development are likely to play a far greater role in determining the pattern of educational access than any strategies based on maximizing the economic contribution of schooling.

Notes

1 There are grave dangers in generalizing about educational growth in developing areas. A glance at countries grouped by levels of resource development in Harbison, Frederick, and Myers, Charles A., *Education, Manpower and Economic Growth*, New York: McGraw-Hill, 1964, 33, reveals enormous variation between countries. In these pages, therefore, we shall be dealing largely with those nations classed as Level I in terms of the rubrics of these authors. Moreover, the focus of discussion will be substantially on sub-Saharan Africa. I shall also eschew any attempt to provide any succinct (and thus unacceptable) definition of modernization.

2 Blau, Peter M., and Duncan, Otis Dudley, in *The American Occupational Structure*, New York: John Wiley & Sons, 1967, provide perhaps the most comprehensive discussion of the relationship between education and mobility in a highly developed Western economy. Chapter 12 provides an excellent summary of the present situation.

3 See, for example, Bolibaugh, Jerry B., and Hanna, Paul R., *Education as an Instrument of National Policy in Selected Developing Nations. Phase 2: French Educational Strategies for Sub-Saharan Africa: Their Intent, Derivation, and Development*, Stanford: Comparative Education Center, 1964, 29–42.

4 See Hennessy, Jossleyn, 'British Education for an Elite in India (1780–1947)', in Wilkinson, Rupert (ed.), *Governing Elites*, New York: Oxford University Press, 1969, 145–8.

5 See McCully, Bruce Tiebout, *English Education and the Origins of Indian Nationalism*, New York: Columbia University Press, 1940, 184–91.

6 See LeVine, Robert A., *Dreams and Deeds: Achievement Motivation in Nigeria*, Chicago: University of Chicago Press, 1966.

7 See Soja, E. W., *The Geography of Modernization in Kenya*, Syracuse: Syracuse University Press, 1968.

8 Haute Volta provides an example of rapid expansion, but primary enrolments still only represent approximately 28 per cent of the relevant age cohort.

9 See Foster, Philip, *Education and Social Change in Ghana*, London and Chicago: Routledge & Kegan Paul and the University of Chicago Press, 1965, 189, and Hurd, G. E., 'Education', in Birmingham, Walter, Neustadt, I., and Omaboe, E. N. (eds.), *A Study of Contemporary Ghana: Vol. II, Some aspects of Social Structure*, Evanston: Northwestern University Press, 1967, 227.

10 *Côte d'Ivoire, 1965. Population. Etudes Regionales, 1962–65. Synthèse*, Abidjan: Ministère du Plan, 1967, 91.
11 See Foster, *op. cit.*, and Clignet, Remi, and Foster, Philip, *The Fortunate Few: a Study of Secondary Schools and Students in the Ivory Coast*, Evanston: Northwestern University Press, 1967.
12 Foster, *op. cit.*, 253.
13 Clignet and Foster, *op. cit.*, 79–85.
14 In the case of both Lesotho and Botswana, female enrolments exceed those of males, in contrast to the situation in the rest of sub-Saharan Africa. It seems likely that the task of cattle-herding performed by younger boys and the pull of occupational opportunities for males in the Republic may account for this unique development.
15 See Foster, *op. cit.*, 240–6, and Clignet and Foster, *op. cit.*, 57–8.
16 See Foster, *op. cit.*, 276–84.
17 Thus in Imperial China the children of the literati were frequently exempt from the initial examination on the educational ladder that provided access to administrative roles.
18 Julius Nyerere, *Education for Self-Reliance*, Dar-es-Salaam: Government Printer, n.d.
19 For example, in the years immediately following the Revolution the Soviets freely utilized differential entrance requirements and quota systems in order to facilitate mobility of the children of workers and peasants into higher education. These efforts were largely curtailed during the thirties in the drive to produce a technological élite.

three

The production process and education

JOHN VAIZEY

References to 'productivity', to 'cost–benefit' and to similar pseudo-economic terms of art are allied to a contempt for artistic and cultural matters which must be alarming indeed for those who believe that education occupies a central place in our society with potential for good or evil effects on the nature of our civilization.

It must therefore be fully understood that in conducting the following analysis of productivity trends in education, the author is by no means conceding that this approach is in itself desirable or necessary; nor that such an analysis should inevitably take a high place in the debate; he is not arguing that culture in these 'hard times' has to take second place—the times are not (in that sense) particularly hard, and even if they were it would seem to be even more important in such circumstances to have culture take the first place.

Inputs, process and output in education

In very many spheres of human life it is possible to divide the activity up into inputs (things that go into a process), the process itself, and the outputs which follow the processing of the inputs. Obviously this is often an analogy for what is seen most clearly in industry and agriculture. In the fields, the seed is sown, fertilization and cultivation take place and the harvest is reaped. In industry, iron ore and coal and various other things go into a furnace; it is all boiled up, and steel emerges. This relationship can be applied to whole processes. For example, we can talk about all the effort which goes into producing, making and selling a product in relation to the final output for the nation as a whole, or for any part of any sector of the nation's economy. It would be perfectly possible to talk about the National Health Service as a system into which the labour of doctors and nurses and many thousands of people, together with the buildings that they use and all the drugs, and sheets, and food, are measured as inputs, the process of dealing with patients is the 'productive process' and the recovery or death of the patients would be the outcome, or 'output'.

Thus it is perfectly proper and perfectly acceptable to talk by analogy about the input, the process and the output of education, though we have to be careful of the limits of analogy. The input into education is the use of the buildings and the equipment that is contained in them, the time of the teachers, social workers, assistants, secretaries, administrators, inspectors, voluntary workers of all kinds, the time of the pupils: all that is the 'input'. The process of education is what goes on while all this 'input' is being used. The 'output' is something that is extraordinarily difficult to be precise about. In one sense the output in any one year is everybody who leaves school in that year. In another sense it is the things that everybody has learnt in that year. In another sense it may be everybody who has passed an examination in that year. In still another sense it may be the general rise or fall in the level of culture—if such a concept has any meaning. It is thus seen that 'educational output' is an extraordinarily imprecise notion. But the fact that a notion is imprecise does not necessarily mean that it has no meaning at all; many of the notions which we customarily work with are imprecise, but they are still essential tools of thought.

Thus, if you accept for a moment the use of such language, the input into education is the services of all the people working in education (including the students), and the services of the capital and equipment with which they work, and the output is the result of what they have done. What they do is the process of production. If it is conceivable that the inputs of education could be measured and related to the outputs, then the comparison of the relationship of these inputs to the outputs using different processes of production would be called the productivity of education. Productivity is an extraordinarily complex and difficult concept to handle without ambiguity—misleading ambiguity. Productivity is a ratio of inputs to outputs, and the ratio changes as the process of production changes, or as inputs change, or as outputs change. Productivity in its original sense involves the notion that if you divide the output of an industry among the number of people employed by that industry you get a productivity per man. Thus, for example, if the coal industry employs 1,000 miners and produces 100,000 tons of coal a year, the output per man in the coal industry is 100 tons. If each ton sells at £10, the output per man is worth £1,000. The marginal product would be the extra output which would be generated by taking on one extra man, and, of course, it might be greater or less than the average of 100 tons. In a manufacturing industry normally the marginal product is greater than average; in other occupations (notably in agriculture and the extractive trades) usually the marginal product is lower than the average.

Now, productivity measured in this way, of course, would imply that the whole output of industry is the result of the work of the people engaged in industry. Yet this is an absurdity. A great many industries (nuclear power is an extreme case) consist of enormous volumes of capital with the odd little white-coated man scurrying around tightening up knobs or pressing buttons. In that case a man's output might easily be £1,000,000 worth a year. To avoid this evident absurdity, the notion of productivity is applied to units of capital. For every £100 worth of capital employed there might be a £100 worth of product. Or for every £1,000 worth of capital you might get £10,000 worth of output. To get a true measure of productivity, therefore, you would have to evaluate all inputs against all outputs in the part of the economy you are analysing: and some means of dividing the output among the people who contribute to it. The problem is made infinitely complex by the fact that inputs and outputs are heterogeneous—coal plus people plus machines gives degrees plus culture plus cookery classes. To add them up you need acceptable index numbers.

Some economists hold that there are such unambiguous

index numbers—the money and price system—and consequently a means of allocating output between labour and capital. Other economists do not see that such a measure is possible. This is the central problem. Be that as it may, it will be seen that productivity is the relationship between input and output. It is, further, normally concluded that if productivity rises, there is more output per unit of input; or the same output with less input. Thus in every conceivable way there would be more as the result of doing less, if productivity were rising.

In the British economy as a whole—not untypically—the rate of growth of productivity—that is, what occurs without any increase of inputs—is positive, and somewhat more than 3 per cent per year, probably, if there is not a statistical error. A great deal of this rise is due to the manufacturing industry, and the reason for the rise in the productivity in the manufacturing industry is generally conceded to be the growing amount of capital with which each man works—this volume of capital per man is increasing and the capital, as it increases, embodies the newer technology and the improvement in technology increases the output faster than inputs increase. There are certain occupations where productivity seems not to rise at all. In traditional agriculture in Asia and Africa it is probable that productivity hardly rises from one year to another over decades. In some places productivity may even fall, as the land becomes exhausted and the capital wears out and the people become increasingly feeble through malnutrition and ill-health.

In some sectors of the economy productivity is stagnant because the productive process could not change, given present knowledge and attitudes. It is in this nebulous area that the question of productivity in education must be considered. In the 'service' sector of the economy—including health, education, social welfare, defence, the civil service and central administration—there are substantial employers of expensively educated manpower, some using little capital equipment (compared with industry or engineering), where the techniques of production do not necessarily change very quickly, and it is extremely difficult to measure the output. It is the growth of this sector which lowers the average rate of growth of productivity in the economy. It is to this 'stagnant sector' that the argument now turns. It could be stagnant for *real* reasons—that output does not rise faster than inputs—or for statistical reasons—that, though output rises, we are not able to measure its rise.

It is difficult to measure output in service industries for two reasons: first, because the output is extraordinarily hetero-geneous compared, for example, with that of the steel industry. To add up the total effects of health or education, social welfare or defence, is extremely complex because of this heterogeneity of output. The index usually used is the value of output—cheap and dear steel are added up, not just by tons of steel, but by tons multiplied by value. Secondly, very little of the service output is sold on the open market. Defence is the supreme example of this, where it is inconceivable that a realistic money value could be placed on the total effect of defence in a modern economy. You could argue that there would be no economy at all if there were no defence; or you could argue that British defence is completely wasted, since the only thing that deters the Russians is the existence of the American nuclear weapons; the main function of the defence forces is to mount guard at Buckingham Palace to attract tourists. The one thing you could not do is to give a numerical value to the output of defence as a whole; and the same certainly goes for education and health, because the great bulk of their output is not sold in the market and has no market value.

Some of the existing work seems implicitly or indeed explicitly to assert that it is possible to measure the output of the education system as a whole in meaningful terms. Certainly if the output is defined by some comparatively simple numerical criterion, such as the number of people successfully passing examinations, and these criteria are not varied over the years, then it is possible to say that output has risen or fallen. But has such a criterion operational meaning? The criterion which is chosen, such as examination results, is only part of the complex results of an immensely complex social process, and it is to be doubted whether any simple overall index has any meaning, since it is bound to be arbitrary and can never be universally acceptable. Assertions about the global output of education are not meaningful if they are intended to be some guide to the efficiency with which resources in education as a whole are used compared with the way resources are used in other parts of the economy.

If we turn away from output to the question of input, it is also the case that the measurement of the inputs into the education system is no simple matter. The most important point to make initially is that the value of the capital which is employed in education is in itself not simple to establish. It is customarily valued in school authority accounts as the payment of the interest on the debt which has been incurred in the creation of the capital goods. But this is only one way of measuring the capital input—capital can be valued at its present market value, or at its replacement cost, or at its original value, and in times when the value of money is changing rapidly and also the type of capital good is changing rapidly, there is no unambiguous answer to this.[1]

Secondly, if it is intended to add to the costs of education, a notion of the costs of the time which is devoted by the students, there are complex problems. What would they have earned if they had been in employment? This requires some rather subtle analysis of the effect of unleashing hundreds of thousands of students on to the labour market. It also requires judgment of the benefits (or pains) immediately enjoyed by the people who are undergoing education: the existing valuation of students' time measured as input avoids all these implications. Thus the measurement of inputs is not free from significant ambiguity.

It is not even unambiguous in the relatively simple field of teachers' salaries. Salaries, broadly, are not determined on the open market. They are administered prices, with all the valuation problems to which that gives rise.

If we then turn to the educational process itself, there is so far absent from much of the discussion any detailed analysis of the way in which education is actually carried on. A lot of loose description is used of conventional as against unconventional methods, and similar phraseology, but when we get down to an analysis of the way in which reading or French or science is taught, I can only say that my own conclusion, drawn from a fairly wide inspection of the evidence, is that at the moment very little is known. For one thing, the educational process rests upon a complete absence of any effective kind of learning theory. It is not really possible to assert unambiguously that one method is better than another on psychological or sociological grounds, and what is true of methods is also true of teacher personality, administrative style, organizational structure and many other things.

Now, where does all this leave us? The resources devoted to education are increasing. How fast they are increasing it is difficult to say without ambiguity. How far output is changing must rest upon work which is not yet done. The way in which the inputs are transmuted into outputs is largely an area of ignorance. This is said quite frankly because much of the present work on the productivity of education rests upon the assumption that inputs, outputs and processes are known and understood. One of the conclusions that should be drawn from what has been said is that educational policies which are advocated because they are likely to lead to rapid rises in the productivity of education should be viewed with great suspicion. Considering the present state of knowledge, it is probably not possible unambiguously to make such an assertion about any major step in education.

But neither should the conclusion be drawn that the investigations with such an end in view are not worth while. If you compare two situations which in all other respects are exactly similar, except for one small variation, then it is possible to use the terms 'input', 'output' and 'productivity' without significant ambiguity. For example, if a school remains in every respect unchanged, except that it gets an additional teacher or that it gets an extra £100 to spend on equipment, a reasonable assumption may be made that a change in what happens to the pupils could, without stretching too much, be attributed to the extra teacher or to the extra £100. However, the unreality of this situation must again be emphasized. In the course of a year, all the pupils become a year older, so do all the teachers; there are always, however, withdrawals from the student body, new entrants, retirements from the teaching force. The general cultural *ambiance* of the school and the pupils' families changes. As anybody who has ever done any educational research knows, it is impossible to say without qualification that one thing has followed from a particular cause rather than from some other unspecified causes—laboratory conditions do not prevail in the social sciences.

The implication here is that where on the whole the situation is fairly stable and there is a gross change, either in input or in output or in the productive process, it ought to be possible to say that the consequent changes, or changes which are related to this, may be attributed to what may be given a fairly clear causal origin.

In summary, the inputs of education are increasing. There is every sign that there will be a mounting number of highly skilled people used in the education service, including teachers at all levels, and a growing number of better-qualified students, particularly at the level of higher education. Thus the 'burden' of education is growing all the time.

Little is known of what is happening to the output of education. The number of qualified people is rising. The general effects of education, both negative and positive, may be increasing (if only in terms of the number of riots caused by students). But as to whether the general trend of all the consequences of education is up or down, can anything be said?

Raising the level of productivity in education

It is not true that the productive process in education is stagnant. The education system can rarely have been in such rapid change as it is at the moment, from changes in the relationships of teachers and taught, in what teachers think they are trying to do, to the introduction of new methods of educational technology (including the computer). The question is whether or not this increase in inputs, the changes in outputs and the changes in productive techniques are causing productivity to rise or fall.

It will be seen that even in the economy at large this is a difficult question to answer unambiguously. Output changes, and as output changes it is possible to say that output is both rising and falling, and for both statements simultaneously to be true. Similarly with inputs. At a relatively unsophisticated level it might seem that this complexity is redundant. If a lecture theatre is used for ten, twenty or thirty hours a week, then one use is surely more 'productive' than another? Up to a point, of course, that is obviously true. One can go too far (lavatories rarely have a hundred per cent occupancy, for example), but in general the higher the use the more 'productive' the capital is.

But the real question of 'productivity' in education applies not to capital, but to teachers. If two teachers of equal ability teach two groups of children of equal ability and one group is larger than the other, and their results are the same, surely the teacher with the larger group is the more 'productive'.

It is this central question that the whole concept of productivity is intended to apply to. It is perfectly obvious that the fall in the pupil–teacher ratio—that is to say, the increased number of teachers per hundred children—has the effect of reducing the number of children taught by each teacher and is therefore *prima facie* cost-raising. It would be argued, I think, that unless this leads to significant improvements in the learning process, this cost-raising effect of improving the pupil–teacher ratio is *prima facie* wasteful. It is for this reason that strong arguments have been used in Britain for allowing the pupil–teacher ratio in higher education to deteriorate. There is one minor and one major point to be made about this. The minor point is that the 'comfort' of the teacher and taught must certainly be taken into account in computing the consequences of the pupil–teacher ratio. Even if pupil learning did not diminish, if the pupil–teacher ratio deteriorated, if the discomfort of the teacher and taught was significantly increased this would be a factor that would have to be taken into account. As far as I understand it, the research into the effects of the size of the teaching group has not taken this into account.

The major point concerns the applicability of the concept of productivity to the educational process. Let me put it like this: Why do people work? They work, obviously, partly to earn money and partly to get satisfaction in their working activity. In a totally non-alienated situation the division between work and leisure would be completely eroded (as it is for many of us in teaching and research). But if we may put a certain amount of the world's activity under the heading of work which is done not for itself but because it enables people to live, one has to ask whether or not the educational process comes into the area of the world's work or into the area of the world's living. Thus, for example, if by a new device one speeded up the rate at which people went round the National Gallery in London looking at the pictures, would this be a rise in the productivity of the National Gallery? In one sense, of course, it would be; it might be possible to get two million people a year around the National Gallery instead of one million, while keeping constant the number of pictures, the amount of heat used to heat the building and the number of guards there to see that the pictures are not stolen. But, you would say, this is a ludicrous concept: you couldn't possibly apply these sorts of concepts to the National Gallery. This seems to be a wholly sensible reaction; it is not therefore necessarily a sign of intellectual immaturity and lack of hard-headedness if an improvement in the pupil–teacher ratio is considered to be desired of itself, whatever its effects on productivity. The reason why there is a national income is to give satisfactory conditions to our children and young people, and to the people who teach them. Education is the end of the activity rather than the means: the national income is the means.

But this is not in itself a sufficient rejoinder. It is not a silly suggestion to make to the Director of the National Gallery: 'Here is an extra £10,000. You can use it on raising the temperature of the National Gallery in the winter, on buying a new picture, on hiring a few extra secretaries or several more attendants.'

There is a hidden point here which is important. If you offered an extra £10,000 to the coal industry and said that your aim was to increase productivity, the answer would be a technical matter. If all the people who were well informed on the coal industry were asked what would raise the productivity of the coal industry, you would probably get an answer which would ultimately be agreed by most of them, that the important thing was conveyor-belts, or railway trucks, or pithead showers.

In education the answers would differ, and differ very much, from the standpoint of people involved: parents might say one thing, teachers another, different kinds of teachers say different things, administrators and politicians and children might say different things. You could not demonstrate that any of the answers was right, any more than the Director of the National Gallery could irrefutably say that what he wanted was to make the National Gallery more comfortable, so that people enjoyed their visit to the National Gallery more, rather than to buy a new Duccio. And this gives us a clue to the nature of the argument about productivity in the education system. You can use the concept of productivity when you are comparing two very minor courses of action: that is to say, comparing two ways of teaching a modern language where the problem is a purely

D

technical one—how fast people can acquire a knowledge of imperfect verbs, say. But if you are asking a broader question which implies judgment as to whether or not people should learn French, or whether in learning French they should acquire a general understanding of French culture, or whether that should be left outside the educational system, these matters are not susceptible at all to any unambiguous answer. We are back indeed to the genuine central problem of how to measure educational output.

Educational productivity in developing nations

Let us now apply some of these ideas to the problems of education in the developing countries. In the first place, the inputs are much lower than in rich countries. For example, in Portugal in 1965 $29 were spent on each primary school child, $192 in England and Wales, $103 in Ireland and $292 in Quebec. Using British price weights, the figure for Portugal becomes $95, for England and Wales $192, for Ireland $110 and for Quebec $244. Despite the levelling effects of a revised price index, the inputs are very different.

It is almost certain, secondly, that the outcomes are much lower. Evidence of drop-out rates, for example, and casual inspection will suggest that the education is far less effective in the lesser than in the more developed countries. (This may be due to lack of family support, the inappropriateness of the education system to the socio-economic conditions, or sheer educational inefficiency. Whichever it is, the cause of the ineffectiveness does not affect the point at issue.) Thus inputs and outputs are relatively low in the developing nations. This is generally true of many sectors of their economies—agriculture, especially— and it reflects both their low level of skills and modern capital. Whether or not the productivity (in the sense of the ratio of inputs to outputs) is higher or lower in the developing or the developed countries it is not possible to say, since unambiguous index numbers of inputs and outputs do not exist. It seems probable that as inputs rise, however, outputs do not rise *pari passu*—there are many reports of falling rather than rising standards. It looks as though developing countries may go through a phase, perhaps a lengthy phase, in which inputs rise but outputs do not, followed by a period of consolidation in which 'productivity' begins to pick up. Behind this idea is a notion that there is a 'critical mass' for education where, after a few years, it begins to 'work': families accept its disciplines, the schools settle into a rhythm which accomplishes, more or less effectively, the goals, high or low, that they set themselves. In such circumstances, easily recognizable to experienced teachers and administrators, though hard to describe, it is not straining language to describe 'productivity' as rising. If the analogy is thought useful, it could be said that fuller utilization of plant and the gradual improvement of staff and students will lead to marked improvement in output, with relatively constant inputs over the years. Thus one answer can be given to those who ask the question: how does productivity change in the developing countries? It is that it falls during rapid expansion and rises during periods of consolidation. The answer in terms of policy decisions is thus essentially a conservative one: consolidation is desirable on productivity grounds. But what of the more radical question: can modern techniques be used to accelerate productivity rises?

To that the answer is more complex and—probably—disappointing. In the first place there is widespread evidence that most pedagogically desirable improvements—better-trained teachers, better buildings, more books and more favourable pupil–teacher ratios—are cost-raising. Modern technology, from the television to the computer, is at best no cheaper than 'conventional' techniques and often more expensive. Yet productivity does not depend on inputs alone, but on the ratio of inputs to outputs. Both pedagogically desired reforms and modern technology certainly improve output. Whether they increase output *pari passu* with the increase in inputs is debatable.

There is a further point. Reforms based on the experience of the advanced countries are usually both skill-intensive and capital-intensive. Since skill and capital are both scarce in developing nations, the new techniques are the opposite of those that the factor-endowment of the developing nations would indicate as desirable. This is part of a wider economic problem: that developing nations (generally speaking) adopt new techniques from the West that are inappropriate to their factor endowments, and there seem to be insuperable practical obstacles as well as some theoretical objections to the adoption of autonomous technologies that use more labour and less capital and skill. Education is by no means alone, therefore; but since its modern techniques are so skill-intensive it is perhaps hardly surprising that it should be especially handicapped by shortages.

The problem is complex. To adopt modern pedagogic methods is to adopt an expensive education system. In a developing country such a system will be even costlier than it seems, because its productivity will be low, owing to the inappropriate backgrounds of the students and of the teachers. Failure rates, for example, will be high.

Note

1 In our recent work for the Nuffield and Gulbenkian Foundations we have tried to tackle this problem. In an international study, *The Economics of Educational Costing*, it was found to be significant because it raises the average cost of educating a child by anything between 20 and 30 per cent of the figures which are currently quoted as the average cost.

four

Productivity and efficiency within education

DANIEL ROGERS

Education is a major industry throughout the world. In 1965 over \$100 billion was spent on formal education. Typically, it accounts for one-thirtieth to one-fifteenth of a country's gross national product (the total value of the goods and services produced in a year). Therefore, the efficiency with which education is produced is important to the overall economic efficiency of countries and hence to their development. In Chapter Seven Professor Zymelman discusses educational productivity from a macro-viewpoint; that is, the effectiveness of educational expenditures in transforming children into productive adults who contribute to the development of the nation. This essay will delineate various aspects of efficiency and productivity *within* the educational industry by looking at the school as a firm which produces education—that is, from a micro-viewpoint.

Efficiency and productivity are closely related concepts. Efficiency is defined as either achieving the greatest amount of output from a given set of inputs or achieving a specified amount of output utilizing a minimum quantity of inputs. Productivity, on the other hand, is the amount of output per unit of input. As Professor Vaizey points out in Chapter Three, productivity in education is a difficult concept to come to grips with largely because there is no agreed upon output measure. Even if an output measure were available, there would still be a different measure of productivity for each input: output per teacher, output per book, output per supervisor, output per dollar spent, output per classroom, etc.[1] In spite of these problems, the concepts of productivity and efficiency are useful in attempts to analyse the performance of the educational industry as will be demonstrated.

The problems and potentials for efficiency in education are quite similar for developed and less developed nations. Therefore, in spite of the emphasis in this volume, much of this chapter will be applicable to all countries; of course, the special aspects of the less developed nations will be brought out at every opportunity.

The potential for one specific sort of contribution to efficiency, economies of size, will be discussed in the first section. Utilizing potentials for economies of size was chosen as a concrete example of a procedure which has successfully increased efficiency in education in many countries. The next section describes various planning and evaluating techniques which can be and are applied to the problem of creating maximum efficiency within the education industry. Some difficult obstacles to efficiency in education which face many developing nations will then be considered. Finally, some possible radical changes designed to effect greater efficiency in education will be discussed.

Economies of size and efficiency

Economies of size is one of the areas in which the efficiency of schools and school systems can be improved. *An economy of size is a decrease in the average cost of producing an item related to an increase in the production of that item.* For example, if the total cost increases by less than a factor of two while the number of the item produced doubles, an economy of size is realized. Economies of size often result from indivisibilities—that is, a certain necessary item may come in a minimum size. For example, one cannot have half a cinema projector. However, as enrolment increases, one does not necessarily need to increase the number of cinema projectors in order to provide the new students with films. Therefore, the average cost per pupil of providing films decreases as the number of students increases.

That is an economy of size. It is also possible for diseconomies of size to exist. As the size of an educational system increases, the point *may* be reached where it is necessary to add administrators at a more than proportional rate, due to the system's becoming more and more complex and difficult to co-ordinate. This would cause the average cost per pupil to increase. The optimum size is the one which captures all economies of size and does not yet reach the diseconomies of size stage.

Next to the individual student, the class is the smallest unit in education. The major cost associated with each class is the salary of its teacher. As a consequence, the number of students per teacher—class size—is the most important determinant of the cost of education. If the optimum student–teacher ratio were known, much of the battle for efficiency in education would be won. Unfortunately, it is quite difficult to specify the conditions which would constitute an optimum ratio. If only costs were considered, the optimum would be to have an infinite number of students for each teacher, as the more students per teacher the less the average cost. However, efficiency requires that costs be minimized for a given quantity and *quality* of output. It is obvious that beyond a certain number of students per class the quality of the education provided declines. The attention given to each of the students by the teacher decreases and overcrowding occurs, which would reduce the students' ability to concentrate.

Theoretically, given some minimum performance requirement, there is a maximum number of students per teacher. The research designed to determine this optimum student–teacher ratio which has been undertaken to date in the United States has yielded inconclusive results. This is due in part to differences among teachers and among students. In the less developed nations, where the quality and training of teachers is even more diverse, these individual variations are a greater problem still. One can argue that a poorly trained and educated teacher might just as well have large classes, since he is not likely to be able to respond to an individual student's problems or questions. One can just as easily argue that a low-quality teacher cannot handle a large class. In any case, very little evidence exists to support the dogma that small classes are generally superior to large ones from an educational point of view. On the other hand, there is no doubt that large classes are superior from a cost point of view.

Taking the school as the unit of observation, clear evidence of economies of size exists in developed countries. The consolidation of several school districts into one in order to achieve economies through the creation of larger secondary schools is a process which has been under way in the United States for decades. It is often found profitable to proceed with consolidation even when students have to be transported at the expense of the school. Costs per student are cut, due to increased utilization of such facilities as libraries, laboratories, shops, cafeterias, gymnasiums and auditoriums. Moreover, more subjects can be offered, so that the quality of the education can be improved at the same time. Another saving often realized with consolidation is a reduction in administrative staff. The administrative staff necessary for a large school may not be as large as the total staff for several small schools, due to elimination of what would be duplication of effort. For example, only one payroll official is necessary in a large school, while each small school might need one.

While several studies of economies of size for schools have been undertaken in developed countries,[2] little work on this subject has been completed for less developed countries (LDCs). The type of economies discussed above can also be of benefit in LDCs, but these nations are faced with particular difficulties in trying to realize them. A general problem confronting LDCs in any attempt to increase the average size of school, which more developed countries do not feel so acutely, is the lower geographic density of children who are to be schooled combined with inferior transportation networks. The relatively lower density is a result of a lower proportion of children attending school, a predominately rural and hence spread-out population, or both. On the other hand, the greater relative scarcity of qualified teachers, especially in the sciences, increases the attractiveness of the consolidated school. In a consolidated school a teacher capable of teaching, for example, mathematics would teach it all day rather than waste his specialized and scarce skill by teaching one or two mathematics classes and three to five classes in other subjects each day.

Economies of size are also available at the national level.

Research and development in education are more efficiently carried out at the national than the school level. The development of new curricula and new materials is especially important for many of the newly independent LDCs, who need to replace materials held over from colonial times. The economies of size which can potentially be realized in this area are obvious when one considers the 'fixed' costs (costs which do not relate to the quantity produced) of research and of some aspects of production, such as the setting of book-plates. These fixed costs do not increase when extra copies are run off on the printing press, so that the larger the unit for which new materials are being developed, the lower the average cost of the materials.

The potential for realizing economies of size at the inter-national regional level exists in higher education for many of the smaller LDCs. Since only a small proportion of the appropriate age-group acquires higher education in LDCs (from less than 1 per cent in sub-Saharan Africa to about 5 per cent in Latin America), many of these nations cannot afford to offer a full range of subjects at their universities. Indeed, many observers would suggest that several existing universities are not viable. One way to overcome the inadequacies of small national universities is the creation of international regional universities. Either one university could serve an entire region or, what is politically more practical, a set of universities could be co-ordinated, with each specializing in different fields.[3] Such co-operation conserves the scarce resources of highly educated manpower. Furthermore, disciplinary groups become large enough for the cross-fertiliz-ation of ideas to take place. Another advantage is the development of a sense of international co-operation which may stimulate further regional co-operation.

There are both political and physical obstacles to this kind of regional activity. On the political side, nations are frequently disinclined to forego the prestige associated with having a com-prehensive university. This is especially true for newly indepen-dent countries. The other difficulty is that conditions and problems confronting one nation may not closely resemble those facing its neighbours. The legal, medical or agricultural con-ditions may be quite different, even in adjacent countries. Such considerations restrict the possible economies, but do not eliminate them. Regional co-operation can increase productivity markedly. In order to have a degree programme in medicine, for example, a certain number of subjects must be taught, necessitating a certain number of instructors. A given country may only be able to afford medical education for twenty students per year. The productivity of the teachers would be markedly increased if several countries joined together, so that the same teachers would teach, perhaps, eighty students per year. While difficulties do exist, there is considerable potential for achieving economies of size through regional operations in higher education.

In sum there is no doubt that potential for economies of size exists at all levels of the educational system. However, very little research has been undertaken, especially in LDCs, to determine the particular class and institutional sizes which are optimal for any country or educational level. Regrettably, we must end with the somewhat unsatisfactory statement that attempts to achieve economies of size seem to be the correct road to follow, but we do not know exactly how far along that road the best stopping-point is.

Micro-educational planning

A second realm in which productivity is central is that of micro-educational planning. Among the techniques being applied to the planning of the educational industry are cost–benefit analysis, programme planning and budgeting (PPB) and simulation. We shall discuss each of these in turn and then look at some factors which are common to all micro-planning for increased efficiency in education.

De facto, planning of one quality and type or another has always been practised. It might take the form of specifying the budget for the next year or informal discussions on the future of the educational system between those responsible for it and other concerned individuals. However, formal planning is a rather new development in education. The techniques of cost–benefit analysis are indispensable for educational planners, whether they are concerned with macro-planning (matching the total educational system to a country's needs for educated people and its ability to furnish education) or micro-planning (determining the most efficient manner of producing the education needed to achieve given goals). Whatever the change or development being considered, one can specify its costs and make attempts at specifying its benefits. If the benefits do not equal or exceed the costs, then the action is not worth undertaking. Of course, when dealing with education, there are many intangible benefits, and even intangible costs, which complicate cost–benefit analysis, making it, perhaps, more of an art than a science. Nevertheless, cost–benefit analysis can assist in the organization and the rational consideration of the difficult problems posed by education in any country.

Programme planning and budgeting is an approach to decision-making which can be utilized in the drive to attain increased efficiency at every level of the educational ladder.[4] PPB has a dual emphasis. First, it emphasizes the *purpose* of an expenditure rather than that which is purchased *by* the expenditure. Second, PPB puts planning and evaluation within a rational economic framework.

A programme has been defined, in the context of PPB, as 'a group of interdependent, closely related services or activities possessing, or contributing to, a common objective or set of allied objectives; a package of sub-programmes, elements, components, tasks and activities'.[5] Programmes for a university might include, for example, instruction for the Baccalauréat degree, instruction for the Master's degree, research, and extension services to the community. These contrast with traditional budget aggregates, such as salaries, materials and buildings. By specifying costs within a framework of programmes, the real cost of achieving a given end is emphasized. This eases the task of assessing alternate means of achieving an end as well as the cost of expanding existing activities.

The planning and evaluating aspects of PPB are aimed at assuring that the programmes undertaken are intelligent and rational methods of attaining the ends desired. A plan extending over several years provides a temporal framework for the programmes making up the education unit. Evaluation is included to assure the testing of programmes within a plan as to their success in achieving ends and their efficiency therein. Cost–benefit analysis can be used in the evaluating step. Simulation, which is discussed next, can be utilized in both the planning and evaluating aspects of PPB.

Simulation is a technique which is increasingly being used in micro-educational planning. First, a model of the school, university or school system is developed, employing information on the workings of the unit in the past, the experiences of similar units and expectations about the future. This is not as difficult as it may sound; for example, the simulation model for the Arts Faculty of the University of Toronto took only nine man-months to develop. Such a model would consist of a set of relationships between courses, students, teachers, buildings, materials, land, administration and time, which together present a simplified version of the way the unit fits together.

Simulation models of educational systems, when combined with modern high-speed computers, can be utilized to determine the many ramifications of alternate policy actions or expected future developments before they are a reality. This is accomplished by entering the change of policy or expected development under consideration into the model of the unit to be affected and then tracing (simulating) with the computer the unit's hypothetical development over many years. The problem might be to determine the specific resources—buildings, teachers, finance—which will be required to meet a projected enrolment ten years hence. It might be to find the effect of making a given course mandatory for all students, of placing a ceiling of one hundred students on the size of lectures, or of specifying the implications of extending the school day by two hours.

The yield in each case is a picture of the unit in each of several years, which includes the costs, material and financial, of attaining that state. Thus the implications of each of a large number of policy choices over long periods of time are made available for evaluation. In this manner the most efficient alternative may come to the fore. All too often decisions are made with only the effects in the following year in mind. While a decision may seem efficient, or even be efficient, for the time horizon of one year, it may be extremely inefficient over longer periods of time.[6]

It might seem that sophisticated methodology employing computers is inappropriate for developing nations. There is much to suggest that such a view is incorrect. Most governments now have computer service available to them. The educational systems of the less developed nations are typically changing very rapidly—much more rapidly than those of developed nations. Employing traditional administrative methods—making *ad hoc* marginal changes from year to year—can easily lead to extremely inefficient situations. Therefore, any technique which can plot out the effect of major changes over several years has great potential for assisting educational administrators at all levels in their work.

The nature of educational planning differs markedly, depending upon whether the educational system being planned for is to be created or is already in existence. In either case one can employ cost–benefit, PPB and simulation techniques. However, if the planner is brought into the picture after the system, school or programme is established, his potential for creating efficiency is proscribed. If the planner is brought in at the outset, the optimal number and size of schools would be built, thereby realizing the economies of size. But if hundreds of thousands of dollars have been invested on a set of new secondary schools which have been designed without considering the possibility of economies of size, the country's potential for achieving such economies may be lost for many years. In this situation the most efficient way to proceed might be to forego a revamping of the system designed to achieve economies of size (its benefits may be less than the cost of the schools which would have to be abandoned in order to achieve them).

Hindrances to educational efficiency

Two of the most prominent hindrances to educational efficiency and productivity in the less developed nations are the high ratio of student years to the number of graduates and the teacher–salary structure. Neither of these is a problem unique to developing nations, but both are more acute there than in developed countries.

High rates of wastage and repeating are responsible for making the ratio of student years to graduates so high in the less developed nations. *Wastage* can be defined as *the number of students who begin a unit of education* (either a year or course of study) *who do not successfully complete it*. In the 1965–6 school year, in all of Africa, the number that successfully finished the sixth grade (typically the end of primary school) was only

32 per cent of the number which had begun school six years earlier. Assuming that the drop-out rate was constant throughout the course, this implies that thirteen and a half years of education were invested for each graduate of the six-year course. Thus, if wastage were eliminated, the same number of primary school graduates could be educated at less than half the cost. This is not meant to imply that the years of education received by the drop-outs are not part of the positive output of the primary schools. Some students benefit from even a short period of school; however, studies have shown that the average individual requires a minimum of three or four years of education before he will retain functional literacy. This means that for many drop-outs the years in school are a complete educational waste. For many jobs a diploma testifying to the completion of a course of study is required; having attended part of the course will not improve one's chance of attaining the position. Because of such institutional rigidities, the completion of only part of an educational cycle may have no effect on the type of job the student can obtain.

Economic difficulties and low-quality education are the two major causes of wastage. Often students or their families cannot meet tuition fees (even primary school is not always free). Even where no tuition fee is charged, the need for a child's labour at home may force him to drop out. In many cases a child will start school only to have to drop out when other children in his family reach school age, as not all the siblings can be supported in school at once. Other major contributors to the high wastage-rate are low-quality instruction and poor syllabuses. The low-quality instruction is particularly characteristic of the primary level, where it is not uncommon for the teacher to have had no more than a primary education himself. Low-quality teaching can lead to drop-outs due to boredom and frustration. In addition, the syllabuses often have little relevance to the lives, present or future, of the mass of the people. For example, a full term is spent on the geography of Australia and New Zealand in a *new* syllabus in Kenya. Primary syllabuses are often directed to a preparation for secondary school, even though only a small minority of students will be able to undertake education at that level (less than a third of the age-group in Asia, about a quarter of the age-group in Latin America, and only a twentieth of the age-group in Africa).[7] Irrelevant syllabuses also lead to student frustration and wastage.

The methods of reducing wastage are suggested by the specification of the problem's causes. Creating a fund to finance the schooling of hardship cases, improving teacher quality and increasing the relevance of syllabuses would all cut down wastage. Each of these has a cost; these costs must be weighed against the benefits of decreasing wastage and/or improving the educational experience for all students.

The phenomenon of repeating also contributes to the high ratio of student years to the number of graduates from primary and secondary schools: The low quality of much instruction is one factor which leads students to repeat. Another is the intense competition for promotion between levels of education. Typically, only a small proportion of the primary or secondary school graduates are admitted to the next higher level of education. For example, in 1968 in Senegal only 30 per cent of the final year primary students of 1967 found places in the secondary schools. Therefore, many students repeat in an effort to score well enough on examinations to be awarded a place at the next level. The size of the overall repeater problem is illustrated by Kenya, where a sample survey of 5 per cent of all primary schools in 1967 found that 8 per cent of the nation's primary students were repeaters. One method of attacking the problem is to make it more costly for a student to repeat. The rationale for this, giving more individuals a first chance before giving some a second chance, is hard to argue with. Increasing the cost for repeaters would have the dual effect of cutting down on repeating and generating revenue for the schools. With both results, output per public dollar is increased.

The second hindrance to educational efficiency in much of the less developed world is the general method of determining the salaries of teachers. Typically, teachers' salaries are determined by their basic educational qualifications and years of experience. Many developing nations have recently passed through, or are in, a stage of rapid growth of the educational system. Therefore, they have a large proportion of young teachers with little experience. For such a system there is an almost automatic downward trend in productivity as measured by number of students per dollar expenditure, because the cost of teachers rises rapidly as they gain experience. As the growth-rate slows down, the average number of years of experience of teachers will increase. In addition, the qualifications of teachers will undoubtedly continue to improve. Both of these tendencies lead to higher payments per teacher. With salaries, which are the major component of educational cost, increasing, productivity decreases. While it is possible that the better-qualified and more experienced teaching staff will compensate for the higher cost per student by improving the quality of each student's education, this will not help ease the financial problem of the governments. On the other hand, if increased teaching quality leads to lower wastage and repeating rates, productivity as measured by expenditure per graduate would not necessarily fall. While the effects on productivity of this trend are unclear, it is certain that continuation of present policies will lead to a greatly increased burden on government finances.

One direction of action which has been suggested for solving the government's problem is to dissociate salaries in teaching from educational qualifications and experience. A move might be made to either merit pay (payment on the basis either of students' examination results or subjective judgment of teaching quality) or simply a system of payments which yielded an equal salary to all teachers at a given level. Either of these would stop the automatic spiralling of costs per teacher. On the other hand, neither is without its own costs. For example, a merit-pay system tied to examination results would encourage teachers to concentrate on preparation for examinations at the expense of other education; merit pay based on personal evaluations would lay open possibilities for favouritism and corruption; and a uniform-salary schedule would discourage teachers from acquiring more training. Finally, it must be remembered that teachers have considerable political power, due to their number and status. Therefore, innovations made at their expense can have serious political repercussions. A government may or may not be in a position to move towards greater productivity under such circumstances.

Possible radical changes in education for increased efficiency

Having assessed several possible ways to increase efficiency and productivity in education which do not require radical action, let us turn to certain proposals of a more radical nature for major improvements in efficiency which have been proposed and debated in the literature. They are: revising the school year, utilizing new technologies and making education an economic undertaking.

A revision of the school year could effect educational productivity and, potentially, the productivity of the entire economy. At present the school year in most countries lasts from seven to nine months. Consequently, school facilities are not being utilized for between one-quarter and almost one-half the calendar year. In addition, the school day is typically only a small fraction of the total time available. There are several forms which revision of the school year could take. One form would be to make school a year-round activity for children, so that they finish a given course of studies in fewer years. Another would be to institute shifts, so that more than one group of children would utilize the school facilities each day. Still another would be to have two different groups of children attend during the year—perhaps one group the first half and another the second. A different tack would be to institute special courses during the time that is at present not being utilized.

School facilities include buildings, materials and equipment, administrative and service staff, and teachers. When school is not in session, buildings are completely idle, except for any *ad hoc* use to which they may be put from time to time. The same is true of equipment. Any of the above reforms would eliminate the squandering of these resources. While some administrative and service staff have vacations free, others work year-round, although even these undoubtedly have very light work loads during vacations. Those staff people who do not work during school vacations may take other jobs if they are available. However, in the less developed nations, which typically have large-scale unemployment, finding white-collar vacation jobs may be difficult, and working, for example, as a labourer in the harvest may be unacceptable to school personnel. Thus the slack in their time very likely will not be taken up by other productive work.

The remaining educational 'facility' is teachers. Teachers at all levels in developing nations have opportunities to fulfil other tasks during vacation periods. University teachers may

E

undertake research and/or consulting work during the time school is closed. Teachers at the lower education levels often perform leadership tasks during vacations—for example, organizing community development projects, such as erecting a new school, digging a well, or building a road. Both types of teachers perform the tasks enumerated during the school year as well. It is not clear, therefore, that the performance of these non-teaching tasks would suffer markedly if the school year were extended. Since the payment to teachers would most likely have to be increased to compensate teachers for the increased work load, there may not be a direct financial benefit here for the government. However, a saving of the scarce resource of teachers would be achieved. This would free high-level man-power to undertake other productive processes or to increase the size of the educational effort.

The final resource which enters into education is the time of the students. At the lower end of the educational ladder students' time has no productive value, except in the case of pastoralites, whose children can perform useful productive herding tasks even when very young. At higher levels of education, students' time is valuable, since educated people are typically a scarce resource. Therefore, to the extent that students at the secondary and higher levels of education cannot find productive employment during their school vacations, the present system is wasteful of these resources.

In total, the effect of increasing the school year would be to conserve scarce human resources and to increase the productivity of education as measured by the cost per time unit of education, due to the more intensive utilization of the capital —equipment and buildings. Unfortunately, the probability of adoption of this innovation is generally rather low for at least two reasons: a large system like that of education has great inertia and the students and teachers would both probably feel that such changes would threaten their interests.

A second area of change which can lead to increased educational efficiency is the introduction of new technologies which are being developed for education. Some of the most promising technologies are not new in terms of age, but are new in the sense that they have not been adopted in a particular place. Examples of such techniques include educational radio and

television.[8] More recent educational innovations include programmed instruction textbooks, teaching machines and video-
taped lectures. Programmed instruction texts and teaching
machines are usable at every level of education. They are
especially beneficial when the quality of teachers is not high, in
that they are designed to require no inputs other than the
student's attention. Video-taped lectures are also usable in all
levels of education. Taped lectures are not designed to provide
self-contained courses. They do require a teacher on the spot to
interpret and supplement them, but the teacher need not be of
the highest calibre. This is another way of conserving scarce
high-quality teachers. Several projects utilizing taped lectures
include co-ordinated programmes of teacher education in their
use. At the university level taped lectures can make it possible
for small institutions to cover a wide range of subjects which
would otherwise be impossible to offer, in that there are simply
not enough qualified people in many specialized areas to go
around. In effect, taped lectures could be a substitute for the
regional universities that were discussed earlier.

A final area of potential change which could have radical
effects on the efficiency and productivity of the educational systems in less developed nations is that of making education more
of an economic good. The most radical manner of achieving
this is simply to charge full-cost tuition for all levels of education.
At present, effectively no country charges tuition throughout
its system. The main argument against doing this is, of course,
that it would have the effect of strongly reinforcing any class
rigidities that exist in the society. Education would be only for
the most well-to-do. To prevent this, any such programme
would have to include a subsidization mechanism to assure a
wide distribution of education through the class structure. One
might ask, 'Why charge tuition and then subsidize?' Part of the
answer is that not everyone would be subsidized. Those who
could afford it would have to pay. Those unable to pay immediately could be provided with educational loans which
would be repaid after completion of their education. In either
case, the fact that individuals are visibly paying for the education would undoubtedly lead to a greater concern on the part
of the consumers about the quality, relevance and efficiency
of production of the education. In addition, it would make

the choice between work and education a clearer one for the community and the individual. At present it often appears that education is a free good, and an individual would therefore be foolish to turn it down in favour of work. If the youngster or his family had to pay the full cost of the education or the government (local or national) had to vote a subsidy to him, the potential benefits of education relative to its costs could and would be more rationally compared to the benefits and costs of other alternatives, such as work, apprenticeships, on-the-job training and correspondence courses.

Looking more carefully at the suggestion that loans be given to students to finance their education, it is seen that this is not only a method of increasing incentives, but also of providing revenue to the government. As the educational loans are repaid out of earnings which are at least partially attributable to the education the loans were used to finance, a balance between the government's educational expenditures and revenue could be established. All studies of educational expenditure show that individuals receive a high rate of return on their investments, so repayment of loans would not be unduly burdensome. Such a situation could be thought of as one of greater efficiency from the government's point of view, since the net cost to the government per student would be markedly decreased. This is not the only way for governments to generate revenue, but it does have the advantage of tying the payments to the government to those who receive the benefits of the services—that is, those who receive the education pay for it.

A scheme which entailed charging education's full costs would have beneficial effects on the efficiency of the production of education. Attitudes would undoubtedly change. For example, instead of having student riots in Kenya when the university asked students to share rooms, one might expect petitions for such cost-saving innovations. It is often amazing how free a person can be with goods he is not paying for and how stingy the same person can be with goods he does have to pay for.

There are two factors which press towards the production of most goods at the lowest cost: pressures from consumers and competitors. Very little competition exists in the education field. Private schools for general education, private vocational and commercial schools, and correspondence courses are typically available in developing nations. However, all these are at a disadvantage *vis-à-vis* the public schools, due to the difference in financing. The competition between schools would be greatly increased if each student were provided with a voucher good for a given number of dollars and usable at any school instead of being assigned to tuition-free public schools by geographic criteria. New incentive for school administrators and teachers to achieve excellence would be created. While this is theoretically a very attractive innovation, it does not appear to be a politically realistic possibility in the immediate future.

Conclusion

In most less developed nations education is a major sector in both its employment of high-level manpower and its use of general resources. As a consequence, the efficiency with which education is produced is extremely important to their development efforts. We have surveyed some of the problems and potential solutions to them in the field of educational productivity and efficiency. There are no easy solutions. Many of the best minds in the world have been working on the problems of development and the role of education in development, often with little success. All of the suggestions for future activities to improve efficiency have various kinds of costs associated with them. In many cases the immediate costs for programmes which are worth while in the long run are too large for the resources at hand, given the many demands on those resources. In other cases the political costs are high. Only so many reforms affecting the vital interests of the people—money and education are two of the strongest—can be undertaken by a regime in power before they are thrown out of power. As a consequence, schemes to increase efficiency may be deemed politically unfeasible, even though they might seem to be worth while when viewed in isolation. None the less, much room exists for improvements in efficiency in education in developing nations.

Notes

1 We shall usually refer to output per dollar when speaking of productivity.

2 See, for example, Riew, J., 'Economies of Scale in High School Operation', *Review of Economics and Statistics*, August 1966.

3 The University of the West Indies is an example of such co-ordination. Potential for regional co-operation at the intra-national level also exists.

4 For an extensive coverage of PPB in education, see Hartley, H., *Educational Planning–programming–budgeting: a Systems Approach*, Englewood Cliffs, N.J.: Prentice-Hall, 1968.

5 *Ibid.*, 256.

6 See Judy, R., 'Simulations and Rational Resource Allocation in Universities', in OECD, *Efficiency in Resource Utilization in Education*, Paris: OECD, 1969.

7 In 1965. Derived from UNESCO, *Statistical Yearbook, 1967*, Paris: UNESCO, 1968.

8 Studies undertaken in 1965 by the International Institute for Educational Planning showed that such techniques can add to the efficiency of education in less developed nations as well as developed countries, having the potential both for cutting average costs and for conserving on scarce resources: IIEP, *New Educational Media In Action: Case Studies for Planners, II and III*, Paris: IIEP, 1967, and Schramm, Wilbur, *The New Media: Memo to Educational Planners*, Paris: UNESCO-IIEP, 1967. Programmes in fourteen developed and less developed countries are discussed.

five

The process of educational technology: a tool for development

ROBERT A. COX

Two of the purposes of this chapter are to present a formal definition of educational and instructional technology and a rationale for acceptance of that definition. An attempt will also be made to clarify at least some of the confusion surrounding educational technology by comparing it with several other terms. A third purpose is to suggest reasons for considering the process of educational technology as a model which may be of practical value for the planning, implementation and evaluation of educational programmes in less developed nations.

Assumptions and definitions

Before presenting a definition of educational technology, it is important to state several basic assumptions:

a Communication is one of the parent disciplines necessary for an understanding of human behaviour. Man, in fact, may be viewed as a communicating biological system.
b When man utilizes any physical object that is not an element of his own biological system to extend his communication—such as sticks, smoke-signals, films, magnetic-tape recording, radio and television broadcasting, computers, laser beams, satellites and other devices—such devices, or systems combining more than one of such devices, are defined as

communication media. Such media have been described as 'extending media'[1] and as 'extensions of man'.[2]

c It is precisely these 'extensions of man', and particularly the newer electronic media, that have become critically pertinent to the basic educational problems faced by all developing nations, but such newer media considered as panaceas to educational problems have often created as many problems as they have solved. Thus an urgent need exists throughout the developing world to systematically plan, implement, analyse and evaluate the newer educational communications media and methods available to the professional involved in educational development.

Many studies of teaching suggest that communication media can facilitate learning. Teachers, advertisers, artists and researchers selectively and systematically organize media into an almost infinite variety of styles for any kind of environment and for any purposes or goals which they may choose. The more highly developed that a particular society happens to be, the more likely it is that the society will attempt to structure the use of media into learning environments by the application of scientifically derived information processes. This application of scientific processes to man's learning conditions is what has come recently to be called 'educational' or 'instructional technology'.

The American economist J. K. Galbraith, in his book, *The New Industrial State*,[3] makes the point very well in his general definition of technology:

> Technology means the systematic application of scientific or other organized knowledge to practical tasks. Its most important consequence . . . is in forcing the division and subdivision of any such task into its component parts.

Galbraith further emphasizes that '. . . the subdivision of task to accord with areas of unorganized knowledge is not confined to nor has any special relevance to mechanical processes'. Restating this general definition more concisely, one may say that the essence of technology lies in the organization of knowledge for systematic application to specific tasks. Thus, when the technological process is applied to the task of extracting minerals from the earth, it may be called 'mining technology'; technology applied to a certain class of transportation task may be called 'aviation technology'; and when applied to tasks of an educational nature it may be called 'educational technology'.

General tasks are commonly divided into more specific subordinate tasks or elements. In the case of education, contemporary terminology reflects this fact by the use of the terms 'educational technology' and its subordinate term, 'instructional technology'.* These two terms will be used throughout this chapter, but the reader should be aware that he may occasionally encounter several other similar 'technology' terms (for example, 'behavioural technology' and 'media technology') in the literature of development. Frequently such terms are sufficiently misused as to cause serious confusion. G. O. M. Leith has noted:

> Educational technology is the application of scientific knowledge about learning, and the conditions of learning, to improve the effectiveness and efficiency of teaching and training. In the absence of scientifically established principles, educational technology implements techniques of empirical testing to improve learning situations.[4]

Leith further states:

> The difference between educational technology and audio-visual aids to teaching lies in the explicit search for the effective contribution to learning of each of the media and methods of teaching, by themselves or in concert. Thus educational technology is concerned to provide appropriately designed learning situations which, holding in view the objectives of the teaching or training, bring to bear the best means of instruction.[5]

A brief practical test may be helpful in clarifying the foregoing definitions and terminology. Consider the following hypothetical teaching situation:

Basic situation An elementary teacher has developed a concise and relatively simple explanation of the fact that the earth is

* In Europe there is a tendency to delimit the use of 'instructional technology' to industrial and other non-school training environments and methods, but the difference between this usage and that of the author appears to be one of semantics rather than of philosophy.

round rather than flat. He has prepared a simple graphic illustration to aid him in the explanation of this concept to his pupils. The reader is asked now to visualize this basic message ('The earth is round') as it might be transformed by communication media in the following variations on the basic situation:

Variation 1   Teacher (outdoors with his pupils) uses a pointed stick to draw a representation of the earth in the dust or sand to accompany his verbal explanation of the concept—the earth is round.

Variation 2   Teacher (inside school) standing before his pupils draws the same illustration on a blackboard.

Variation 3   Teacher uses a globe or map to further illustrate the basic concept.

Variation 4   Teacher and pupils holding printed sheets or books with the same graphic illustration, but the related verbal explanation is being heard via broadcasts received from a radio in the classroom.

Variation 5   Repeat of Variation 4, but visual and aural message is obtained from a television receiver which the teacher operates in front of the pupils.

Variation 6   Teacher and several pupils clustered around an electronic computer terminal which displays the basic visual illustration and accompanying verbal message.

Other variations using different types of educational media and combinations of media can easily be visualized.

Question   Do the foregoing scenes necessarily demonstrate the application of educational or instructional technology?

Answer   The scenes do not necessarily represent the application of educational or instructional technology; however, several of the scenes may be said to depict 'media technology'. The following general components should be present in any educational project or programme to warrant the use of either of the terms 'educational' or 'instructional technology':

1 Goals and behavioural objectives.
2 Analysis of the characteristics of the learner(s).
3 Organization of the educational, or subject-matter, content.
4 Mediation of the educational content and resources for presentation to and utilization by the learner.

5 Measurement and evaluation of the learner's performance.
6 Feedback among the other components.

The above components are stated in a communications context, which is considered the larger context or discipline within which all teaching and learning may be viewed. The first five components in the above process are not necessarily in their natural sequential order, but they tend to occur in most applications in the approximate sequence presented here. It must be stressed, however, that the sixth, 'feedback', is a continuous sub-process which must occur among the preceding five components. If, as quoted earlier from Galbraith, the most important consequence of technology 'is in forcing the division and subdivision of any such task into its component parts', then in the above process the most important consequence of feedback may lie in facilitating dynamic interrelationships among all of the components of the process. One might say that the process and its essential elements constitute a communications system characterized by continuous feedback.

The distinction between educational technology and instructional technology may be made clearer by comparing their major components:

Educational technology	*Instructional technology*
(Goals or behavioural objectives)	
1 Selecting the functional priorities of the curricula for the nation or geographical regions within that nation. Statement of the classes of skills and other behavioural competencies in terms of regional or national needs (e.g. agriculturalists, book-keepers, machine-operators, carpenters, mechanics, teachers, nurses, etc.).	1 Selection of local curricular priorities in terms of availability of resources and needs of the learners. Specification of behaviours which the pupils are expected to perform at the end of the lesson, unit of study or year's curriculum (e.g. 'On completion of the unit the pupil will be able to dissect a frog and name the bones in its skeletal structure'). Test and analysis of behaviours desired.

Educational technology	*Instructional technology*

(Analysis of the characteristics of the learners)

2 Specification of the present skills and competencies of the pupils within the age-ranges for which the goals are possible. Determination of the special testing that may be prerequisite to validating the total plan's feasibility.	2 Discovering the existing levels of the pupils' knowledge and skills in given areas (for example, in biology, 'Can the pupil identify the bones of a frog?'). Development and administration of appropriate pre-test to determine the best entry point into learning the content and performance required by the terminal behaviour. Consideration of the pupil's learning styles.

(Organization of the educational content or subject-matter)

3 Curriculum review: Analysis of relationships between similar courses of study to determine what revisions are necessary. Up-dating of content where feasible, elimination of obsolescent information and unnecessary skills. Survey of persons at present performing the behaviours for which the pupils are to be taught.	3 Analysis of the content of the particular subject in order to select and organize that which is to be included in the lesson or unit of study. Addition or elimination of inappropriate provision of amounts sufficient for fast, average, and slow pupils, or provision of alternative content, if appropriate, for a group of pupils where great differences exist in pre-entry behaviours.

(Mediating the educational content and resources for presentation to and utilization by the learner)

4 Selection of the educational media which will most efficiently and effectively permit simultaneous teaching and learning of the required	4 Selection of instructional media (i.e. charts, books, films, television, etc.) which are most appropriate for the types and conditions of

skills and knowledge (behaviours) to take place in numerous schools. Economic, political, geographical and social factors must be weighed in relation to the level of priority the educational plan may be accorded by the populace. Decisions to undertake large-scale production of books, films, programmed instruction materials, television or radio courses, etc. Here many factors of indirect influence on national development goals must be examined before adopting new systems or changing old ones.

learning to take place. Preparation of content in sequential steps which allow various presentation styles to be adopted as required by the pupils for achievement of the objectives. Development of reinforcement experiences at appropriate points in the learning sequence. Teacher and pupil preparation of teaching or learning media with locally indigenous materials.

(Measurement and evaluation of the learner's performance)

5 Constant monitoring of the achievement levels of pupils in all of the schools, national (regional or district) evaluation by testing. Surveying the output of personnel with the skills or other behavioural competencies specified by the goals (see point No. 3, above). Comparison with gains (or losses) for similar efforts and expenditures in other districts, regions, or nations. Evaluation should lead to continued revision to increase efficiency of future efforts.

5 Testing for the criterion, i.e. the terminal behaviour (see point No. 1, above). Evaluating the influence of specific parts of the content as presented by the media of instruction to find what may have most (and least) influenced pupil learning (behavioural change). This step may lead to teacher's revision of content or change of media to produce more efficiency and effectiveness in future instruction.

(*Feedback among the other components*)

6 Feedback must occur throughout the components of the process of educational or instructional technology in order to maximize both efficiency and effectiveness and to be certain that the established educational goals or specific behavioural objectives are still valid and, in fact, are being achieved.

Some applications of educational technology

The comparison above describes the idealized model of the process of educational technology. In actual practice many existing development projects which are primarily based on educational technology have shortened the process by assuming, but not guaranteeing, that adequate attention would be given to all of the components. However, over-emphasis on one component (frequently the mediation component) at the expense of appropriate concern for another has often caused serious imbalances to occur in educational development projects. The following are cases in point:

Case 1

Late in 1961, on the small group of islands called American Samoa, the United States Government undertook a massive educational development programme in which broadcast television is used to provide the principal mediating component (the pupils receive televised instruction between 20 and 30 per cent of the school day) for a new school curriculum. The new curriculum is based primarily upon a lock-step method, teaching English, developed by George Pitman, an Australian. This method stresses the necessity of presenting language concepts in an order of 'rational difficulty', which, translated into the Samoan programme, means proceeding in a carefully controlled progression from oral comprehension to reading, dictating exercises, patterned sentence writing and finally, to paragraph composition. (Paragraph composition is not to be reached prior to level 5, i.e. grade 8.) In applying this method, teachers are particularly discouraged from making any alterations in the sequence of subject-matter and materials, since their own weakness in English might render it impossible for them to correct resulting errors. The major objective of the programme is to raise the instructional quality of American Samoan education by effecting a higher level of competency of the teachers and by improving curriculum and methods of instruction. The single most important objective of the curriculum is proficiency in the English language. In aiming towards achievement of this objective, primary education has received the greatest priority for development; secondary education, which was seriously neglected at the outset, has more recently received greater attention. However, adult education remains badly neglected. Few plans for other types of development activities in the American Samoan islands have been initiated, and, outside of tourism, there have been few attempts to exploit the natural resources of that area. As a consequence, and as a part of the island's tradition, a growing number of Samoans travel to Hawaii to seek employment.

After six years of operation, recent estimates indicate that achievement of the project's objectives is progressing at a much slower rate than had been anticipated. Although the results were not statistically significant, the use of the Michigan Test of English Language Proficiency to evaluate student achievement revealed that only 10 per cent of American Samoan students scored at a level of seventy or above, in comparison with 14 per cent in Western Samoa. It is likewise interesting to note that the distribution of test scores of American Samoan students was skewed in such a manner that there was no tail, i.e. few scores existed at the upper end of the distribution. Prohibition of student use of materials to supplement the Pitman sequence could serve to explain this lack of high-level achievement in the distribution, for it discourages students from attempting to explore beyond the prescribed level, methods and materials. The end-result might be a tendency to produce people with a very limited ability to express themselves creatively. So much emphasis to date has been placed on the production of television programmes (more than 200 television lessons per week, of which only a few have been video-taped for use at a later date), and on the development of related materials that several other components of the process of educational technology have been seriously neglected. For example, although dramatic and obvious changes have taken place since the project's inception, there is an insufficient amount of critical evaluation and comparative data to analyse the precise nature and significance of the educational change which occurred. Not until recently was a specialist trained in educational measurement brought on to the staff. Consequently, the effective contribution of the medium of educational television to learning and its exact cost may never be fully calculated, due to the failure to apply a development model which contained an evaluation component. Had the process of educational technology described earlier been employed as the model, short-circuiting of the 'feedback' component would have signalled an early warning of the critical aspects of both the amount and the type of evaluative information required to make adjustments needed among other components of the programme. Another area of neglect which may have serious longer-range consequences is the failure of the project to prepare more than a small number of Samoans to replace the teaching and high-level administrative positions currently held by mainland United States personnel. Although the American Samoa project is attempting to overcome these and other problems, at this point in time it would not appear to be a useful model for adoption in the case of other developing nations.

Case 2

A project which appears to be potentially more successful in the application of educational technology is at present occurring in the Central American country of El Salvador. The Minister of Education initiating the reform had been very favourably impressed by educational television (ETV) in Japan while serving there as his country's Ambassador. Several years ago he initiated a study in depth of El Salvador's educational system, which revealed numerous sources of weakness and wastage within the system. It had become painfully obvious to the Minister and other leaders in El Salvador that it was urgently necessary to provide an educational output more closely congruent with the political, social and economic development requirements of the entire country.

In land mass El Salvador is a small country, and particularly fortunate in that the geographical terrain, though mountainous, lends itself to the economic utilization of a television distribution system. Approximately 97 per cent of the population can be reached by using one centrally located transmitter and two broadcast translators (systems for rebroadcasting signals from the central transmitter) at each end of the country. Thus, from the outset television was considered to be the only medium by which effective widespread change could be obtained in a relatively short time and at a cost which was viable for a nation with its population density, social problems and economic development needs.

Essentially, the national study indicated that the *Plan Básico* (PB) level, which include grades 7 through 9, was in greatest need of expansion and improvement. It was also concluded that the reform of the PB level would facilitate the major expansion and improvement of the total educational system. The study discovered that the qualified teachers available at the PB level were too few in number. Moreover, it was felt that a 'globalization' was critically needed, and that it could be partially accomplished by grouping the teaching of a number of subjects which had been previously distinct courses into three major and integrated areas of study. The three areas include the humanities, science and mathematics, and another area which encompasses physical education, music, art, etc.

Another objective to be incorporated into the reform was the elimination of the use of part-time teachers at the secondary and higher-education levels. It is traditional in Latin America for many teachers to hold positions in more than one school, moving about much like itinerant salesmen. Such positions have long been the bane of quality education in most Latin American countries by exempting such teachers entirely from any type of inservice training and administrative or professional direction from within the school system.

It was quickly recognized as a critical factor that the reform would require the retraining of all the teachers in the system. A year-at-a-time phasing plan was developed whereby all the teachers from one grade level would be retrained in the year preceding the start of televised instruction for that grade. A training centre was established at the same location (San Andréas) as the central television production facility, thus

F

enabling curriculum development, media production and teacher training to be closely integrated. The PB teacher specialized in one of the three new subject areas will henceforth be a full-time teacher in the school to which he is assigned.

In February 1969 the seventh grade began implementation of the televised instruction curriculum on a pilot basis within about twenty-seven schools. In 1970 the entire country's seventh-grade classes received televised instruction while the pilot programme moved into the eighth grade. This year-at-a-time phasing cycle will continue until all grades in the public schools are utilizing ETV. Televised inservice training of teachers will also be initiated, and eventually programmes for literacy and adult education will be offered.

Both short- and long-range plans are constantly being reviewed and revised on the basis of feedback as to the day-to-day progress obtained from teachers by their supervisors.

An evaluation component was begun well before the start of the televised instruction and continues to effectively develop continuous testing and measurement procedures for the feedback of information to the teacher training, curricular and production components of the project.

A number of other studies and physical developments related to the reform were undertaken. These included the design and construction of many new school buildings, the development of production facilities for teaching materials correlated with the televised lessons and the modification and construction of television production and teacher-training facilities adequate to permit the large-scale concentrated effort, which the reform required. Several other governments including Japan, the United States and the United Kingdom, as well as UNESCO, are providing technical and financial assistance to El Salvador in the planning and operation of the project. It is anticipated that the experiences gained in El Salvador may be of great value to other countries which are considering mass-media technology in the expansion and improvement of their educational systems.

Case 3

The preceding examples dealt with the application of technology on a large scale—educational technology as compared to instructional technology. Although narrower in scope, attempts to improve the quality of instruction within a single institution have many of the basic problems of similar regional or country-wide projects. A brief example from Latin America may be useful to consider.

The University of San Carlos in Guatemala is an old and well-established institution which, like most universities, is experiencing growing pains resulting from the 'knowledge explosion' and growing student enrolment. A number of the faculty at San Carlos felt that an injection of new teaching techniques coupled with newer educational media would improve the quality of instruction and also permit more effective teaching to larger numbers of students. Members of the faculty in biological sciences were particularly anxious to establish such a development project, and consequently initiated a series of exchange visits and correspondence between their faculty and the faculty of the University of Pittsburgh. Within eighteen months a proposal was developed, and late in 1968 the Guatemala office of the United States Agency for International Development (AID) agreed to financially support a co-operative development project between the University of San Carlos and the University of Pittsburgh for an initial period of two years.

The detailed plan of the project incorporated all of the components of the instructional technology process as described above. The thrust of the project was aimed at the establishment of an Instructional Materials Centre (IMC), wherein the project's professional staff could assist the San Carlos faculty in the development, preparation, production and evaluation of new instructional media and techniques. Another objective of the IMC was to develop an instructional media resources collection to be used by faculty and project staff for extensive curriculum development within the various departments of the university. An additional specific objective of the project was to bring to San Carlos the appropriate expert consultants whom the faculty could call upon to assist them in revising and improving the teaching/learning effectiveness of their classes. In spite of the care taken in detailing the objectives, the problems which developed during the early implementation of the project made it apparent that they contained an element of ambiguity that the sponsors did not recognize. Apparently, the representatives of the two institutions and AID did not effectively validate the project's objectives with a broad representation of the faculty throughout the host institution, San Carlos. As a consequence there was an insufficient amount of feedback in the development of the project's specific objectives.

The establishment of the IMC was not greeted with the level of enthusiasm anticipated, and its services were seldom requested by the faculty outside of the biological sciences. When the IMC personnel attempted to publicize their services they were always politely received, but the services were not sufficiently utilized to justify the existence of nor the expenditure for the IMC.

Consequently, when the time arrived for the planned expansion of the IMC and the required financial appropriation, there was insufficient faculty support for the project and it was slowly phased out.

The point of the example is that the objectives of a development project are useless, no matter how complete and well articulated they may be, unless they are acceptable to a large enough segment of those in the institution who will be affected by them. Feedback within the institution is an essential component from the beginning of the development of an innovative project, and can serve to force attention on potential problems before they become major deterrents to later components of the project. It is not unfair to say that this was one of the main reasons why the San Carlos/Pittsburgh project never got far enough in its development to demonstrate a level of impact on the institution's faculty which might have ensured its continuance and expansion.

The examples above have examined the use of mass media in educational technology development projects of great current interest. It should be recalled from the descriptive definition of educational technology presented earlier that the process does not depend upon the use of machines or electronic mass media. Paper-and-pencil programmed instruction presents a very important example of the process and offers potential to resolve educational development problems in a wide range of subject areas. Programmed learning can also be combined with any other type of media, ranging from simple graphic illustrations on blackboard, paper or flannel-board, through highly sophisticated simulations via television, teaching machines or computer-assisted instruction for individually prescribed learning experiences.

The potential of programmed instruction was recognized by the workshop conference directed by Komoski and Green in 1963 and 1964 in Africa and the Middle East.[6] Although the results have stimulated some continued programmed instruction activity, no vigorous thrust has been made, due mainly to lack of support on the scale required to produce widespread impact. Perhaps one reason for this lack of continued emphasis grew out of a misunderstanding of the term 'teaching machine', which tended to obscure the true value of programmed instruction.

Hawkridge, while directing the Centre for Programmed Instruction in Rhodesia,[7] reported on a number of commercially produced programmes which had been evaluated and some which were locally developed to train workers in the Zambian copper-mines, as well as other programmes concerned with the usual academic disciplines. The Centre is apparently now defunct, for little has been heard from it since the recent alterations on the Rhodesian political scene.

Probably the greatest contribution of the programmed instruction movement has been to the development of educational technology as a recognized process and specialized area of importance in the field of educational development. For example, such recognition was apparent at the Seminar on Programmed Instruction held in August 1968 at Varna, Bulgaria.[8] The participants in the seminar recommended that it would be more appropriate for future seminars to incorporate the term 'educational technology' into the seminar title rather than the term 'programmed instruction'.

Another noteworthy development in the application of the process of educational technology to future systems of mass education is revealed in the plans of several nations to incorporate the potential of satellite television into their systems. In India several such proposals to this effect, developed by the United States Aeronautics and Space Administration, UNESCO and various other organizations, are under consideration, involving the initiation of pilot projects as early as 1971.[9] Similar experimental projects with communications satellites are being contemplated in the near future in Latin America and Africa.

The potential utilization of computers should also be mentioned, for, although such may be an expensive undertaking, it is probable that the introduction of satellite television will facilitate their extended use. A number of agencies, including the World Bank and UNESCO, have begun to study the potentials and problems associated with the use of computers.* As planning is undertaken for the introduction of sophisticated, advanced educational communications systems, it becomes evident that consideration of the role of educational technology in providing a basic process model is becoming increasingly more important.

Many development projects have in fact probably had to be considered as 'failures' simply because of the lack of even the crudest form of a model for the planning and implementation of innovations. Even 'common sense' appears to have been absent in some cases. For example, the author, on a trip to Africa to study the use of innovative teaching methods and media technology, visited three teacher education institutions in West Africa. All had sophisticated and expensive language laboratories ranging in size from twelve to thirty student positions, yet none of the language laboratories was being used, simply because they had been provided by an outside donor agency who had failed to recognize the consequences of the fact that adequate technical service was unavailable at the location of the institution. Even worse, two of the three installations had never functioned properly, due to improper original installation and failure of the equipment supplier to subsequently correct the errors. The third laboratory has been sporadically usable for about one-fifth of the time since it was installed nearly four years ago. One of the three must now be completely replaced, as the tropical weather has destroyed any possibility of economically repairing it.

It has been suggested that the process of educational technology offers a practical and generally applicable model for projects of educational change. It has a communications bias

* The first UNESCO conference called to investigate the feasibility and applicability of computers in the educational systems of developing nations was held in Paris during March 1970.

which tends to make it particularly relevant to projects in which a major component depends upon the use of electronic communications or media technology. Perhaps there is no one model or process which can effectively accommodate all of the possible variables which are directly related to the specific characteristics of a given geographical region, country or cultural group. However, from the panorama of educational development that can be found in the literature, and from the experiences of the growing body of professionals from many disciplines who have worked throughout the world, some lessons have been learned which appear to have constant relevance. The following list is offered as a guide-line to those who are initiating a broad programme of educational change, or to those who are analysing their previous or current efforts.

Some key lessons from development experience

1 Political support from the highest possible level is usually more important than grass-roots acceptance at the beginning, or at the implementation phase, of a project. The nature of developing countries, and particularly of those with a high level of nationalistic zeal, is such that the politicians and leaders of the country are instrumental in determining the general acceptance of its ideas and programmes. This has been particularly critical in programmes which depend upon broadcast media.
2 Public relations both within the country and without are important to many development projects. There may also be conditions and times when dissemination of information about a planned project should not be widely diffused until other factors have been given adequate consideration. In some instances prematurely rising expectations can be nearly as damaging as unfulfilled promises at the end of the project. The whole area of public relations has sometimes been ignored, to the detriment of well-conceived projects, and it deserves far more attention than is found in the initial plans of many development schemes.
3 Time-schedules must be based upon realistic considerations which involve different time estimations based on a variety of assumptions. It is a well-evidenced fact that unrealistic time-tables have been the hallmark of most unsuccessful development

projects. Such miscalculated time can also destroy what may originally have been well-conceived budget projections for a given project.

4   Experimentation within development projects is, of course, desirable; however, 'experimentation' should not become the label for large-scale operational efforts. A clear distinction should be made between a programme's operational methods and its experimental methods. The danger in not developing such boundaries lies in the possibility of the total project being publicly viewed as merely an 'experiment', and of little practical value.

5   Evaluation by qualified local and 'external' professionals should be considered. The results of such evaluation must feedback throughout the components of the project to become a self-correcting system.

6   Budgetary support for a project must be capable of relating to all central as well as peripheral personnel and physical facilities. It is useless, for example, to provide development funds for a language laboratory, a science laboratory or a new school building if there are no recurrent funds available from the outset of the project for their maintenance and operating costs. Likewise, personnel associated with the secondary or peripheral support activities must be as adequately provided for in the budget as are the primary personnel in the project. This is a frequent problem area which must be given careful attention if the project is to succeed.

7   Educational technology based upon the use of mass media (i.e. radio and television) has been found to be financially feasible only where it has been employed on a relatively large scale, such as with a country-wide project, or on a regional basis involving several countries.

8   Personnel employed for the initial planning phase of a project should be as competent and rigorous in their special disciplines as the personnel hired to work at the operational level. To guarantee the quality of the latter at the expense of the former may build in problems which cannot be overcome during the life of the project.

9   It is a well-documented fact that educational development projects which do not directly involve the teachers affected have had a tendency to fail to achieve their objectives. More than

mere public relations efforts are required where curriculum reform introduces new teaching methods and materials into a traditional school system. Political and social leadership is put to a strong test when attempting to change traditional attitudes about the teaching/learning process, particularly where such attitudes may be linked to a rigid examination system. One would do well to recall Beeby's dilemma when trying to convince a group of Maori chiefs and village elders in New Zealand to accept a new secondary school intended to introduce needed technical courses instead of the classical studies with which they were familiar. One of the chiefs, on learning that the distinguished Australian educator had studied Latin, quickly used the information to reinforce his argument for classical studies by explaining to Beeby, 'And look where you got to!' Beeby noted, 'The proper answer still eludes me.'[10]

The preceding list purports to be neither hierarchical nor exhaustive, but it does contain some of the most relevant lessons drawn from a wide variety of projects based upon modern communication methods and educational media technology. These lessons appear deceptively obvious when distilled to a few words, but the application of the 'obvious' is frequently the most difficult to implement.

Notes

1 Doob, Leonard W., *Communication in Africa: a Search for Boundaries*, New Haven: Yale University Press, 1961, 97–9.

2 McLuhan, Marshall, *Understanding Media*, New York: McGraw-Hill, 1961.

3 Galbraith, J. K., *The New Industrial State*, Boston: Houghton Mifflin Co., 1967, 12.

4 Leith, G. O. M., 'New Media and Methods', in Robinson, John, and Barnes, Neil (ed.), *New Media and Method in Industrial Training*, London: BBC, 1967, 42, 43.

5 *Ibid.*

6 Komoski, Kenneth P., and Green, E. G., *Programmed Instruction in West Africa and the Arab States*, Educational Studies and Documents, No. 52, Paris: UNESCO, 1964.

7 *Newsletter of the Centre for Programmed Instruction*, Salisbury: University of Rhodesia.

8 United Nations Educational, Scientific, and Cultural Organization, *Seminar on Programmed Instruction: Final Report*, Varna, Bulgaria: 19–29 August 1968.

9 Schramm, Wilber, and Nelson, Lyle, *Communication Satellites for Education and Development—the Case of India*. ii, Washington, D.C.: Agency for International Development, August 1968.

10 Beeby, C. E., *The Quality of Education in Developing Countries*, Cambridge, Mass.: Harvard University Press, 1966, 30–1.

six

Alternatives in education

EVERETT H. REIMER

In the summer of 1968 Ivan Illich and the author decided to formalize, through a seminar, a dialogue on education which had been going on, intermittently, for ten years. Both the reasons for this decision and its results after two months of systematic work appear in subsequent paragraphs. While our personal experience of schools is confined to Western Europe, North and South America and parts of Africa, we believe the analysis to have worthwhile validity. Secondary sources suggest that the schools of Communist countries, Japan, Israel and the rest of Asia do not constitute significant exceptions.

Today's school system requires basic reform or replacement for the following reasons:

1   Two-thirds of the world's population cannot be provided education at present unit costs.
2   The school system fails in its attempt to educate most students of the lower class. They drop out before they become literate.
3   The school system also fails in part to educate most of its nominally successful students, stultifying rather than nurturing their lifetime capacity and desire for learning.

The plethora of educational projects and experiments currently being attempted show little promise of making a significant impact on the problems outlined above. In the typical case such projects succeed initially, but, once special support is withdrawn, their influence within the larger system gradually dissipates, leaving no discernible effects upon it. The system rejects them almost in the manner of an organism rejecting a foreign substance. Furthermore, none of these promises economies of the order required to make education universally available in the foreseeable future. Developing nations, on the other hand, show every indication of placing major reliance for the education of their people in the institutional patterns of the wealthier nations. Perhaps the major hope of avoiding this eventuality is not only to demonstrate the economic contradictions involved, but also to illustrate possible hope of discovering fruitful directions for change.

Definition of the school system

The present school system may be defined as the institutional union of four social functions:

1 Custodial care: provision for the safety and well-being of children, adolescents and young adults; to some degree serving *in loco parentis*, and thereby maintaining the dependent status even of persons who are legally adult.
2 Selection for social roles and social status: determining and certifying eligibility for progress within the school system and eventually for employment, for the exercise of certain basic rights of citizenship and for other kinds of social roles and status.
3 Value formation: teaching the socially approved values.
4 Cognitive education.

While these social functions can never be wholly separated, the present form of their institutional union in the school system is largely responsible for the major shortcomings attributed above to this system. Specifically, these functions are given priority in the present system approximately in the order in which they are listed above. The relatively low priority thus accorded to cognitive education accounts in considerable part for the high costs and low student achievement characteristic of most schools.

Conflicts among the listed functions also account, in part, for the unsatisfactory benefit–cost ratios of schools. For example, the way the selection and education functions are now combined makes school a failure experience, and thus a punishment system, for half the students. Most of the other half are forced to adopt educationally sterile forms of answer-getting behaviour in order to avoid the punishment of falling into the left-hand tail of the grade distribution.

Alternatives to the present school system

The discussion of alternatives took three directions:

1 The commercialization of the present functions of the school system, i.e. the marketing of custodial care, selection and certification, indoctrinational and educational services.
2 The redistribution of these functions to non-specialized agencies, e.g., custodial care to the home, selection to employers, indoctrination to religious groups, education to guilds.
3 Radical reform of the present system, i.e. retention of the four functions in one institution, but with a reduction in the conflicts between them and with a higher priority for the educational function.

These directions were explored by making an inventory of specific alternatives actually available.

In order to do this, the clientele for the services of the school system was first divided into four age-groups and three social classes. Then tables like the following were filled out:

Educational services commercially available

		Class		
	Upper	Middle	Lower urban	Lower rural
Age 2–5				
6–12				
13–18				
19				

The contents of a table like the foregoing, filled out as completely as possible, gave an overview of the educational services and materials which households of different social class and geographic location could purchase for members of various ages.

Similar tables were filled out for indoctrination, custodial care and selection, not only for services commercially available but also for those provided by homes, employers, unions and other non-commercial, non-educational institutions.

From these tables the following generalizations could be made:

1   Similar educational experiences are available to upper-class children of pre-school age, to middle-class elementary-school children, and to lower-class high-school children, i.e. there appears to be a lag of about six years from one class level to another in the availability of such educational experiences as trips, music, books or theatre of a given kind.

2   Such selection and certification services as tests, advanced placement and provisional admission are little utilized by the upper class, are seldom at the option of the lower class, and thus serve almost exclusively the upwardly mobile middle class.

3   Individualized services, i.e. tailor-made education, indoctrination and custodial care, are the prerogative of the upper class, the use of mass-produced services characterizes the middle class, while the lower class, which has only marginal access to mass-produced services, has a range of informal educational opportunities which the other classes do not fully share.

4   All of the functions performed by schools are also available independently, and in almost any combination, either commercially or as functions of non-educational institutions, somewhere in the world, if not in any one country.

The results of this exercise suggest the idea of large-scale empirical surveys which would establish the actual availability, from alternate sources, of the services now provided by the school system.

When attention is turned to reform of the school system there is a need to be more specific about what kinds of changes would constitute reform. First, top priority should be given to the cognitive development of the individual. The importance of providing for the general well-being of the young, of selection for social roles and of the transmission of cultural values is recognized. Any change in the school system will have to make provisions for the performance of these functions, but is not uniquely qualified to perform them. Schools are, on the other hand, the only institutions which have ever specialized in the cognitive development of individuals and, at this stage of world history, nothing appears more crucial than to try to provide optimum conditions for the development of all men's minds. Thus, even if it should be determined that schools must continue to give priority to functions other than cognitive development, this would require that other institutional means be developed to achieve the cognitive aims of education.

A basic guide from which norms for reform could be derived seems to be required. The following attempt to define education may not succeed in saying much that is new, but, hopefully, may help develop a vocabulary general enough to accommodate some conflicting views. Note, first of all, that much learning is unplanned. Learning directly from nature is unplanned unless the student is deliberately studying nature. Learning directly from the culture, unless it is research, is also unplanned. Not even all planned learning is education. Learning directed towards the performance of non-learning tasks is better called training. Only planned learning which has future learning as its objective is defined as education. The paradigm can be summarized as follows:

Learning

---

1 Learning
    A   from nature
    B   from culture

2 Planned
    A   for performance (training)
    B   for learning (education)

Education defined as planned learning implies, at least in the case of young children, a two-person relationship between 'teacher' and student. In terms of the commonly held theories of learning, the role of the 'teacher' is to select the learning task, to select the appropriate reinforcement schedule and to supervise the learning process. Since, however, the aim of education is further learning, the best education is that which maximizes lifetime learning. A programme for lifetime learning can be written only piecemeal, and it appears, intuitively, that the later stages of an optimum programme can be written only by the learner himself. One objective of education, therefore, is that the student becomes his own teacher. The timing and other aspects of the procedure by which the 'teacher' role shifts to the student is obviously one of the critical aspects of education.

The content of the educational curriculum can be derived from the goal of maximizing lifetime learning, if it is accepted that all of man's learning tools can be defined as codes, i.e. as ways of encoding sensory inputs. Man's major code is natural language, which, in its oral form, is learned at home. Encipherments of natural language, such as reading and writing, appear to be the next most important learning tools, basically because they provide those who master them with a secondary long-term memory system which is collective as well as individual. At some future date, computer language may become as important as reading and writing, for similar reasons.

Next in importance, after these encipherments, come the major sub-languages of mathematics, the sciences and the arts, and the major meta-languages, such as linguistics, philosophy of science, etc. Finally, along with code learning and encipherment, several value systems bound up with cognitive learning must be effectively transmitted through formal education. One is the set of values attached to coding and encipherment themselves. Another, less easily specified, is that set of values which maintains the right relationships between facts and values.

The preceding paragraphs define, in a very general and preliminary way, the priorities which should govern a reformed school system.

Possibilities for economy in education

One of the problems cited at the outset is that most of the world's population cannot be afforded education at even the lowest cost levels associated with present school systems. It is clear that, regardless of the other reforms, economies in education must be achieved if the world's masses are not to remain 'ignorant', economically and politically impotent, and rapidly increasing in number.

Educational economies must fall into one of the following classes:

1 Reduction in the time required to achieve educational goals.
2 Reduction in the unit costs of inputs required to achieve those goals.
3 Reduction in the inputs per student or, inversely, an increase in the number of students served per unit input.

Under (1), for example, the time required to achieve educational goals can be reduced by:

a Setting fewer or lower educational goals.
b Setting fewer or lower goals for associated custodial care, selection or indoctrination.
c Achieving goals more efficiently.

Setting fewer educational goals implies reducing the curriculum, which is not only possible, but highly desirable on many counts. The typical elementary school-teacher today has six subjects to teach, with from six to twelve learning objectives per subject per semester. With thirty students, if individualized instruction is given more than lip-service, this teacher has at least 1,080 specific learning objectives to achieve per semester, an obviously impossible responsibility as schools are now organized.

Lower educational goals, on the other hand, are not indicated. Goals for the learning of basic codes and encipherments need to be raised to levels which will guarantee use of the skills in question as tools for further learning. This will be feasible only if offsetting economies can be made—if, for example, the number and level of goals for custodial care, selection and indoctrination can be reduced. This would appear to be possible. Students would probably be better off with fewer hours spent in class, in less elaborate space, with fewer tests, gradings and sortings, and with less planned value-teaching, most of which is mutually cancelling in today's school situation.

Re-scheduling of learning tasks offers other great opportunities for achieving educational goals more efficiently, especially if the lifetime of the learner is used as the base for re-scheduling.

G

Adults learn to read, for example, in one-tenth the school-time it takes to teach children, although children might learn as rapidly if one waited until they were ready or else used different techniques at an earlier age.

Incentives for specific achievement also promise great reductions in the time required for learning. Bonuses for learning to read at a given level of skill, payable to teacher, parent or pupil, whoever is responsible for the learning, might work well even in the context of the present school system. Daily reading to very young children might be a means not only of earning such bonuses, but also of sending all children to school literate.

Reduction in unit costs, the second type of economy cited above, can be attained by substituting lower-paid personnel for professionally trained teachers in the performance of non-professional tasks. They can also be obtained by mass-media instruction and by shifting the instructional load from teachers to materials, which are subject to economies of scale.

As an example of the third class of economies listed above, using students as the English Lancastrian System and now again in a version of the English Primary Lancastrian System achieved pupil–teacher ratios of 250, and such ratios are not inconceivable in a modern system free of the defects of the original.

Enough examples have been cited to make clear that educational economies of very great scope are possible. Whether they are also practicable is to ask what sacrifices they entail and whether strategies exist capable of securing their successful adoption.

Outline of strategy variables

In a discussion of strategy, four tasks may be distinguished:

1 Identification of the interests served by the existing school system.

2 Identification of groups whose interests would be served by changes in the present system and of the motives to which an appeal might be made.

3 Identification of relevant beliefs about the present school system.

4 Survey of possible tactics.

In relation to the first task, the present school system serves primarily to ensure the succession of middle-class children to status levels no lower than those of their parents. It relieves middle-class parents of all but routine decisions about the future of their children and also relieves them of partial responsibility for their custody. The older generation are also relieved by this school system of some of the impact of the young upon the political process. Older members of the labour force are also partially protected from the competition of the young. Other examples of the interests of specific population groups served by the present school system might only elaborate the general theme stated above, but this cannot be said for certain until a systematic inventory is made of such population groups and the interests relating them to the school system.

Turning to the second task listed above, positive strategy planning would consist in a similar inventory of such population groups as students, parents, teachers, school administrators, employers, etc., identifying for each which of their interests could be served by replacement or reform of the present school system. The interests of students, as judged by themselves, would be served, for example, by cutting class hours in half or by payment for school attendance and might be served in a variety of other ways. The interests of at least some parents would be served by an increase in the learning rate of their children, by increased enjoyment of school work, etc. Some of the potential interests of taxpayers, employers, etc., are equally easy to identify. The first step in serious, positive strategy planning would be to compile and verify a detailed list of such interest-potentials for the significant population groups.

Task 3 involves another, but parallel, kind of planning concerned with beliefs rather than with the interests of client groups. Most parents, for example, believe that their children learn more as a result of attending school than they actually do. Many employers put more faith in years of schooling as a selection device than is warranted. Most students believe it is harder to learn mathematics or a foreign language than it actually is. A systematic inventory of such beliefs, in relation to their truth value, would suggest another array of tactics comparable to those related to interests.

Task 4 goes beyond research to the interpretation of research results for action planning. Tactics would follow directly from such an array of strategy potentials as are outlined in the preceding paragraphs. To serve the economic and power interests of lower-class parents, for example, one might propose that an educational account be established for each child at birth, from which parents could spend for educational goals and services of their choosing. Such a proposal would also, of course, appeal to the interests of potential purveyors of such goods and services. Offering bonuses for specific learning achievements, assignment of teaching roles to children, expanding the market for direct purchase of professional services by parents from educators, are other examples of tactics which suggest themselves as means of appealing to the specific interests of particular groups.

Outline of future work

In the planning outlined above, obviously, no more has been done than to develop an over-view. The present school system has been defined and the roots of its difficulties have been discovered. It has been demonstrated that various kinds of alternatives to the present system exist. Finally, a systematic strategic and tactical approach to the realization of alternatives has been outlined. It may be equally important to summarize what has not been done. There has been no commitment to a theory of learning, child-development or pedagogy. Also avoided has been any explicit 'world view', i.e. any theory of education derived from values other than that of 'learning' itself. So long as alternatives to the present school system have lower unit costs, serve more people effectively and promise more learning over the lifetime of students, they are acceptable. Furthermore, a variety of alternatives may not only be easier to achieve, but may in the long run result in better education than an 'ideal' solution.

To elaborate and further study alternatives on education over the next two years, the author and his colleagues, through a continuing seminar, plan to do the following:

1 Repeat, more thoroughly, some of the work that has been done. For example, a continued survey of the literature will be undertaken in an effort to get a more complete and documented

listing of the availability, from schools and from alternate sources, of the goods and services now provided by the school system.

2   Carry out the planning outlined above. A systematic analysis will be attempted of the economic, political and status interests associated with the present school system and with possible alternatives to it. A similar analysis will be attempted of the beliefs held concerning the present school system and concerning possible alternatives. These analyses would be based upon the knowledge and judgment of participants in the seminar and upon a survey of the literature.

3   Develop tentative designs and recommendations for empirical studies which would discover, from appropriate population samples, respondents' actual sources of educational goods and services, their knowledge of other sources, their beliefs about and their interest involvements in the present school system and possible alternatives to it.

Such population samples would probably be stratified, not only by age, sex and social class but also by such functional categories as student, parent, teacher, administrator, taxpayer, employer, etc.

4   Extend the analysis of planned and unplanned learning, training, and education. Pursue the idea of expressing educational objectives in terms of codes, encipherments and immediately associated value systems. The concern is not with formal theory, as an end-product, but with guides for the improvement of educational practice.

5   Try to answer systematically such questions as the following:

a   Why does the teacher–classroom–homogeneous student group remain the structural module of the school system?
b   Why do these modules continue to be organized in ranked layers?
c   Why do teachers remain the major direct source of instruction?
d   Why is schooling increasingly regarded as the full-time occupation of youth, over an expanding period of years?
e   Why are schools taking on an increasing number of training functions?
f   Why do employers give increasing weight to schooling?

Such concepts as cultural lag do not adequately explain these phenomena. Rather, the answers may lie in as yet unexplored aspects of the above functional analysis of the school system. It may be, on the other hand, that this analysis will have to be expanded to include additional functions, or otherwise modified or replaced. Again, the reason for working towards a more adequate theory of the school system is not because of any interest in formal theory as such, but because a better understanding of the system will be an effective instrument for orderly change.

6 Try to define and spell out the essential characteristics and implications of a limited number of alternatives to the present school system. Until this is done, only vague assessments of corresponding availabilities, interests and beliefs can be made. This task, however, is as difficult as it is important and no more than limited success can be expected.

7 Develop specific recommendations for research and for legislative, government-administrative, entrepreneurial and political action. It is probably not very profitable to try to guess what the substance of these recommendations might be. Possible examples, most of them already referred to in the preceding text, include:

1 Promotion of schools operated for profit.
2 Transfer of training functions to employers.
3 Educational accounts, e.g. extension of 'GI'-type educational benefits (benefits offered to veterans by the U.S. Government) to the general public and to all levels of schooling.
4 Bonuses paid to individuals for specific educational achievements.
5 Concentration of the teaching of coding and encipherment skills.
6 Transfer of the instructional function from teachers to didactic materials.
7 Institutional separation of custodial care, selection, indoctrination and cognitive education.
8 Taking teachers out of schools and substituting the kind of relationship that exists between doctors and hospitals.

These ideas are not original; neither have they been subjected to critical analysis. One purpose of continuing the seminar is to subject such ideas to the critical scrutiny of persons capable of improving them, rejecting them or substituting others, and also capable of promoting the adoption of those ideas which manage to obtain a reasonable consensus.

Ideas can neither be evaluated nor applied, however, in the summary form in which they are stated above. Everything depends, for example, on the kinds of schools which are run for profit, what they teach, who runs them, how they are promoted and what else is done. A second reason for continuing the seminar is to get such ideas into a shape which makes evaluation and adoption possible. Much depends, also, on whether a set of recommendations constitute merely a list or a coherent pattern. Only a systematic analysis and an integrated set of recommendations has a chance of coping with the problem. It is obviously not possible to make such a set of recommendations on the basis of what has been done to date.

seven

Labour, education and development

MANUEL ZYMELMAN

At the beginning of the twentieth century H. G. Wells remarked that humanity was engaged in a race between education and catastrophe. The events of the last decade bear witness to this race. On the one hand, the developed nations that reaped the fruits of the Industrial Revolution during the nineteenth century and the early part of the twentieth are confronted with an unprecedented increase in the rate of scientific activity and technological progress, with its concomitant rapid changes in the composition and educational requirements of the labour force. On the other hand, the developing nations, late arrivals to the scene of economic bounty, are confronted with the protean task of bridging the gap between the affluent and the needy, a task that requires a basic transformation of the economic structure, a change in the occupational mix of their labour force and educational attainments of the population.

The problems of the developing nations are not, however, identical to those faced by the present developed countries during their industrial revolution. The first phase of the Industrial Revolution was characterized by factories replacing home production and workers becoming appendices to complicated machinery. The process was accompanied by an accelerated pace of urbanization. The urban proletariat was constantly fed by the continuous flow of population from agriculture, who also witnessed an unprecedented technological revolution. During that period skill requirements for the vast majority of the labour force remained low. Moreover, the initial effect of the Industrial Revolution was to replace craftsmanship with semi-skilled labour. Therefore the pressure to provide education was minimal. Secondary and university education was confined to a small élite ordained and destined to govern and hold power. Elementary education, if provided at all for the labouring masses, was promoted by the ruling classes for humanistic reasons, and viewed mainly as a tool for sustaining social balance and social responsibility.

Now the situation is different. Unlike the burden put on developed countries when they were at similar stages of economic development, the present technology and available knowledge demand ever-increasing technical skills and education of the labour force. If a country is to advance economically and participate actively in international trade, it must educate its population. Additionally, international political developments coupled with a popular idea that education is a right rather than a privilege are exerting tremendous pressures on governments to expand educational systems at unprecedented rates.

How can the developing nations respond to the challenge? Should they follow in the footsteps of the now developed countries and labour under the same historical assumptions, or should they strike out into new directions and different forms of education and training? To answer these questions it is useful to analyse employment trends, occupational changes in the labour force, changes in the skill and educational requirements of occupations and the role of education in economic development.

Sectoral employment and economic development

Economic development can be viewed as a continuous shifting and reallocation of resources. Historically the shift has been from agriculture into industry, and thence into services.[1] So consistent has been the direction of the shift that the sectoral distribution of employment has been used widely as an indicator of economic development. For example, the proportion of the labour force engaged in agriculture is highly correlated with many economic development indices, such as literacy, death rates, school-enrolments and so on. For every country for which historical records are available over long periods, they show that the percentage of the labour force engaged in agriculture has fallen over time (see Table 1). A similar conclusion is obtained

Table 1 *Historical trends in the distribution of the labour force by type of economic activity in some countries*

Country	Year	Agriculture	Industry	Service
Great Britain	1881	13	50	37
	1921	7	49	44
	1961	4	49	47
France	1886	51	26	23
	1906	43	30	25
	1957	26	37	37
Italy	1881	57	26	17
	1921	56	24	20
	1961	28	39	33
Japan	1880	82	6	12
	1920	55	17	28
	1961	33	28	39
U.A.R.	1907	71	11	18
	1937	71	10	19
	1960	58	12	30
U.S.A.	1870	53	22	25
	1910	32	31	37
	1960	8	39	53

Sources: LLO Publications

from an analysis of the data for different parts of the world for the years 1950 and 1960 (the only years for which data are available for most countries). If we classify the regions of the world into two groups, developing and developed countries,[2] we can observe the following facts during the decade of the 1950s (see Table 2).

While the absolute numbers of workers engaged in agriculture increased for the world as a whole, the relative distribution shows a decrease *vis-à-vis* the other two sectors. While in the developing countries the absolute number of labourers engaged

Table 2 *The labour force in the less developed group of regions and the more developed group of regions by broad economic sector, 1950 and 1960*

Year and group of regions	Total labour force	Agriculture	Industry	Service
	Absolute numbers in millions			
1950				
Less developed	744	553	71	121
More developed	393	139	127	127
1960				
Less developed	849	615	96	138
More developed	447	130	155	162
	Percentage distribution by sector			
1950				
Less developed	100·0	74·3	9·5	16·2
More developed	100·0	35·5	32·3	32·2
1960				
Less developed	100·0	72·4	11·3	16·3
More developed	100·0	29·1	34·6	36·3

Source: Baum, Samuel, 'The World's Labour Force and Its Industrial Distribution, 1950 and 1960', *International Labour Review*, xcv, No. 1–2, January–February 1967, 99.

in agriculture increased, in the developed countries the absolute number decreased.

At the same time the industrial sector gained relative to the service sector for the world as a whole. Yet in the developing part of the world the percentage of people engaged in services remained the same, while in the developed group the proportion of the labour force engaged in services has had the largest increase.

The trends therefore indicate: (1) a decrease in relative

employment in agriculture for developed and developing nations, (2) an increase in the employment in industry for developed and developing nations, (3) a rapid increase in employment in services in the developed countries and (4) a small increase, or a stationary percentage, of employment in the services sector in the developing nations.[3]

Of course, within these broad sectoral groups there are constant shifts that produce changes in the relative proportions of employment in the different industries comprising these sectors. For example, as manufacturing as a whole develops there is a tendency for the relative share of employment in textiles and food-processing to drop *vis-à-vis* employment in the chemical or electrical machinery industries.

There are two main reasons for these shifts: changes in the consumption patterns of the population related to income increases, and technological progress.

As income goes up, the proportion spent on food and necessities goes down (income elasticity of necessities is less than 1) while the proportion spent on durable goods and services goes up (income elasticity for these goods is higher than 1).

At the same time technological progress demands the introduction of new methods of production to produce increases in productivity. These in turn are based on the development of industries that provide some of the inputs required to increase productivity in other sectors, such as machinery and equipment for processing industries, chemicals and fertilizers for agriculture, better transportation and communications, etc. These two effects, the change in consumption patterns and technological progress, are mutually reinforcing, since the same industries that propel modernization also produce durable consumption goods whose proportion in the consumption budget increases as income rises. The end-result is a further accelerated shift among industries and sectors.

Trends in the occupational changes of the labour force

The relative shift of employment from one sector to another affects the composition of occupations of the labour force because the working force of each industry has its particular occupational structure. For example, most of the labour in agriculture consists of unskilled and semi-skilled labourers, while in industry we find a larger variety of skills, e.g. professional, technical, clerical and blue-collar workers. If there is a relative shift of employment from agriculture to industry, the proportion of farmers and unskilled labourers will go down while the proportion of white-collar occupations will go up.

The process of change in the occupational distribution of the labour force is also reinforced by the ongoing technological change in each industry considered separately. Historically the increase of invested capital per worker, with its consequent increase of productivity, occasioned changes in the occupational composition of the labour force. But the pattern of change was not uniform for all sectors and industries; in some industries the increase of machinery increased the demand for skilled workers, while in others the increase of machinery had the effect of abolishing crafts. Moreover, the effect of modernization varied at different stages of the industrialization process. At the beginning of the industrial revolution the appearance of the factory system and mass production brought about an increased demand for semi-skilled workers whose tasks were to tend an assembly line and to perform repetitive routing operations while at the same time eliminating the demand for some specialized crafts. Later the increase of mechanization demanded higher skills, especially technicians, clerical workers and managers.

Analysis of more recent reliable and detailed data for the years 1950 and 1960 on productivity and occupational distribution in different industries confirms that there is still a direct and unique relationship between the occupational profile of a particular industry and productivity in the same industry.[4] It must be stressed, however, that the nature of the relationship is not the same for each industry. Each seems to have its own pattern of occupational change related to productivity changes. Therefore one cannot generalize from one industry to another, or from one industry to a whole sector. For example, the data show that for the textile industry, as productivity increases the proportion of operatives in the total work force decreases. In contrast, in printing, publishing and allied industries the number of operatives increases as productivity increases. The change in occupation structures is also compounded by technical innovations which cause the abolition of some occupations and the creation of new ones. For example, the welder is slowly replacing the blacksmith, and the tape-recorder the telephone operator, while the numbers of computer programmers, key-punch operators, and space engineers—jobs never in existence before—are increasing constantly.

However, in spite of the uniqueness of the effect of technological progress on the occupational structures of specific industries, the combined effect of the introduction of new production techniques in industry and the relative shift of employment between industries is, in general, to increase the demand for more skilled and better-trained workers, and decrease the demand for the unskilled and uneducated. For example, in the United States the proportion of unskilled labourers in the total labour force decreased from 12·5 per cent in 1900 to 5·5 per cent in 1960, while at the same time the proportion of white-collar workers increased from 17·6 per cent to 43·1 per cent. In the less developed countries of the world in 1960 the proportion of white-collar workers is seldom over 15 per cent, while the unskilled may reach more than 90 per cent of the total labour force (occupational patterns at different levels of productivity for selected countries can be seen in Table 3).

Changes in the skill requirements and educational requirements of occupations

The introduction of technological change also has an effect on the content of occupations. In the recent past, as productivity increased, the required level of theoretical knowledge necessary to perform successfully in a job became higher. Less physical effort and slower reaction time were required of workers for the performance of an occupation. Precision was supplanted by instruments. Whereas before a high degree of skill was synonymous with manual dexterity, the introduction of modern methods of production demanded a better understanding of the principles involved in the production and distribution processes, the skill to control and repair machines and the ability to combine manual and mental work. The complexity of equipment and its high cost imposed a higher responsibility, coupled with the ability to communicate with the written word for continuity of operations and evaluation of results. Finally, the advance of

Table 3 *Occupational structure of the total labour force and output per worker: by country*

	Year	Pro-ductivity US $	0	1	2	3	4–9	Total
U.S.A.	1960	7,080	10·8	8·3	13·3	8·9	58·7	100·0
Canada	1961	5,120	9·7	6·3	12·9	8·9	62·1	100·0
Sweden	1960	3,410	11·6	2·0	8·5	9·5	68·4	100·0
Norway	1960	2,930	8·1	3·2	7·0	7·6	74·2	100·0
France	1961	2,820	9·7	2·0	7·1	9·1	72·2	100·0
U.K.	1961	2,670	8·7	2·7	13·1	9·8	65·8	100·0
Costa Rica	1963	1,090	5·2	1·3	5·2	8·0	80·2	100·0
Greece	1961	890	4·0	0·5	3·6	9·8	82·1	100·0
Peru	1961	740	3·7	1·3	3·3	7·7	84·0	100·0
Japan	1960	730	4·9	2·3	10·4	10·4	71·8	100·0
Portugal	1960	660	2·8	1·3	4·5	6·4	85·0	100·0
Egypt (UAR)	1960	520	3·2	1·1	3·7	8·2	83·9	100·0
Korea (Rep. of)	1962	250	2·4	1·3	2·6	8·3	85·5	100·0
India	1961	160	2·8	0·6	1·6	4·2	90·8	100·0

0 = Professional, technical and related workers
1 = Administrative, executive and managerial workers
2 = Clerical workers
3 = Sales workers
4–9 = All others
Source: Yearbook of Labour Statistics, Geneva: ILO, 1965.

technology required workers to take on additional tasks; first, the ones relating to their immediate occupation and later branching out into quite different ones. This broadening of occupational profiles necessitated more knowledge on the part of employees in each occupation.

All these new requirements for new occupations or modified traditional ones demanded increased education and training. The greater demand for better training and greater knowledge found its expression in the ever-increasing formal educational attainments of workers in different occupations all over the world.

Data on the formal educational attainments of people in different occupations from the years 1950 to 1960—years for which data on education and occupation are available—show that levels in 1960 were in all cases higher than in 1950 (see Table 4).

Table 4 *Percentage distribution of formal years of schooling in selected occupations*

Occupation	Year	Years of schooling		
		0–8	9–12	13+
		United States		
Secretaries	1960	2	72	26
	1950	4	70	26
Postmen	1960	12	70	18
	1950	23	62	15
Plumbers & pipefitters	1960	38	67	5
	1950	46	50	4
Labourers	1960	58	39	3
	1950	69	29	2
		Canada		
Secretaries	1961	5	72	23
	1951	5	77	18
Postmen	1961	39	55	6
	1951	48	48	4
Plumbers & pipefitters	1961	49	47	4
	1951	55	42	3
Labourers	1961	76	23	1
	1951	80	19	1
		United Kingdom		
Secretaries	1961	15	83	2
	1951	29	70	1
Postmen	1961	73	27	
	1951	84	16	
Plumbers & pipefitters	1961	49	51	
	1951	81	24	
Labourers	1961	66	24	
	1951	81	19	

Source: Zymelman, M., *op. cit.*

However, one has to be very careful not to attribute the increase solely to higher demands for formal education due to an upgrading of occupational traits, because this increase is in part the outcome of an 'upward educational drift' produced by social and demographic changes.

As the economy develops there is a change in the structure of the labour force, i.e. there is a tendency towards increasing the proportion of white-collar workers *vis-à-vis* blue-collar workers, and among the blue-collar workers for increasing the proportion of skilled *vis-à-vis* unskilled workers. This change in the composition of the labour force affects the social structure of society, since social class is usually related to occupational membership. Different social classes have different propensities to 'consume' education. ('Consumption of education' is the use of education for other than productive purposes in the economic sense.) When the change in the proportion of the different occupational groups is in the direction of increasing the proportion of those groups with a higher propensity to 'consume' education, there is an overall increase in the demand for formal education even by those who do not enter into the labour force. But the increase in the educational levels of those that do not participate in the labour market puts pressure on their peers that do go into the labour force to acquire at least the same level of formal education, even though the successful performance of their jobs may not actually require so much formal education.

Besides, the new entrants to an occupation, by having usually a higher level of formal education than the existing older members, because there is a trend of increasing the years of compulsory education over time, provide a 'floor' of formal education levels for succeeding entrants. This floor has a tendency to 'drift upwards', since in general employers demand higher formal education levels during times when there are surpluses in the labour market, and are reluctant to lower the educational requirements during labour shortages in the same degree.

Education and development*

The changes that occur in the sectoral composition of output, in the occupational structure of each industry, and in the formal

* Part of this section is based on 'The Relationship between Productivity and the Formal Education of the Labour Force in Manufacturing Industries' (paper prepared for UN Industrial Development Organization, November 1967), by M. Zymelman.

H

educational attainments of workers in occupations as the economy develops give rise to a direct relationship between productivity (production per worker) and the formal educational attainments of the labour force.

Economists have long ago focused on the role of education in economic development. The approaches ranged from a general defence of education as a major force in shaping a desirable society 'prone' to development to the 'precise' econometric measurements of residuals and rates of return to education of the 1950s and 1960s.

The attempts to quantify the role of education in economic growth had a flourishing era, starting with S. G. Strumilin[5] in 1925. On the micro-economic level there were studies trying to relate earnings to years of schooling. The works of Walsh,[6] Friedman and Kusnetz[7] prepared the ground for many other works that appeared in the 1950s and 1960s, such as the works of Schultz,[8] Becker,[9] Blaug,[10] Mincer[11] and many others. The implications that can be derived from these studies for the importance of education to economic development can be summarized as follows:

a Wherever relative earnings reflect the free interplay of market forces—a very 'iffy' proposition—we may expect that a higher education,[12] with its corresponding higher earnings, reflects higher productivity from the national point of view.

b Rates of return from investment in education, however measured, compare favourably with rates of return from other types of investment.

Conclusions to the effect that education is responsible for a large proportion of the rate of economic growth were also provided from other quarters.

The appearance of 'The Residual' in a flourishing economic literature, based on the works of Abramowitz,[13] Solow,[14] Aukurst[15] and Kendrick,[16] promoted economists to try to label the residual, hitherto known as 'the measure of our ignorance',[17] and lay claim to it. The attempts ranged from making estimates of the contribution of everything, including education, to physical production,[18] to attributing the unexplained rise in productivity to such esoteric influences as 'Learning by Doing'[19] and the Horndal Effect.[20]

Another tack, trying to relate education and national income *per capita*, was attempted mostly in order to determine relationships needed for planning purposes. Many of these planning models[21] assume fixed coefficients between manpower and income, and manpower categories are defined according to educational attainments, thus providing fixed coefficients between income and different educational levels.

Others embarked directly to find the relationship between income and education. In general, the approach consisted of correlating income with current or lagged levels of educational activity on an inter-temporal[22] or on an inter-country comparison basis. In the latter type of study the authors try to find a relationship between stages of development and enrolments in primary, secondary and university levels. (These are, presumably, proxies for education.)

Harbison and Myers,[23] for example, report good correlation coefficients between GNP/*capita* and different levels of enrolments. Lewis[24] found relationships between secondary education and development. Peaslee[25] found that a threshold of 10 per cent of primary-school enrolments, as a proportion of total population, is needed to achieve any 'significant' rate of growth. Kaser[26] tried to relate levels and growth rates of national product *per capita* to quantity and quality of education.

McClelland[27] investigated the relationship between levels of development and the educated stock, and also between the achievement level with higher levels of education. The introduction of lags in the analysis by Curle, Anderson and Bowman, and Kaser[28] was an attempt to relate enrolments and expenditures of education of one period to increased rate of growth or income *per capita* of a later period.

All of these studies and similar ones relating expenditures of education and economic growth[29] show a relationship between increases in educational expenditures or enrolments and economic growth.

Economists, educationists and politicians have used this statistical relationship as supporting evidence for policies designed to increase expenditures in formal education in developing and developed countries. This relationship, however, does not imply causality. Formal educational attainments of the labour force may be only a dependent variable. The independent agents in this process are the occupational structure of the labour force and education of workers in specific occupations.

A statistical analysis of all relevant variables—education, occupation, and productivity of a large sample of industries in different countries[30]—reveals that, although there is a positive correlation between education of the labour force and the productivity of an industry, this relationship is due more to the occupational structure of the labour force rather than to the formal educational attainments of workers in the different occupations.

For example, productivity in a given industry located in country A is higher than productivity of the same industry in country B because in country A the labour force has a higher occupational mix—a higher percentage of skilled workers—and probably more modern equipment than country B, and not because skilled workers in country A have more formal education than skilled workers in country B.

It is the variation in the proportion of specific occupations in the total labour force rather than the variation in the years of schooling of the same occupations that is the major determinant in the variation of productivity.

A corollary of these findings is that an increase of productivity in a given industry does not come about by increasing the amount of education in general, but rather by increasing the proportion of those workers with a specific type of higher education. If, for example, we provide more education for salesmen it will probably not affect the productivity of industries very much, although there will be an upward shift of the educational attainment of the labour force in the industry. Productivity may, however, go up if we increase the proportion of technicians—people with higher educational levels—*vis-à-vis* blue-collar workers.

A comparison of formal educational attainments of workers in specific occupations across countries at different stages of development confirms that, in general, the relationships between formal educational attainments of specific occupations and income *per capita* of different countries is very weak or nonexistent.

The major forces shaping the *formal* educational levels of

education of workers in a given occupation are related to cultural, social and legal norms of the particular country.

In countries where compulsory education ends at the sixth or seventh grade, and in countries where formal vocational schools are not looked upon with favour, the education of most manual workers tends to concentrate around the sixth or seventh year, unless some requisite skills cannot be acquired solely with 'on-the-job training'. In countries where the formal vocational system is highly developed and universally acceptable we find a large proportion of workers with some years of formal education after the minimum legal requirements. In countries where the level of compulsory education is high, even those engaged in menial tasks have a relatively high level of formal education. For example, the proportion of those with eight years or less of education working as unskilled labourers in the United States is smaller than the proportion of electricians with eight years or less of education in Argentina. The proportion of those with twelve years and more among semi-skilled labourers in the United States is higher than the proportion of electricians with more than twelve years of education in Yugoslavia.

In analysing the data of formal education by occupation in industrially advanced societies, one is impressed by the diversity of paths through which skills can be acquired and the vast possibilities of substitution and trade-offs between formal education, apprenticeship programmes, on-the-job training, experience and other available forms of skill-acquisition.

Why, then, is the formal educational level the traditional index of the qualifications needed for an occupation, and why do economists and educators, especially the latter, tend to stress formal education and not other important informal ways for acquiring skills? There are probably many reasons for this predilection. Foremost is that little concrete information is available about how people acquire specific skills of a non-professional sort. Second, traditionally too much attention, relatively, has been paid and continues to be paid to the education of professional and technical occupations where the gestation period is relatively long and where the way to become proficient in these types of jobs is singular and generally fairly well defined. The less conspicuous but yet important skilled manual workers, until recently, have drawn much less attention from educators and economists, despite their numbers and their role in production. We should not forget, however, that although the way to become a skilled worker is not clearly delineated, training a craftsman may require years of formal schooling in addition to on-the-job training and work experience. In some cases training may be substituted for schooling and vice versa, and skills appropriate to one occupation may be transferable in varying degrees to other occupations. In short, there are multiple paths of skill acquisition leading to the same objective: the production of an individual who can responsibly meet the requirements of an occupation.

In view of the many alternatives of producing occupations needed for economic development, should the developing nations emulate the more advanced countries by replicating their educational and training institutions?

At present most developed nations are saddled with educational systems that derive from epochs and environments unlike the ones existing today. It cannot be denied that there was a continuous evolution from the times when apprenticeship and informal training provided the only avenues for most occupations, and when the formal school provided a general type of education to enable students to further their education in higher institutions of learning and help them adapt socially to their preconceived role in an élitist society. Unfortunately, the general attitude today is still to consider formal education as general education while relegating formal vocational training to a less desirable type of educational endeavour. This attitude is shared by educators, parents and students alike. The reasons are obvious: general secondary schools have always acted in most countries as a selective mechanism. Those lucky enough to have been selected proceed to universities and other institutes of higher learning to become leaders of industry, government, education, etc. Employers perpetuate the system by choosing those already selected by the educational system in preference to those that may have as much relevant training, but lack the formal credentials. The result is a vicious circle where vocational training becomes less and less prestigeful; its students, in the main, are the rejects of the academic streams, as are the teachers.

This historical burden that is rapidly becoming dysfunctional in the developed countries is especially detrimental in developing nations where conditions of under-development are combined with the dubious effects resulting from unquestioned copying of foreign institutions and where the educational system proceeds independently and unrelated to the developments of the labour markets.

A few examples will clarify this point. There is no doubt that, after many developing nations became independent, there were broad-based political pressures to increase formal education, frequently at the expense of other types of education. Parents raised in a culture where formal education was the only avenue to success logically demand it for their children. Educators and politicians with vested interests and a desire to increase their power and influence play on popular sentiments. Businessmen are happy to shift the burden of selection from their enterprises to the schools. But where existing educational avenues for a limited number of preferred occupations expand faster than the number of jobs available, there is a tendency on the part of graduates to queue and wait for an opportunity, small as it may be, to get the sought-after traditional positions instead of taking a lower-paying job, where most workers have inferior education. We thus find the unfortunate situation of unemployed educated people in societies where education is in short supply.

In some other cases where wage differentials do not reflect market forces an insistence to preserve rigid formal educational requirements transmitted from abroad causes distortions in the supply of people into occupations. For example, in most developing countries we find that there is a greater lack of good technicians rather than a short supply of professionals. The reason for this is simply that the professional commands a much higher wage than a technician, even though the discrepancy in number of years of training required by traditional curricula is not commensurate to the wage differential. A student who reaches the level of a secondary school in a country where secondary schooling is already an élitist prerogative, acts very much rationally when he decides to forge ahead for a professional degree rather than remain a technician.

A similar problem exists when, after providing more years of formal schooling to the new entrants to the labour force, many of the graduates are reluctant to enter occupations where the mean years of schooling is much lower.

In view of the grave problems associated with (*a*) providing education to respond to an increased popular clamour for more general education, (*b*) the changes that must be introduced in the content of training in order to satisfy technological requirements and (*c*) the particular conditions of the labour markets in developing nations, it might be more profitable for these countries to think of new approaches to educational problems rather than to copy the old moulds of the developed countries.

If, for political reasons, a larger proportion of young people are to go into the formal educational system, education will have to broaden its horizons beyond the general education presently offered. It will have to include also elements of occupational education. Formal education will have to reach out from its present academic narrow straits and adapt some of the functions outside academia. It will have to offer a variety of alternatives to those who by their intellectual abilities, interests, background and job opportunities cannot profit from a prolonged general education.

But just the inclusion of vocational curricula in the general school is no panacea for the problem. With a continuous change in the content of jobs, brought about by an accelerated pace of technological progress to which the developing nations have to adjust, there is the necessity to change the content of existing vocational curricula in order to increase theoretical knowledge, intellectual flexibility to adapt to unforeseen changes and transferability of skills of the students.

Most profitable of all, societies should start thinking of education in broader terms. The old forms of elementary, secondary and tertiary education, and the traditional dichotomy between the world of work and the world of school require careful critical examination.

Educational planners who think of education in terms of schools and of the place of work in terms of production, under the assumption that theoretical knowledge is better imparted in formal schools, and work habits, industrial behaviour and acquaintance with specific machinery and tasks are provided better in places of work, might find it useful to combine these separated concepts. We must think of the place of work as an educational institution and view formal schooling partly as a vocational instrument for preparing people for productive occupations.

This marriage is not easy. Employers lack the will and the capacity to transform their productive units to include educational functions. Educators are zealously defending their role as the sole purveyors of knowledge. But it will surely pay to think in terms of new structures, regardless of the political risks involved and existing vested interest. We dare not perpetuate known failures or limited successes.

What kind of institution can effectively combine productive units with education, their effect on the whole social fabric of society, and on the whole pattern of development are questions whose answers can only be left to a bold imagination. Nevertheless, the possible social and economic benefits of novel approaches in this area, if successful, are too large to be ignored. In the developing countries, where the pace of change is outrunning the ability of existing institutions to adapt to new realities, there appears to be little choice.

Notes

1 For the sake of simplicity, we shall use only three major sectors: agriculture, comprising agriculture, forestry, hunting and fishing; industry, comprising mining and quarrying, construction, electricity, gas and water and manufacturing; and services, consisting of commerce, transport, storage and communication, and other public and private services.

2 The developed group comprises North America, Europe, the U.S.S.R., Southern Africa, Japan, Australia, New Zealand and temperate South America. The developing group comprises Africa (excluding Southern Africa), Latin America (excluding temperate Latin America) and Asia (excluding Japan and Melanesia).

3 The high proportion of employment in the service sector in developing nations is of a different character than that of the increasing proportion of employment in services in the developed countries. In the developed nations the shift is a direct consequence of consumption patterns; in the developing nations the service sector is partly residual. Migrants from the rural areas find temporary service jobs in the cities, swelling the ranks of the disguisedly unemployed. The high proportion of employment in the service sector is mostly a reflection of inefficiency

and of atomization of trade and personal services rather than a reflection of the desire of the people for more services.

4 See Zymelman, Manuel, 'Skill Requirements in Manufacturing Industries', *Industrialization and Productivity*, Bulletin 12, New York: UNO, 1968.

5 'The Economic Significance of National Education', reprinted in *The Economics of Education*, Robinson, E. A. G., and Vaizey, John (eds.), New York: St Martin's Press, 1965.

6 Walsh, J. R., 'Capital Concept applied to Man', *Quarterly Journal of Economics*, February 1935.

7 Friedman, Milton, and Kusnetz, Simon, *Income for Independent Professional Practice*, New York: National Bureau of Economic Research, 1946.

8 Schultz, Theodore, *The Economic Value of Education*, Columbia University Press, 1963.

9 Becker, Gary S., *Human Capital*, Princeton University Press, 1965.

10 Blaug, Mark, 'Private and Social Rates of Return to Education', *Manchester School*, September 1965.

11 Mincer, Jacob, 'On the Job Training Costs Returns and Some Implications', *Journal of Political Economy*, Supplement, October 1962.

12 A pernicious side-effect of this plethora of publications was, unwillingly, to submerge many human aspects under the general title of 'education'. The term 'education' became an all-embracing concept in which the meaning of formal and informal education, learning by doing, learning by osmosis from environment, tradition, value, systems, social structure, and so on, became indistinguishable one from another.

13 Abramowitz, M., *Resource and Output Trends in the United States since 1870*, New York: National Bureau of Economic Research, Occasional Research Paper 52, 1956.

14 Solow, Robert, 'Technical Change and the Aggregate Production Function', *Review of Economics and Statistics*, xxxix, August 1957.

15 Aukurst, O., 'Investment and Economic Growth', *Productivity Measurement Review*, February 1959.

16 Kendrick, John W., *Productivity Trends in the United States*, Princeton University Press, NBER, 1961.

17 Abramowitz, M., *ibid.*, 11.

18 See Denison, Edward E., 'Measuring the Contribution of Education (and the Residual) to Economic Growth', in *The Residual Factor and Economic Growth*, Paris: OECD, 1964. Schultz, T. W., 'Capital Formation by Education', *Journal of Political Economy*, December 1960. Griliches, Zvi, 'The Sources of Measured Productivity Growth in U.S. Agriculture, 1940–60', *Journal of Political Economy*, xxxi (4).

19 Arrow, Kenneth, 'Learning by Doing', *Review of Economic Studies*, xxxiv, June 1962.

20 This name was derived from the Steel Mill in Horndal, Sweden. A rising trend in labour productivity was noticed at this particular mill with no new investment. (Commented by Erik Lundberg in *Productibitet och Rontibilitet*, Stockholm, 1961.)

21 Tinbergen, Jan, and Bos, H. C., *Econometric Models of Education*, Paris: OECD, 1965. Correa, H., *The Economics of Human Resources*, Amsterdam: North Holland Publishing Co., 1963. Parnes, Herbert S., *Forecasting Educational Needs for Social and Economic Development*, OECD, 1962.

22 Schultz, T. W., 'Education and Economic Growth', in *Yearbook of the National Society for the Study of Education*, 1961.

23 Harbison, F., and Myers, C. A., *Education, Manpower and Economic Growth*, New York: McGraw-Hill, 1964.

24 Lewis, W. A., 'Secondary Education and Economic Structure', *Social and Economic Studies University of West Indies*, Jamaica, xiii, June 1964.

25 Peaslee, Alexander L., 'Primary School Enrolments and Economic Growth', *Comparative Education Review*, February 1967.

26 Kaser, M. C., 'Education and Economic Progress Experience in Industrialized Market Economies', in Robinson, E. A. G., and Vaizey, John (eds.), *op. cit.*

27 McClelland, David C., 'Does Education Accelerate Economic Growth?', *Economic Development and Cultural Change*, xv, No. 3, April 1966.

28 Curle, A., 'Education, Politics and Development', *Comparative Education Review*, vii (1964). Bowman, M. J., and Anderson, C. A., 'Concerning the Role of Education in Development', in Geertz, C. (ed.), *Old Societies and New States*, The Free Press, 1963. Kaser, M. C., *op. cit.*

29 Edding, F., 'Expenditures on Education Statistics and Comments', in Robinson, E. A. G., and Vaizey, John (eds.), *op. cit.* Blot, Daniel, and Debeauvais, Michel, 'Educational Expenditures in Developing Countries: Some Statistical Aspects', in *Financing of Education for Economic Growth*, Paris: OECD, 1966.

30 See Zymelman, M., *op. cit.*

eight

Population, education and modernization

ROBERT M. BJORK

During the 1940s and 1950s most of the writers who touched on the relation of population to development were content to treat population as a dependent variable. The modernization of the less developed areas would, it was thought, automatically bring birth rates down to rough equivalence with the much-reduced death rates. Something like this had happened in most Western countries as they industrialized, and a similar 'demographic transition' could be sanguinely expected in the under-developed world as progressive economic and social trends took hold. This being so, one could avoid delving very far into such touchy questions as the state of contraceptive technology, policies towards abortion and sterilization and the possibilities of mass educational campaigns in the need for and the use of various birth-limitation methods. William Vogt, long-time President of World Population–Family Planning, met with but scant sympathy in the educated world when he wrote in 1948 that 'unless population increases can be stopped, we might as well give up the struggle'.[1]

During the 1960s much had changed in this regard. Extensive treatment was commonly given to the need to spread birth control, and discussions of the sociological, economic, political and technological dimensions of limiting births were often set forth. In short, there has been a shift in intellectual perspective: population is now perceived by most writers as an independent variable in the analysis of development problems. In company with only a small number of social scientists, Harvey Lieben-stein anticipated in the mid-1950s the need to shift perspective on the relation of population to development. He wrote:

> One cannot argue . . . that [since], on the basis of historical evidence, fertility decline is a consequence of economic development, we need not worry about birth rates. The reason why this approach is fallacious is that the economy might not have experienced sustained development if fertility rates had not declined at some crucial stage during this experience. One need not impute the absence of a barrier simply because the race is of such a nature that the barrier cannot be seen when it is successfully overcome.[2]

The increasing concern with population as a crucial independent variable in the development has led to a number of studies attempting to relate aspects of fertility control to other social conditions. Some of the factors which have been advanced as being correlated with fertility include degree of urbanization, income *per capita*, religious attitudes, and education.

In the following discussion an attempt is made to summarize, interpret, and synthesize a number of empirical studies and theoretical speculations concerning the relationship of education to fertility. On the educational side of this relationship, con-sideration will be given to such measures as literacy, school years completed, and percentage of school-age people in school. Some attention will also be given to the effects of adult education in the field of birth control. The measures we shall consider on the fertility control side of the question will include crude birth rates (number of babies born per 1,000 population), fertility rates (number of babies born per 1,000 women, 15–45 years old), child–woman ratios (number of children 4 years of age or under per 100 women aged 15–45), contraception use, attitudes con-cerning birth control, and attitudes concerning 'ideal' number of children.

Before turning our attention to more recent findings and speculations in this field, it should be noted that some Western scholars have had much to say on the subject. A number of thinkers have assumed that increasing amounts of education tend to reduce fertility among those groups which are its beneficiaries. For example, Thomas Malthus, writing in the early nineteenth century, was of the opinion that few plans to ameliorate the conditions of the poor had any long-range prospect of success. However, he did entertain a modest hope that education could help the poor by making them more prudent and therefore more cautious in entering into early marriage. Since the provision of adequate education could only be provided by the State, Malthus overcame in this regard his repugnance to the extension of the functions of the State and became dedicated to a system of national education. At one point he displayed some vehemence in his support for public education:

> We have lavished immense sums on the poor, which we
> have every reason to think have constantly tended to
> aggravate their misery. But in their education and in the
> circulation of those important political truths that most
> nearly concern them, which are perhaps the only means in
> our power of really raising their condition, and of making
> them happier men and more peaceable subjects, we have
> been miserably deficient. It is surely a great national
> disgrace that the education of the lower classes of people
> in England should be left merely to a few Sunday schools,
> supported by a subscription from individuals, who can give
> to the course of instruction in them any kind of bias which
> they please. And even the improvement of Sunday schools
> (for, objectionable as they are in some points of view, and
> imperfect in all, I cannot but consider them as an
> improvement) is of very late date.[3]

Malthus' friend and sometime intellectual opponent, David Ricardo, shared with Malthus the idea that an inculcated change of motive could bring about reduced fertility which would allow an improvement in the economic rewards of the great majority of the population. His general position is summarized in this passage:

> The friends of humanity cannot but wish that in all
> countries the labouring classes should have a taste for
> comforts and enjoyments, and that they should be
> stimulated by all legal means in their exertions to procure
> them. There cannot be a better security against a

super-abundant population. In those countries, where the labouring classes have the fewest wants, and are contented with the cheapest food, the people are exposed to the greatest vicissitudes and miseries.[4]

Thus Ricardo felt that any effort, educational or otherwise, which converted, in the minds of labouring people, former luxuries into present necessities would reduce fertility. While Malthus dwelt on the direct effect of education on prudence and economic understanding, Ricardo emphasized the indirect effect of education in whetting the appetite for goods which would make a large family a greater psychological burden and discourage, therefore, the creation of such families. In Ricardo's way of thinking, one might speak, for example, of the 'educational' effect of all modern advertising on fertility.

Some, but by no means all, of the currently available statistical material concerning the relationship between educational levels achieved and fertility seems to bear out Malthus and Ricardo in their belief that education has a depressing effect on fertility. A survey of some of the available data on this subject suggests a division of this particular topic into three areas of interest: (a) the relation of differential fertility to education among various nations; (b) the relation of fertility to education among various regions within nations; and (c) the relation, within nations, of differential fertility to education within particular classes, races and religions.

Education and fertility

According to the available data it appears that those countries which are able to school the great majority of their people for an extended period of time are also the countries with the lowest birth rates. Using literacy-rates as a measure, it is true that virtually all nations of the world which have achieved literacy rates of 85 per cent or above (31 countries) now have birth rates below 20 (with a mean of 18 and a median of 18), while practically all of those nations with a literacy rate below 40 per cent (34 countries) have birth rates above 40 (with a mean of 46 and a median of 46).[5]

Of course, the countries with a high proportion of their

Table 1 *Education, national development and population**

Level of countries by composite index of educational development[1] (country means, medians and ranges generally rounded to whole number)	% of population literate (15 years and over)	Enrolment ratios (circa 1960)				National Income per capita US $ (circa 1965)	% in agriculture	Death rate (circa 1967)	Birth rate (circa 1967)	Population estimate (mid-1968, in millions)	Recent yearly rate of population increase
		1st level unadjusted (ages 5–14)	1st & 2nd levels adjusted (ages 15–19)	2nd level adjusted (ages 15–19)	3rd level unadjusted (ages 20–24)						
Level I.[2] 17 countries. Total pop. = 200 mil.											
Mean	15	22	20	2·7	0·15	94	83	24[a]	48[a]	12	2·3
Median	11	20	18	2·8	0·1	78	85	24[a]	49[a]	8	2·3
Range	3–43	3–49	3–44	0·3–6·2	0·0–0·53	38–188	59–90	19–33	43–53	1–62	1·7–3·0
Level II.[3] 21 countries. Total pop. = 1,225 mil.											
Mean	46	42	45	12·4	1·6	220	65	16	44	58	2·9
Median	43	39	45	11·8	1·6	211	67	15	44	9	3·1
Range	17–82	19–69	21–71	5·3–21·9	0·3–3·8	56–636	53–81	8–27	34–50	2–728	1·8–3·6
Level III.[4] 21 countries. Total pop. = 916 mil.											
Mean	74	62	66	27	4·6	498	52	10	30	44	1·8
Median	84	62	69	26	4·4	509	49	10	32	14	2·2
Range	23–99	24–94	35–89	11–51	2·2–8·9	86–1453	26–85	6–16	13–50	2–523	0·3–3·6

* See p. 123 for sources and for notes.

Level IV.[5] 16 countries. Total pop. = 810 mil.										
Mean	98	93	89	59	11·0	1484	23	9	19	51	1·1
Median	99	70	90	57	9·2	1442	20	9	18	18	1·1
Range	88–100	62–88	70–104	31–95	6·1–33·2	696–2893	5–50	6–12	14–25	3–239	0·5–2·2

Sources: For all population, national income and literacy data: Population Reference Bureau, Population Information for 136 Countries (Washington, D.C., March 1968). For other information: Harbison, Frederick, and Myers, Charles A., Education, Manpower, and Economic Growth, New York: McGraw-Hill, 1964, 45–8.

1 The Level I countries have composite indexes between 0·3 and 7·5, the Level II countries between 10·7 and 31·2, the Level III countries between 33·0 and 73·8, and Level IV countries between 77·1 and 261·3. See p. 124 for a description of the procedure for deriving the index.
2 The Level I countries in ascending order by composite index are: Niger, Ethiopia, Malawi, Somalia, Afghanistan, Saudi Arabia, Tanzania, Ivory Coast, Zambia, Congo (Leopoldville), Liberia, Kenya, Nigeria, Haiti, Senegal, Uganda, Sudan.
3 The Level II countries in ascending order by composite index are: Guatemala, Indonesia, Libya, Burma, Dominican Republic, Bolivia, Tunisia, Iran, China (mainland), Brazil, Colombia, Paraguay, Ghana, Malaysia, Lebanon, Ecuador, Pakistan, Jamaica, Turkey, Peru, Iraq.
4 The Level III countries in ascending order by composite index are: Mexico, Thailand, India, Cuba, Spain, South Africa, Egypt, Portugal, Costa Rica, Venezuela, Greece, Chile, Hungary, Taiwan, South Korea, Italy, Yugoslavia, Poland, Czechoslovakia, Uruguay, Norway.
5 The Level IV countries in ascending order by composite index are: Denmark, Sweden, Argentina, Israel, West Germany, Finland, U.S.S.R., Canada, France, Japan, United Kingdom, Belgium, Netherlands, Australia, New Zealand, United States.
[a] Data available for only eleven of the seventeen countries in Level I for birth and death rates.

population literate are characterized by a number of other, and possibly more significant, attributes which contribute to their relatively low birth rates, e.g. much higher *per capita* production, much greater urbanization, and a greater proportion of middle-class people.

In order to take some account of a variety of educational and other factors related to population, Table 1 presents data on seventy-five countries which are divided into four levels of educational development: Level I, Under-developed; Level II, Partially Developed; Level III, Semi-advanced; and Level IV, Advanced. The criterion for the placement of countries in the four levels was worked out by Harbison and Myers by computing a second level enrolment ratio for each country (percentage of population aged 15–19 in school), which was adjusted for structural differences in secondary and post-secondary school organization arrangements in different countries. This was weighted by one. Unadjusted third-level enrolment ratios (percentage of population aged 20–24 in school) were computed, weighted arbitrarily by 5 and added to the adjusted second-level enrolment ratio to get a composite index of educational development. The four levels were then delimited by this composite index, the arbitrary division being at 10, 32 and 75 on the index. To relate population to the various levels of educational development, birth rates, death rates, total population and recent annual rates of population increase have been added to the Harbison and Myers data. Literacy rates, recent *per capita* national income figures and the percentage of population in agriculture are also included.

It is to be noted that birth rates in Level I countries are high, and do not fall significantly when general educational development reaches Level II accomplishment. There are thirty-eight countries in Level I and II combined; not one of them has a birth rate below 34, and thirty-five have birth rates above 40. When development reaches Level III, there is some decline in the mean and median birth rate (30 and 32 respectively). Among these Level III countries there is great variability of birth rates (range, 13–50). Finally, in Level IV countries the mean and median birth rate drops below 20, and the range of variation is much smaller (14–25). Until Level III is reached there are no countries with low birth rates. The Level III countries with low birth rates are in Eastern or Southern Europe; the high birth rate Level III countries are in Latin America or East or South Asia. The Level IV countries are in Europe or European settled areas, plus Japan.

In order to see the relationship of birth rates to those countries in the Harbison and Myers data where educational advance has been relatively more rapid than urbanization, and also the relation of birth rates to those countries where educational development has been relatively less rapid than urbanization, Table 2 presents data on countries which seem most characterized by such uneven trends. The number of countries in Table 2 number only sixteen out of seventy-five countries in the Harbison and Myers array. The data in this table seem to indicate that, at certain stages of development, educational advances might be more significant than urbanization in depressing fertility.

Contrary to the data found in Table 2, a study of twenty Latin American countries (data from the early 1950s) indicated that educational measures were much less related to reduced fertility when degree of urbanization was controlled than vice versa.[6] The partial correlation of illiteracy and the birth rate dropped from a simple correlation of 0·61 to 0·03 when urbanization was controlled, while partial correlation of urbanization and the birth rate (illiteracy controlled) dropped only from a simple correlation of −0·80 to −0·65. The seeming contradiction between Table 2 and findings of this study is probably accounted for in the following way:

In most under-developed areas of the world, if any degree of fertility decline is to be found, it will be in the cities, even though those cities may for a time be behind or only slightly ahead of rural areas on certain measures of educational development. For example, Singapore, with an illiteracy rate of about 45 per cent, has a much lower crude birth rate (about 27) than the rural Philippines (crude birth rate, 50) with an illiteracy rate of only a little over 25 per cent. Urban Hong Kong, with about the same illiteracy rate as rural Thailand, has a birth rate of about 25 compared to one of about 45 in Thailand. Only when rural literacy (or other measures of educational progress) and economic development are very advanced (as in East Europe) do we perhaps see education more closely related to further

Table 2 *Urbanization, educational development, and birth rates*

Countries (37–55% of population in agriculture) below Level III median composite index of educational development

Country	% in agriculture	% of population over 15 illiterate	Composite index	Birth rate
Venezuela	41	33	47·7	41
Costa Rica	55	15	47·3	45
Portugal	48	38	40·8	21
South Africa	47	68	40·0	46
Spain	49	15	39·6	21
Cuba	42	20	35·5	27
Jamaica	55	18	26·8	40
Ecuador	53	33	24·4	45
Paraguay	54	23	22·2	45
Colombia	54	35	22·6	45
Median	51	28	37·5	45
Mean	49·8	30	34·7	37·1

Countries (37–55% of population in agriculture) above Level III median composite index of educational development

Hungary	53	3	53·9	15
Czechoslovakia	38	3	68·9	15
Uruguay	37	9	69·8	21
Finland	46	1	88·7	17
USSR	50	1	92·9	18
Japan	39	1	111.4	19
Median	46	3	69·8	17·5
Mean	44·2	5	76·3	17·5

Sources: Harbison, Frederick, and Myers, Charles A., *Education, Manpower, and Economic Growth*, New York: McGraw-Hill, 1964, 45–8. Population Reference Bureau, *Population Information for 136 Countries*, Washington, D.C., March 1968.

fertility decline than urbanization. For example, the more rural, but highly educated and economically developed, Japanese population has much lower fertility than the more urban, but much less well-educated, people of Singapore or Kuwait.

In any case, as was pointed out in Table 1, it would appear that general educational advance is not very closely associated with general fertility decline until the level of such advance is well beyond what it is at present in most of Asia, Africa and Latin America. In general, it may be hazarded that in the early and middle phases of development one might expect urbanization to be more associated with a small degree of depressed fertility than modest educational advances. But in relatively developed countries educational gains may be more significant than further urbanization as factors reducing fertility levels to truly low levels. For example, it is clear that for the fifty-year period from 1880 to 1930 almost all European countries were characterized by a close parallel in their declining fertility and declining illiteracy. The parallel was much less clear in these countries in this period between declining fertility and increasing urbanization or increasing industrialization.

For the near future, it would not appear that educational development in the countries of the world with present low enrolment ratios and literacy is likely to have much influence on fertility. It is evident that educational development of a magnitude that would quickly push the less developed countries into advanced Level III or Level IV positions cannot be expected very soon. If some general educational development in the seriously under-developed countries (most of the Level I and II countries) is not likely to affect fertility, the disturbing possibility arises that unless some more direct manner of depressing fertility can be found, many of these countries may never be anything but backward. Without fertility decline at some point, it is clear that development may be halted and reversed.

Fertility and education within various regions and within nations

The relation of education to differential fertility can be looked at from two regional points of view: (1) the degree to which general fertility differences among regions are to be associated with differences in average educational achievement in the whole population of the different regions; and (2) the degree to which regions differ as to the relation of education to differential fertility within them.

In an extensive study of regional differences (by political sub-units) within eleven Latin American countries,[7] it was discovered that the percentage literate in the various regions of the particular countries had a relatively high negative correlation with the child–woman ratio (number of children 4 years of age or under per 100 women aged 15–45) in Nicaragua, Guatemala, Costa Rica, Colombia, Chile and Argentina. In Honduras, Mexico, Panama and Venezuela there was a slight negative correlation, and in Bolivia a positive correlation. Most of the results were in accord with common expectation to find lower fertility in the better-educated regions. However, when partial correlations were computed with the level of urbanization in the regions held constant, it turned out that the high negative correlations in Guatemala and Nicaragua were changed to slight positive correlations in Costa Rica and Colombia and a sharper reduction in Chile. But the high negative correlation in Argentina was unchanged when urbanization was controlled.

Correlations were computed between literacy and the child–woman ratios among the regions in each country with a high level of urbanization and among the regions in each country with a low level of urbanization. High negative correlations were found among urban regions in Argentina, Chile and Guatemala, and moderately high negative correlations in Mexico, Costa Rica and Venezuela; there was a low negative correlation in Nicaragua, but low positive correlations were noted in Panama and Honduras. High or moderately high negative correlations were found among less urban regions in Argentina, Honduras, Chile, Costa Rica and Panama, but moderately high positive correlations were found in Venezuela, Nicaragua, Mexico and Guatemala. Very high positive correlations were found among both urban (0·84) and rural (0·83) regions in Bolivia.

The fact that high negative correlations between literacy and fertility exist in Argentina, whether urbanization was held constant or not, may reinforce the hypothesis that in countries which are quite well developed, both educationally and economically, like Argentina, one might generally find educational advances related to reduced fertility. But in Bolivia, which is under-developed, both educationally and economically, there was a complete absence of such inverse relationship, and, in fact, positive correlations were found. An observation might be hazarded that, as the process of educational development advances, the likelihood of inverse relationships, on a regional basis, between educational indices and fertility increases.

However, even if countries reach educational levels where inverse relationships are noted in both rural and urban regions, it still does not follow that general fertility will have fallen very much, if at all. The birth rate in Costa Rica is still among the world's highest (45) and that of Chile has fallen only to 34·2.

In Japan, about 1950, the agricultural prefecture of Nagano was the prefecture with the highest rate of induced abortion (at that time, Japan's major birth-control technique). Nagano was also the prefecture with the highest proportion of the relevant age group in senior high school and is renowned for the prestige accorded the scholar. It would appear that the reduction in fertility came sooner in Nagano than in other agricultural regions with less emphasis on education.[8]

A study of regional differences in fertility in Spain from 1900 to 1950 indicated that provincial differences within broad regions could be explained to some degree by educational differences (level of literacy). The correlation was −0·457 for provincial differences within regions, but provincial differences across all Spain in 1950 did not correlate highly with literacy.[9] Within regions, urbanization and industrialization measures did not seem to be related to fertility differences. The author concludes that cultural differences between broad regions in Spain seem most significant in explaining fertility differences. However, Spain now has relatively low birth rates in all regions.

Another question of interest relating to regional differences concerns the pattern of differential fertility among the women of different educational achievement in one region compared with this pattern in others. There are data from the 1960 United States Census which indicate some regional comparisons of this sort.[10] In making generalizations about the variation among states as to the degree of differential fertility–education level relationship within them, it should be remembered that all these states would rank high on any world-wide scale of educational and economic development and have generally low fertility. The following observations summarize some of the most interesting facets of this aspect of American regional comparisons:

1   There are only a few states, largely in the West, South-west, and Appalachia, where the fertility of white women with less than eight years of schooling is much above those with eight years.

2   In much of the Middle West and East the fertility of those white women with less than eight years of schooling is about the same or less than that of women with eight years.

3   Non-white women with less than eight years of schooling have higher fertility than those with eight years in nearly all regions except in a few states in the Middle West, but the difference is small everywhere.

4   In the South, Negro women with a college education are much less fertile than Negro women with less than eight years of schooling. This is due in part to the high fertility of the less-educated rural Negro in the South, and in part to the strong motivation of college-educated Southern Negroes to avoid doing anything, such as bearing more than one or two children, which will endanger their precarious economic and social status. In other regions fertility differences between the least-educated Negro women and the college-educated are much less marked than in the South.

5   White women with some college education have slightly higher fertility than high-school graduates in New England and some parts of the Middle West and the Rocky Mountains.

6   In general the regions with the lowest average fertility, the highest degree of urbanization, and the greatest *per capita* income evidence the smallest inverse relationships between education levels and fertility.

The high inverse relationship of schooling and fertility among Negroes in the United States South (1960) compares to the high intra-rural and intra-urban regional correlations which were found in Argentine data of about 1950, using literacy and the child–woman ratio. Both Argentine and American Southern Negro educational levels are fairly advanced by world standards and probably not too dissimilar. When very high educational development has taken place, as in much of the urban, white, non-South United States, then the high inverse relationship between educational levels and fertility seems to decline or become direct.

Education and differential fertility within selected countries and within sub-groups

Data exist concerning the relationship of education to fertility within particular countries, in particular economic classes (within those countries), in rural and urban settings in a number of countries, and in racial or religious groups. After a careful analysis of a sizeable number of these studies, some general observations seem valid.

First, when one considers the differentials in fertility associated with people with no schooling as compared to those with only a few years (one to four or one to six) in elementary school, the studies indicate little or no relation of education to the degree of fertility. Rarely does the difference in the number of children born differ by more than a fraction of a child, and in a surprising number of instances those with no schooling were less fertile than those with a modicum of elementary training. The following observations should make this clear:

1 White women in the United States (1940) with no schooling had the same number of children born per married woman aged 35–39 as did white women with one to four years of schooling. In 1960 those with no schooling had 0·4 more children.[11]

2 Non-white women in the United States (1940) with no schooling had 0·1 fewer children than those with one to four years of schooling. In 1960 those with no schooling had 0·2 more children than those with one to four years of schooling.[12]

3 In Yaukey's Lebanon study (1958–9) illiterate village Moslem couples married before 1929 had 1·54 fewer live births than couples who had at least one member literate, but with less than five years of schooling; illiterate older village Christian couples had 0·26 more live births than couples who had one member literate, but with less than five years of schooling.[13]

4 In the Lebanon study, illiterate city Moslem couples married before 1928 had 0·56 fewer live births than those couples with at least one member literate, but with less than five years of schooling; illiterate older city Christian couples had 1·50 fewer

live births than couples who had at least one member literate, but with less than five years of schooling.[14]

5   In the Lebanon study, illiterate village Moslem couples married after 1928 and interviewed in the village had a lower fertility rate (by 0·18) than village couples with at least one member literate, but with less than five years of school; younger illiterate Christian couples had a higher fertility rate (by 0·50) than couples with at least one member literate, but with less than five years of schooling.[15]

6   In the Lebanon study, illiterate city Moslem couples married after 1928 had a higher fertility rate (by 0·38) than couples with at least one member literate, but with less than five years of schooling; illiterate city Christian couples married after 1928 had a higher fertility rate (by 0·25) than couples with at least one member literate, but with less than five years of schooling.[16]

7   In Puerto Rico data compiled by Stycos (1960) indicated that all Puerto Rican women over 45 with no schooling had 0·525 more births per woman that those with one to four years of schooling; in rural Puerto Rico women over 45 with no schooling had 0·204 more children per woman than those with one to four years of schooling; in urban Puerto Rico women over 45 with no schooling had 0·589 more births per woman than those with one to four years of schooling.[17]

8   In a Taichung, Taiwan, study (1962) those women, 35–39, with no schooling had had 0·5 more children per woman than those with some primary schooling.[18]

9   In a Poona District, India, study (1951) illiterates and those with only a few years of schooling both in city and village were not significantly different as to their fertility patterns.[19]

10   In Godley's study of Puerto Rican birth-order (1962) by women giving birth that year, women with no schooling had a less than 10 per cent higher mean birth-order than those with one to four years of schooling.[20]

11   In a Santiago, Chile, survey (1959) women, 35–50, with no schooling or one year of schooling had had 0·5 more live births than women with two to three years of schooling and 0·7 more children than women with four to five years of schooling.[21]

12   In a rural area (Pro-tharam Amphur) in Thailand (1964), wives, 35–39, with no schooling had 0·1 more children born than those with one to four years of schooling; wives, 40–44, with no

schooling had 0·7 more children born than those with one to four years; wives, 30–34, with no schooling had 0·1 fewer children than those with one to four years.[22]

13 In Tunisia (1964), women, 30–39, whose husbands had primary education had borne 0·2 more children than women whose husbands had had no schooling.[23]

14 In the largely rural Nagpur District of Central India (1962), women with no education and over 45 years old had had 6·5 children, while the figure was 6·8 for those with primary schooling.[24]

Thus only small inverse relationships seem to exist between fertility and the achievement of a small number of years of schooling, and in a few cases the relationship disappears altogether and becomes direct.

Secondly, the level of education which probably has to be reached to reduce fertility sharply when compared with those with little or no education is relatively high (ten to fourteen years of schooling). In other words, in developing areas meaningful reduction in fertility, as related to education, does not occur until people have come close to or exceeded what is a high-school education in the United States. The following observations illustrate this generalization:

1 In Puerto Rico, 1962, only those wives with twelve years or more of school achieved birth-order means which were over 33 per cent lower than wives with no schooling.[25]

2 In Puerto Rico, 1960, the number of live births per married woman over 45 did not fall below 4 until the group with at least one to three years of secondary schooling was reached.[26]

3 In the United States South, 1960, the number of children born per non-white woman, aged 35–44, did not fall below 3·5 until the group with twelve years or more of schooling was reached.[27]

4 In rural Puerto Rico, 1960, the number of live births per married woman over 45 years of age did not fall below 4·4 until that group with twelve or more years of school was reached.[28]

5 In Santiago, Chile, 1959, the number of live births per married woman, aged 35–50, did not fall below 3·1 until the group with nine or more years of schooling was reached. These are urban women, and many had years of fertility left.[29]

6 In Taichung, Taiwan, 1962, among women 35–39 years of

age, the number of live births did not fall below 4·5 until the group with nine years or more of schooling was reached.[30]

Thus, in those nations or groups with relatively high average fertility, education is not associated with meaningful declines until the educational strata with a rather substantial number of school years behind them is reached.

Third, in groups where the small family is well-established and economic development and general educational level is very high, e.g. Sweden (1930s),[31] West Germany (1958),[32] American white Protestants (1960),[33] American white urbanized (1960),[34] Great Britain (1949),[35] it appears that there is a tendency for those with more years of school to have very similar or, in some cases, slightly higher fertility than those with fewer years. Thus, when all classes have achieved a certain high minimal level of schooling and economic well-being (usually in an urban and industrial setting), then all participate in the small family pattern.

From all the data thus far presented in this chapter, it would seem that an increase in the median years of schooling of a population from a low figure (e.g. one to two years) to a somewhat higher figure (e.g. four to five years) is not likely in itself significantly to decrease fertility. It is only in those groups, areas, or countries where the median years of schooling is already fairly high (e.g. six or seven years) that an advance to the educational standards typical in fully developed countries (median years, nine to twelve years) might be in itself a fertility depressant. It is obvious folly to depend on whatever educational advance can be expected in the seriously under-developed countries as a major factor in rapidly bringing about adequate fertility control. For example, if India (which had 40 per cent of its children from 6 to 13 in school about 1960) is to enrol 100 per cent of its children, 6–13, by 1980, places will have to be found for 81,000,000 children. There were only 32,000,000 children in school in 1960.[36] Much the same situation prevails in under-developed and populous countries, such as Pakistan and Indonesia. To achieve levels of education (as measured by median school years completed) which in themselves perhaps inhibit fertility seems quite impossible for such countries in the foreseeable future.

Education and 'idealized' family size

There have been many surveys which have asked such questions as 'What is the ideal number of children you would like to have?' or 'If you were to advise people on the ideal number of children, what would you say?' and so forth. Most of the studies in the high fertility, poorly educated areas have revealed that the average number of children desired or idealized is in range of 3·5 to 5·0. In the developed and highly educated areas the usual figure in Europe is from 2·0 to 3·0, and in the United States, Canada and Australia from 3·0 to 4·0. Some of the data on ideal family size in both developed and under-developed countries have been broken down by the educational level of the respondents. In these studies the differences in preference are small when related to educational level. No differences at all were found in West Germany, 1958, where the 'ideal' number for all respondents was 2·6. In rural Thailand, 1964, those wives with no schooling idealized 4·0 children, while those with five or more years considered 3·4 children 'ideal'.[37] In Taichung, Taiwan, 1962, the number idealized by all wives was 4·0 and 3·9 by husbands. The variation from these figures was small whether the husbands and wives had no schooling or a considerable number of years in school.[38] The same tendency for respondents to specify similar idealized numbers of children regardless of educational level has been noted in Lebanon, 1958–9,[39] Santiago, Chile, 1959,[40] Detroit, 1952.[41]

In general, it does not appear that differences in educational achievement within the same country have much influence on the idealized size of family. However, nations which are more educationally developed do, as a whole, idealize smaller size families than do less developed countries.

The effect of education on family planning attitudes and the use of contraception

We have seen that countries or classes of people with substantially more education do, in fact, have lower fertility. However, it has also been pointed out that idealized family size within countries is little affected by education, although different 'ideal' size families among nations are probably influenced by education levels in the nations. Obviously, within many countries the better educated are having about as many children as they idealize (in a number of cases fewer), while those with little or no education are having substantially more children than they idealize. For example, a survey of 2,500 women (20–39 years of age) was made in 1962 in the city of Taichung, Taiwan. In this survey, women with no schooling wanted about 4·3 children and had had about 5·7; women with some primary schooling wanted about 4·2 children and had had about 5·2; women with a primary-school diploma wanted about 4·2 and had had about 5·3. However, women with eight years or more of schooling wanted only 3·3 children and had had about 3·6. The difference must lie in differential use of birth-control technique as related to educational level.

Some surveys have been conducted in widely scattered parts of the world to determine the attitude of people towards family-planning efforts and their willingness to use conception control. In general, most of the surveys indicate majority approval, and in some cases overwhelmingly so. More education seems, according to these surveys, to incline people towards a slightly stronger position of approval.

When it comes to actual use of birth-control techniques, those with substantial amounts of schooling seem, in most cases, to be much more likely to use some type of birth control than those with little or no education.

Tunisian data are available from the 1964 survey on the use of any method of contraception by level of education of husband and wife, and by the age of the wife. The areas for this information include two: one a coastal area including Bizerte, Beja, Sfax, Monastia, Nabeul and Ariana (these six areas are relatively urban and have a much higher proportion of clerical workers than the interior); the other a poor suburb of Tunis which has a high proportion of unemployed and recent poorly educated migrants from the rural interior. In all cases, the level of education is positively associated with greater use of contraceptive methods. Table 3 presents the findings.

In Puerto Rico, surveys of a group of health-clinic and hospital out-patients and pre-maternal clinic clients were made in 1953–4. The clients were primarily lower-income people, and 888 wives and 322 husbands were interviewed in a stratified

Table 3 *Education and the use of contraceptive methods, Tunisia, 1964*

	Age of wife			
	Less than 25% using	25–29% using	30–34% using	35–39% using
a Coastal areas				
Education of husband:				
None	6	16	13	14
Traditional	18	23	24	23
Primary	16	22	32	24
Higher	35	45	31	55
Education of wife:				
None	11	18	20	19
Some	22	43	38	35
b Poor suburb of Tunis				
Education of husband:				
None	4	5	6	4
Traditional	2	13	9	0
Primary	10	10	34	4
Higher	*	*	*	*
Education of wife:				
None	4	7	9	4
Some	12	41	65	48

Source: Morsa, Jean, 'Tunisia: a Preliminary Analysis', *Background Papers*, International Conference on Family Planning Programmes, Geneva, Switzerland, 23–7 August 1965, 16–18.
* Too few cases.

(by rural-urban, history of contraception, and length of marriage) sample, while an out-patient study interviewed 3,000 (2,667 married females and 304 married males) throughout Puerto Rico. In both surveys people who had more education were much more prone to have used or be using some birth-control method. Results are presented in Table 4.

When these low-income people had achieved as many as nine years of schooling they were very likely to have used or be using birth-control methods. A small amount of schooling (one to

Table 4 *Use of birth-control method, lower income group, Puerto Rico, 1953–4*

Ages	|	Years of education of respondent						
	0		*1–4*		*5–8*		*9+*	
	%	No.	%	No.	%	No.	%	No.
a Stratification sample								
20–29	13·6	8	36·5	22	42·0	25	72·7	33
30–39	32·0	17	44·2	75	54·2	144	76·5	77
40–49	52·9	28	37·5	57	53·2	154	88·0	53
50–59	30·5	32	29·2	46	33·3	60	60·0	30
60+	19·0	61	26·3	106	25·0	48	41·8	12
	0		*1–3*		*4–5*		*6+*	
	%	No.	%	No.	%	No.	%	No.
b Out-patient sample								
15–24	39·5	84	37·5	200	40·8	204	46·7	289
23–34	54·0	159	55·7	355	58·0	347	69·0	289
35+	37·6	260	51·5	348	61·0	289	70·0	137

Source: Hill, Reuben, Stycos, J. Mayone, and Back, Kurt W., *The Family and Population Control*, Chapel Hill, N.C.: University of North Carolina Press, 1959, 165.

four years or one to three years) generally did not seem particularly to increase the incidence of birth-control use over the incidence found among those with no schooling, although the effect of a little schooling did seem significant among young people in the stratification sample.

About 63 per cent of the out-patient sample and 48 per cent of the stratification sample had used or were using mechanical–chemical means (sterilization, condom, diaphragm, jelly–cream-foam); educational achievement was associated with a higher incidence of the use of mechanical–chemical means. However, of those practising birth control at the time of the interview, only about one-quarter were using mechanical–chemical means; the rest were using abstinence, rhythm or withdrawal. Educational achievement seemed to increase the likelihood of the use of rhythm among those who were not using chemical–mechanical birth control, while those with no education were not likely to use abstinence, rhythm or withdrawal.[42]

In a 1962 pilot study of 241 couples in Taichung, Taiwan, with wife aged 25–29, it was found that education was an extremely significant positive factor in the use of some method of family planning. Table 5 illustrates the impressive difference education made in Taichung.

Table 5 *Practice of family planning, Taiwan, 1962*

	Number of couples	Percentage who have practised some form of family planning
Education of husband:		
None	10	0
Some primary	19	16
Completed primary	89	15
Junior school	49	41
Senior level graduate +	74	62
Education of wife:		
None	33	9
Some primary	49	20
Completed primary	85	26
Junior school	50	60
Senior level graduate +	24	71

Source: Freedman, Ronald, 'Changing Fertility in Taiwan', in Greep, Roy O. (ed.), *Human Fertility and Population Problems*, Cambridge, Mass.: Schenkman, 1963, 122.

As in Puerto Rico, it was only among Taichung people who had more than a few years of primary schooling that actual use of family planning methods was widespread.

It would appear that some minimal amount of schooling is imperative if direct birth-control education and contraceptive dispensing programmes are to have much success. It is true that current programmes are having some success in relatively well-

K

educated South Korea,[43] Taiwan,[44] Hong Kong,[45] Singapore,[46] Puerto Rico,[47] Chile[48] and Ceylon,[49] while little evidence of success is evident in the largely illiterate populations of India,[50] Pakistan,[51] Egypt,[52] or in most African countries.[53]

In other words, the argument, often heard, that education is the answer to excess fertility is probably not true in the direct sense. In most under-developed countries, a modest improvement in enrolment ratios or in median years of school completed will not, in itself, adequately depress fertility. However, any extensive birth-control education and contraceptive-dispensing programme will probably have success only in those countries and regions where such minimal gains in education have been recorded.

In countries too depressed in educational development adult education related to fertility control has little effect, and the results may not justify the cost. Stycos considered poorly educated Haiti to be an area where family-planning education would probably not justify the cost. He commented:

> When one's general lot in life is determined by vague
> forces extraneous to the individual, and when numbers of
> children are viewed in the same context, there is simply
> no solid foundation on which to build a program of family
> limitation. The only hope lies in raising educational levels
> ... to a certain minimum point at which self-improvement
> seems both possible and desirable. Indeed, it is precisely at
> this point that general programs are most needed and make
> most sense. At one end of the continuum population-
> control programs are impracticable, at the other end largely
> unnecessary.[54]

Thus, modest gains in education in very under-developed areas may contribute to the imperative need to control fertility, but only if these gains are thought of as the necessary foundation for truly extensive, imaginative and forthright programmes of youth and adult birth-control education.

Concluding remarks

From the evidence we have available, it appears that Malthus was much too sanguine when he argued that a few years of education emphasizing prudence and economic understanding might be the major force in resolving the population dilemma. Only in those countries where the vast majority of youth stay in school for a considerable number of years does there appear to be some significant tie between controlled population growth and educational achievement *per se*. Of course, in the countries with controlled population, education is but one of an interrelated set of factors which act to reinforce the small family pattern.

The child in a society with higher educational levels, more urbanization, and greater *per capita* income will, for many reasons, enter the labour force later, and any income he can contribute is less imperative. Parents in the more developed societies often can provide for their own old age, and the likelihood of adequate State assistance increases also. Education becomes more relevant to occupation, and in such societies the opportunity costs of a child of any birth-order may become greater, particularly if women can, through education, find remunerative careers outside the family. Also there is likely to be an increased awareness that the occupational possibilities of the child are tied to ever-increasing educational demands. Some recent data from Japan seem to illustrate how increasing social development reacts to raise conventional minimums concerning the cost of raising children in the area of education. Two questions in a 1964 survey of 20,000 people in a random sample of the Japanese population asked about the desired size of family and also about the educational level desired by people for their children. Table 6 presents results of this survey (16,698 responses). Comparing these results with earlier surveys (1951 for desired number of children and 1960 for level of education desired for children), we see that people are rapidly upgrading their wishes for their children's education and also are desirous of much smaller families than formerly. Of course, Japan has moved to a very high rank on any index of social development.

Concerning the pleasures of child-rearing, an urbanized and educated population probably finds a greater range of competing pleasures. Also, the drag of cultural tradition and biological ignorance on the actualization of motives to limit births is surely less in the well-educated societies.

Most of these interrelated conditions characteristic of

Table 6 *Number of children desired and level of education desired for children, Japanese surveys, 1951, 1960, 1964*

	Desired no. of children (%)				
	0	1–2	3	4	5 or more
1951	1	1	51	24	15
1964	5	27	53	11	4

	Level of education desired (%)				
	Junior high	Senior high	2 years college	Univer-sity	Don't know
1960 survey (boys)	9	41	0	38	12
1960 survey (girls)	17	57	0	13	13
1964 survey (boys)	1	28	6	56	9
1964 survey (girls)	4	58	15	14	9

Source: Japan Information Service, *Japan Report*, ii, 15 February 1965, 3.

developed countries are present to only a moderate degree in partially developed countries, and almost totally absent in the most backward societies. Educational advance of the kind which can reasonably be projected in most developing countries must be seen as a kind of lever which will help women to see more clearly that children are now more likely to live, to comprehend the simple but basic facts of reproduction and contraception, and to be more open to viewpoints and values which proclaim the virtue of the two- or three-child family and the use of contraception. Compared with what happened in their own histories, the developed countries have helped to bring the mortality levels of the under-developed countries down at an artificially accelerated rate. They must now try to help match that performance in the realm of birth rates.

Notes

1 Vogt, William, *Road to Survival*, New York: William Sloane, 1948, 279.
2 Liebenstein, Harvey, *Economic Backwardness and Economic Growth*,

New York: Wiley, 1963, 168–9. The original edition was published by Wiley in 1957.

3 Malthus, Thomas Robert, *On Population*, New York: Modern Library, 1960, 541.

4 Ricardo, David, *On the Principles of Political Economy and Taxation*, 2nd ed., v, 95. Quoted in Haney, Lewis A., *History of Economic Thought*, New York: Macmillan, 1949, 301.

5 For literacy rates this information is based on: Russett, Bruce M., et al., *World Handbook of Political and Social Indicators*, New Haven: Yale University Press, 1964, 222–4. For birth rates: Population Reference Bureau, *Population Information for 137 Countries*, Washington, D.C., April 1969.

6 This material has been made available by Professor J. Mayone Stycos, Director of the International Population Program at Cornell University.

7 *Ibid.*

8 Dore, R. P., 'Japanese Rural Fertility: Some Social and Economic Factors', *Population Studies*, vii (July 1953), 79.

9 Leasure, William J., 'Factors involved in the Decline of Fertility in Spain, 1900–1950', *Population Studies*, xvi (March 1953), 283.

10 U.S. Bureau of the Census, *U.S. Census of Population*, 1960. *Subject Reports. Women by Number of Children Ever Born*. Final Report, PC (a) – 3A, U.S. Washington, D.C.: Government Printing Office, 1964, Table 50.

11 Population Reference Bureau, 'New Patterns in U.S. Fertility', *Population Bulletin*, xx (September 1964), 127.

12 *Ibid.*

13 Yaukey, David, *Fertility Differences in a Modernizing Country*, Princeton, N.J.: Princeton University Press, 1961, Table III, 35, Table F–10, 175, and Table F–12, 179.

14 *Ibid.*

15 *Ibid.*

16 *Ibid.*

17 Stycos, J. Mayone, 'Education and Fertility in Puerto Rico', paper given at the United Nations World Population Conference, Belgrade, Yugoslavia, 30 August 1965 to 10 September 1965, 5.

18 Berelson, Bernard, and Freedman, Ronald, 'A Study in Fertility Control', *Scientific American*, 210 (May 1964), 34.

19 Dandekar, V. M., and Dandekar, Kumudini, *Survey of Fertility and Mortality in Poona District*, Poona, India: Gokhale Institute of Politics and Economics, 1953, 65.

20 Godley, Frank, 'Fertility and Education Attainment in Puerto Rico', paper presented to Population Association of America Meetings, 23 April 1965, Chicago, Illinois, Tables 3 and 5.

21 Tabah, Leon, and Samuel, Raul, 'Preliminary Findings of a Survey on Fertility and Attitudes toward Family Formation in Santiago, Chile', in Kiser, Clyde V. (ed.), *Research in Family Planning*, Princeton, N.J.: Princeton University Press, 1962, 282.

22 Hawley, Amos H., and Prachuabmoh, Visid, 'Family Growth and Family Planning in a Rural District of Thailand', *Background Papers*, International Conference on Family Planning Programmes, Geneva, Switzerland, 23–7 August 1965, 11.

23 Morsa, Jean, 'Tunisia: a Preliminary Analysis', *Background Papers*, International Conference on Family Planning Programmes, Geneva, Switzerland, 23–7 August 1965, 3, 12.

24 Driver, Edwin D., *Differential Fertility in Central India*, Princeton, N.J.: Princeton University Press, 1963, 101.

25 Godley, *op. cit.*

26 Stycos, *op. cit.*

27 U.S. Bureau of the Census, *U.S. Census of Population*, 1960. *Subject Reports. Women by Number of Children Ever Born*, *op. cit.*, Tables 26 and 27.

28 Stycos, *op. cit.*

29 Tabah and Samuel, *op. cit.*

30 Berelson and Freedman, *op. cit.*

31 Edin, Karl Avid, and Hutchinson, Edward P., *Studies of Differential Fertility in Sweden*, London: P. S. King & Son, 1935, 78.

32 Freedman, Ronald, Baumert, Gerhard, and Bolte, Martin, 'Expected Family Size and Family Size Values in West Germany', *Population Studies*, xiii (November 1959), 145.

33 Population Reference Bureau, 'New Patterns in U.S. Fertility', *op. cit.*

34 Freedman, Ronald, and Slesinger, Doris P., 'Fertility Differentials for the Indigenous Non-farm Population of the United States', *Population Studies*, xv (November 1961), 1970.

35 Berent, Jerzy, 'Fertility and Social Mobility', *Population Studies*, v (March 1952), 252.

36 Miner, J., and Solomon, E. S., 'Implications of Population Trends for First-level Educational Programmes', United Nations, Asian Population Conference, New Delhi, India, December 1963.

37 Hawley and Prachuabmoh, *op. cit.*, 11.

38 Freedman, Ronald, 'Changing Fertility in Taiwan', in Greep, Roy O. (ed.), *Human Fertility and Population Problems*, Cambridge, Mass.: Schenkman Pub. Co., 1963, 122.

39 Yaukey, *op. cit.*, 65–75.

40 Tabah and Samuel, *op. cit.*, 293.

41 Hawley and Prachuabmoh, *op. cit.*, 19.

42 Hill, Reuben, Stycos, J. Mayone, and Back, Kurt W., *The Family and Population Control*, Chapel Hill, N.C.: University of North Carolina Press, 1959, 159–70.

43 Cha, Youn Keun, 'Development of the Korean National Family Planning Program', *Background Papers*, International Conference on Family Planning Programmes, Geneva, Switzerland, 23–7 August 1965, 6. Also see Kim, Taek Il, 'South Korea: Enlightened Leadership and Enlightened Parents', in Berelson, Bernard (ed.), *Family-planning Programs: an International Study*, New York: Basic Books, 1969, 26–34.

44 Hsu, T. C., and Chow, L. P., 'Family Planning Health Program in Taiwan', *Background Papers*, International Conference on Family Planning Programmes, Geneva, Switzerland, 23–7 August 1965, 3–9.

45 Chun, Daphne, 'Experience with Family Planning Program—Achievements and Problems, Hong Kong', *Background Papers*, International Conference on Family Planning Programmes, Geneva, Switzerland, 23–7 August 1965, Table 1.

46 Lim, Maggie, 'Malaysia-Singapore', *Background Papers*, International Conference on Family Planning Programmes, Geneva, Switzerland, 23–7 August 1965. Also see Kanagaratum, K., 'Singapore: Meeting the Test', in Berelson, *op. cit.*, 53–66.

47 Kantner, John F., and Stycos, J. Mayone, 'A Non-clinical Approach to Contraception', in Kiser, Clyde V. (ed.), *Research in Family Planning*, *op. cit.*, 589. Also see Torres, Antonio, 'Puerto Rico: Achievement in the Northeast', in Berelson (ed.), *op. cit.*, 114–22.

48 Romero, Hernan, 'Experience with the Family Planning Programme in Chile: Achievements and Problems', *Background Papers*, International Conference on Family Planning Programmes, Geneva, Switzerland, 23–7 August 1965, 2.

49 Kinch, Arne, 'A Preliminary Report from the Sweden-Ceylon Family Planning Pilot Project', in Kiser, Clyde V. (ed.), *Research in Family Planning*, 86.

50 Gopalaswami, R. A., 'Family Planning: Outlook for Government Action in India', in Kiser, Clyde V. (ed.), *Research in Family Planning*, *op. cit.*, 73. Also see Bhatia, Dipak, 'India: a Gigantic Task', in Berelson (ed.), *op. cit.*, 67–80.

51 Adil, Enver, 'Experience with the Family Planning Programme in Pakistan–Achievements and Problems', *Background Papers*, International Conference on Family Planning Programmes, Geneva, Switzerland, 23–7 August 1965, 5. Also see Adil, Enver, 'Pakistan: a Large Effort in a Large Nation', in Berelson (ed.), *op. cit.*, 81–91.

52 Husein, Hasan M., 'Experience with Family Planning Programme in the U.A.R.—Achievements and Problems', *Background Papers*, International Conference on Family Planning Programmes, Geneva, Switzerland, 23–7 August 1965, 4.

53 Caldwell, John C., 'Experience with Family Planning Programmes: Achievements and Problems—Africa', *Background Papers*, International Conference on Family Planning Programmes, Geneva, Switzerland, 23–7 August 1965, 5–13.

54 Stycos, J. Mayone, 'Experiments in Social Change: the Caribbean Fertility Studies', in Kiser, Clyde V. (ed.), *Research in Family Planning*, 316.

nine

Emigration, education and development[1]

ROBERT G. MYERS

Education offered beyond the borders of a nation can be considered as a part of or as an extension of a national system of
education. Nationals can be, and are, trained abroad for employment at home, and a nation can influence (within limits) the
extent to which foreign education plays a greater or lesser role
in the total process of educating nationals (see Table 1, col. 7).

For many nations, particularly the so-called developing
nations, foreign training is still a principal means of educating
nationals at the university level. Accordingly, policies have been
fashioned governing migration for study (sometimes involving
regulation of visas, monetary exchange, duration of stay, etc.),
suggesting that relative advantages and disadvantages of study
abroad have been weighed. However, if one looks carefully at
most national educational plans or manpower assessments,
education abroad is seldom incorporated directly, even when it is
numerically and qualitatively important. Estimates of trained
individuals who will be available for particular types of employment and estimates of educational facilities that will have to be
built to produce 'needed' human resources seldom take account
of the option to migrate for study. And, although there have
been attempts to assess utilization of foreign-trained resources,
most of such efforts have been restricted to myopic looking at
the kind of job held by only those individuals who have returned

home after training abroad under particular programmes. Comparisons with similar individuals trained at home, in university settings or on the job are missing. Furthermore, productivity on the job and costs and benefits of study at home as compared with study abroad have been neglected.

Complicating assessments of alternative educational strategies is the fact that education, whether acquired at home or abroad, can be, and often is, utilized abroad; associated with each educational strategy is a potential for subsequent emigration. Although the effects of this emigration or 'brain drain' on development have been vigorously debated, the question of how to incorporate losses (and gains) through emigration into assessments of educational pay-offs remains unclear.

To understand conflicting interpretations of gains and losses through emigration and to explore the manner in which emigration is tied to development in different national settings, it is necessary to sort out the many perspectives brought to bear on the problem. There are, of course, the more popular, sometimes xenophobic treatments of brain drain which can, for the most part, be disregarded. More difficult to deal with are complementary or conflicting research results stemming from different disciplinary approaches to brain drain (sociological, economic, historical, demographic, etc.), each involving a particular set of assumptions about what constitutes a loss or gain.[2] We cannot deal with all of these in the short space allotted. However, there is also disagreement within disciplines among scholars and among practitioners, as, for instance, among economists, whose conflicting approaches will be touched upon in this chapter.[3]

Within the broader topic of emigration, education and development, then, the problems encountered in measuring and interpreting the economic effects of study abroad and related brain drain (non-return) among foreign students will be stressed. First, a migration paradigm will be presented in which individuals are classified by locus of education and employment. From the paradigm, several ways of indexing emigration through foreign student non-return emerge that can be used in cross-national comparisons relating non-return to levels of development. Next the application of 'human capital' concepts to measuring gains and losses through migration and as associated with alternative educational strategies will be examined. Finally,

Table 1 Enrolments at home and abroad, education at the third level, selected countries, c. 1965[a]

Country	Total: students (foreign and national) (1)	Foreign students (2)	Nationals studying abroad (3)	Total: nationals only (1)−(2)+(3) (4)	Total non-returnees[b] (5)	% foreign (2)÷(1) (6)	% nationals abroad (3)÷(4) (7)	Manpower loss index[c] (8)	Rate of non-return from U.S.[d] (9)
U.S.A.	5,526,325	82,709	13,865	5,457,481	—	1·5	0·3	—	—
Canada	283,907[4]	11,284[4]	11,311	283,934	1,440	4·0	4·0	50	14·1
Europe									
Albania	11,937[4]	93	98	11,942	—	0·8	0·8	—	—
Austria	49,382	9,368[4]	1,171	41,725	75	19·0	4·1	17	37·3
Belgium	75,489[4]	5,000[4]	1,146	71,635	56	6·6	1·6	7	21·1
Bulgaria	100,102	1,048[4]	1,028	100,082	—	1·0	1·0	—	—
Czechoslovakia	141,687[4]	3,303	218	138,602	71	2·3	0·2	16	32·6
Denmark	43,731[4]	643[4]	514	43,602	42	1·5	1·2	10	20·1
Finland	38,775	133[4]	1,069	39,731	215	0·3	2·7	5	22·8
France	455,111[4]	35,584[4]	7,370	426,897	816	7·8	1·7	22	41·4
German FR[e]	373,099	26,225	10,491	357,365	253	7·0	2·9	40	15·6
Greece	55,334	1,681	9,053	62,706	—	3·0	14·4	—	—
Hungary	51,002	691	1,555	51,866	5	1·4	3·0	34	8·6
Iceland	1,038[4]	31[4]	423	1,430	156	3·0	29·6	87	46·3
Ireland	20,634[4]	3,364	563	17,833	257	16·3	3·2	9	33·9
Italy	261,358[4]	3,800	3,356	260,914	2	1·5	1·3	11	25·0
Luxembourg	580[4]	48	1,180	1,712	248	11·8	68·9	16	41·0
Netherlands	148,590	1,242[4]	2,134	149,482	128	0·8	1·4	55	25·9
Norway	19,528	274[4]	3,623	22,877		1·4	15·8		
Poland	251,864[4]	1,364	799	251,299		0·5	0·3	9	—
Portugal	32,115[4]	155[4]	811	32,771	31	0·5	2·5	9	20·8
Romania	130,416[4]	508[4]	193	130,101	—	0·4	0·1	—	—
Spain	111,133[4]	7,489[4]	2,225	105,869	115	6·7	2·1	10	24·4
Sweden[f]	61,222[4]	—	1,159	61,222	81	—	1·9	13	24·4

Switzerland	30,488[4]	8,649	1,690	22,877	79	28·4	7·4	34	24·8
United Kingdom[g]	225,960[4]	16,396	7,801	217,365	740	7·3	3·6	34	30·8
Yugoslavia	184,923[4]	1,816	966	184,073	—	1·0	0·5	—	—
U.S.S.R.	3,608,000[4]	21,000[4]	—	—	—	0·6	—	—	—
Oceania									
Australia	122,620[4]	6,960	1,390	117,050	72	5·7	1·2	6	10·1
New Zealand	47,425[4]	1,056[4]	734	47,103	22	2·2	1·6	4	9·3
Caribbean									
Haiti[h]	1,705[h]	—	672	2,377	71	—	28·3	298	31·8
Jamaica	1,902	675	1,605	2,832	88	35·5	56·7	311	7·2
Trinidad	910	186	1,580	2,304	—	20·4	67·5	—	—
Central America									
Costa Rica	6,600[4]	254	616	6,962	43	3·8	8·8	61	14·9
El Salvador	3,624	64	517	4,077	71	1·8	12·7	174	26·6
Guatemala	7,673	243	406	7,836	44	3·2	5·2	56	17·1
Honduras	2,578	180[4]	399	2,797	39	7·0	14·3	139	18·4
Nicaragua	3,343	70[4]	657	3,930	46	2·1	16·7	117	16·1
South America									
Argentina	225,653[h]	13,060	1,310	213,903	168	5·8	0·6	7	22·4
Bolivia	11,090	82	899	11,907	83	0·7	7·6	69	24·3
Chile	36,503[4]	257	977	37,223	74	0·7	2·6	19	14·8
Colombia	37,462[4]	686[4]	2,381	39,157	207	1·8	6·1	52	15·8
Ecuador	12,486	480	761	12,767	64	3·8	6·0	50	15·1
Indian sub-continent									
India	1,310,000[3]	4,540[4]	10,863	1,316,323	475	0·3	0·8	3	6·9
Pakistan	229,003	366	2,897	231,534	33	0·2	1·3	1	3·0
Ceylon	12,485	16	970	13,439	12	0·1	7·2	8	11·6
Middle East									
Afghanistan	3,451[4]	12[4]	501	3,940	3	0·3	12·7	6	1·7
Iran	26,000	92	9,834	35,742	679	0·4	27·5	189	17·9
Iraq	24,662[4]	1,020	3,724	27,366	104	4·1	13·6	38	11·1
Israel	30,273	898	2,626	32,001	199	3·0	8·2	62	12·3
Jordan	2,755	17	15,901	18,639	103	0·6	85·3	55	14·9
Lebanon	20,345	10,798	3,249	12,796	86	53·1	25·4	67	11·8
Saudi Arabia	1,568[4]	242[4]	1,683	3,009	32	15·4	55·9	106	5·5

Table 1—_cont._

Country	Total: students (foreign and national) (1)	Foreign students (2)	Nationals studying abroad (3)	Total: nationals only (1)−(2)+(3) (4)	Total non-returnees[b] (5)	% foreign (2)÷(1) (6)	% nationals abroad (3)÷(4) (7)	Manpower loss index[c] (8)	Rate of non-return from U.S.[a] (9)
Syria	31,993	7,488	7,150	31,655	69	23·4	2·6	21	15·4
Turkey	91,198[4]	3,325	3,727	91,600	98	3·6	4·1	10	8·9
Asia									
Burma	22,399	16	358	22,741	13	0·1	1·6	6	9·9
Cambodia	5,851	104	410	6,157	4	1·7	6·7	6	2·1
China (Taiwan)	85,346	478	8,660	93,528	525	0·6	9·3	56	11·1
Hong Kong	10,189[4]	390[4]	4,836	14,635	460	3·8	33·0	314	13·6
Japan	1,085,119	8,266	4,087	1,080,940	289	0·8	0·4	2	8·3
Korea	141,635	107	6,988	148,516	308	0·1	4·7	20	11·5
Malaysia	8,960	106	6,875	15,729	38	1·2	43·7	24	7·0
Thailand	52,037[4]	50	2,973	54,960	65	0·1	5·4	11	3·9
Vietnam	23,457[4]	34	3,851	27,274	22	0·1	14·1	8	5·5
S. Africa	53,849	2,913[4]	1,475	52,411	52	5·4	2·8	10	12·5
N. Africa									
Algeria	8,177	1,873	1,681	7,985	0	22·9	21·1	0	0
Libya	1,936	110	753	2,579	2	5·7	29·2	8	2·0
Morocco	8,996	998	2,773	10,771	8	11·1	25·7	7	8·5
Sudan	7,701	271[4]	2,179	9,609	4	3·5	22·7	4	2·4
Tunisia	6,230	519	3,592	9,303	3	8·3	38·6	3	3·5
U.A.R.	175,245	16,789	3,572	162,028	105	9·6	2·2	6	12·5
Sub-Saharan Africa									
Burundi	188	79	111	220	0	42·0	50·5	0	0
Cameroon	1,164	25	1,111	2,250	0	2·1	49·4	0	0
Dahomey	39	8	782	813	0	20·5	96·2	0	0
Ethiopia	2,256	115	811	2,952	8	5·1	27·5	27	3·0

	(1)	(2)	(3)	(4)					Manpower index
Ghana	4,788	158	1,401	6,031	11	3.3	23.2	18	3.7
Guinea	585[a]	22[a]	558	1,121	2	3.8	49.8	17	1.5
Ivory Coast	1,566[a]	828[a]	505	1,243	0	52.9	40.6	0	0
Kenya	2,758[a]	398	2,433	4,793	5	14.4	50.8	10	0.6
Liberia	685	60[a]	371	996	10	8.8	37.2	100	3.0
Madagascar	2,418	112	734	3,040		4.6	24.1	0	0
Mozambique	555	2	13	566	1	0.4	2.3	138	6.7
Nigeria	8,933	204	3,844	12,573	21	2.3	30.6	18	1.5
Senegal	2,755	1,437	348	1,666	0	52.2	20.9	0	1.0
Sierra Leone	930	182	473	1,221	3	19.6	38.7	31	1.7
Somalia	61[a]	9[a]	372	424	3	14.8	87.7	58	2.4
S. Rhodesia	639[a]	129[a]	310	820	9	20.2	37.8	109	4.3
Tanzania	115[a]	61[a]	1,477	1,531	3	53.0	96.5	19	1.1
Uganda	1,127[a]	650[a]	1,168	1,645	0	57.7	71.0	0	1.0

[a] Source: UNESCO, Statistical Yearbook, 1966, Paris: UNESCO, 1967. Column (1) figures were taken from pp. 155–69 (Table 2.10, Education at the third level: teachers, students and number of students per 100,000 inhabitants) or from pp. 170–202 (Table 2.11, Education at the third level: distribution of students by field of study). Columns (2) and (3): figures were taken from pp. 251–4 (Table 2.15, Education at the third level: number of foreign students enrolled and number of national students enrolled abroad).

[b] Calculated from: Institute of International Education (I.I.E.) Census forms, Fall, 1964. For details, see Myers, Robert G., 'Study Abroad and Migration of Human Resources', unpublished Ph.D. dissertation, University of Chicago, Department of Education, 1967, ch. 3. The rate of non-return among respondents was imputed to non-respondents as well in estimating the total number of non-returnees. If non-return from other areas could be identified and added, the figures are for non-return following United States study.

[c] The manpower index = (5) ÷ (4) × 10,000.

[d] Calculated from I.I.E. Census forms, Fall, 1964. Non-respondents were excluded from the calculation.

[e] Includes West Berlin.

[f] The most recent figure presented by UNESCO for foreign students in Sweden was a 1960 figure of 1,195. It was assumed, for purposes of calculating a manpower-loss number, that the number of foreign students enrolled approximately equalled the number of Swedish students abroad; the enrolment in column (1) is repeated in column (4).

[g] Includes Ireland and Scotland.

[h] Figures for Haiti were taken from UNESCO, Statistical Yearbook, 1965, Paris; UNESCO, 1966, pp. 253, 308, 309. The column (3) total is for Haitian students in fifteen countries: Australia, Austria, Belgium, Canada, Czechoslovakia, France, Germany (Federal Republic and West Berlin), Italy, Japan, Spain, Switzerland, Syria, U.A.R., U.K., U.S.A.

a comment or two on implications for policy will be offered. Most of the examples refer to foreign study in the United States, the so-called 'sink-hole' of high-level migration flows.

Study abroad, non-return and the brain drain, in perspective

A migration paradigm

To link discussion of study abroad v. study at home with discussion of the brain drain in a context of economic development, it is convenient to crudely divide brain drain into two components: emigration of talent that has been educated at home (sometimes called the 'trained brain drain'), and emigration of talent through non-return of foreign students (sometimes called the 'untrained brain drain').[4] By thus relating locus of study and employment, we have the simple paradigm presented in Fig. 1.[5]

Locus of employment

	Home	Abroad
Home	I	II
Abroad	III	IV

Locus of education

Fig. 1   A migration paradigm

In the first category of Fig. 1, the group consists of all individuals who do not migrate for education or for employment; the category defines a base group of non-immigrants against which migrating individuals can be compared. Categories II and IV represent the 'trained' and 'untrained' components of brain drain respectively. Category III individuals represent a potential brain gain, having studied abroad (at least partially at the expense of another nation), and returned home for employment. The classificatory scheme might be applied retrospectively to individuals at present in the labour force, in which case we would need to know level and locus of prior education; or we might take as our population all individuals at present enrolled in institutions of higher education at home and abroad, using projections about future employment to complete the classification.

The paradigm lends itself to calculating gains and losses associated with each of the education–employment sequences and to making comparisons. Talent losses and gains may be defined in many ways, the simplest being in terms of the numbers of individuals in each of the categories. Alternatively, a 'value' might be assigned to individuals within the various categories, such as their 'human capital' value.[6] Our focus will be on category IV, study abroad and non-return.

National and cross-national perspectives

Most information about global patterns of international migration, including student migration, is derived piecemeal from national statistics. But even at the national level, there is seldom agreement about the magnitude of high-level immigration and emigration. And, even at the national level, it is often impossible to obtain the necessary disaggregations by sex, age, type of employment, etc., that give meaning to the aggregate figures. The global dimensions of our topic, then, remain imprecise at best. Nevertheless, the following general statements seem to be supported by most researchers:

1   The option to migrate for study is exercised by only a small percentage of all individuals in the world who study at the university level (less than 3 per cent),[7] but there is broad variation by country (see Table 1, col. 7), by field of study, and by level of study.

2   A relatively small percentage of all individuals employed in high-level positions migrate across international borders for employment, but again there is broad variation by country, field and level.

3   Although high-level migration flows occur among developed nations and among developing nations, the major flows are (increasingly) from developing to developed nations.[8]

4   A handful of developing nations seem to provide most of the emigrating talent.[9]

5   The United States is the nation hosting the most foreign

students (110,000 or more)[10] and is the final resting-place of the largest number of high-level migrants, both trained and untrained.

6 Most high-level migrants are doctors, engineers or scientists.[11]

While such global glimpses of migration flows may be useful as background and as a needed reminder that nations exist in a world setting, the diversity among nations renders world overviews relatively meaningless, unless they include cross-national comparisons. And, as will be evident below, dividing the world into developing and developed nations is not enough.

Let us assume for the moment that reasonably accurate statistics are available, allowing us to categorize high-level immigrants and non-immigrants at the national level according to the migration paradigm. We are then in a position to compare numerical losses and gains cross-nationally. Several bases for comparison are possible, however, and what is chosen strongly influences the conclusions to be drawn about, for instance, loss or gain associated with study abroad and non-return.

Consider the three hypothetical countries of Fig. 2. For each country, individuals at present enrolled in higher education have been classified by locus of education and employment. To aid comparability, each country is assumed to be training only 100 individuals at the higher education level (hence the number in each education–employment category is also the percentage of the total population in that sequence).

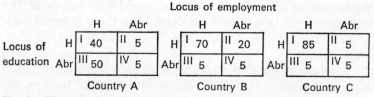

Fig. 2 Hypothetical distributions of individuals among education–employment categories of the migration paradigm

The country A configuration in Fig. 2 might be that of an African nation, still highly dependent on study abroad (55 per cent are studying abroad = categories III + IV). The pattern for country B more closely approximates a developed nation training most of its manpower at home (90 per cent = categories

I + II), but exporting skills at a relatively high rate (25 per cent = categories II + IV). Country C could be a large developing nation such as India or perhaps a nation such as Argentina that trains most of its manpower at home (90 per cent in the example) and that has a relatively low rate of emigration (10 per cent in the example).

Focusing on emigration through non-return of nationals trained abroad (category IV), let us look at four bases for comparing numerical 'losses' cross-nationally.

1 If we compare the absolute number of non-returnees across nations (category IV alone), the numerical losses in Fig. 2 are the same for all three countries. Applying this standard to non-returning students in the United States would result in the conclusion that Canada, Germany, the United Kingdom, Iran, Taiwan, India, Hong Kong and Korea are the principal loser nations[12] (see Table 1, col. 5).

2 The picture changes if we compare cross-nationally the ratio of non-returnees to total brain drain (i.e. category IV divided by categories II plus IV), as is sometimes done by writers with a nearsighted fix on the brain drain. Presumably, the higher the ratio, the greater the cause for alarm and the greater the blame attached to programmes of foreign study as promoters of brain drain. In Fig. 2 foreign student non-return constitutes 50, 20 and 50 per cent respectively of total brain drain for countries A, B and C. The tempting conclusion is that the losses to A and C through non-return are 'greater' than for B. But even if we accept the validity of the base for comparison, several extenuating circumstances must be considered before drawing that conclusion.

First, whether the untrained brain drain (non-return) is relatively larger or smaller depends in part on whether other avenues for migration are open. There is a 'trade-off' between the untrained and trained portions of brain drain. For many 'students' the decision to migrate for study is also a decision to migrate for employment. The fact that emigration occurs through non-return does not imply that study abroad causes migration or that the host nation somehow seduces foreign students on a large scale after they arrive. The degree to which untrained and trained components of the brain drain are substitutes and under what conditions substitution occurs should be examined. Second,

L

when a less developed nation has few or no facilities for training nationals at the university level, it follows that little of its high-level brain drain is likely to be of the home-grown variety.

It should not be surprising, then, that while less than 5 per cent of all immigrants to the United States from developed nations are non-returnees, approximately 40 per cent of all immigrants from the developing nations are 'untrained' when they arrive.[13] Unfortunately, the United States Government and international agencies use such a statistic to express concern about the greater loss of manpower from developing nations through foreign student non-return. But the larger percentage does not automatically signify a greater loss through non-return; the relative loss is affected by the particular limited perspective chosen for viewing non-return.

3 ˙ Another, and probably the most frequent, means for providing perspective on the relative numerical gains and losses associated with non-return is to compare *rates* of non-return among students abroad from each country. To obtain a rate, the number of non-returnees is related to the total number of students abroad, country by country (category IV divided by categories III plus IV). In the hypothetical cases of Fig. 2, the non-return rates are 9, 50 and 50 per cent respectively for A, B and C. Presumably, the higher the rate of non-return, the greater the relative loss through foreign student non-return and the less desirable it would be for a nation to pursue a programme of study abroad for its nationals. The emphasis has shifted from the brain drain to one of evaluating study abroad, taking migration into account. Note that whereas 'losses' were greater for country A than for B by the previous standard, they are reversed when a rate of non-return is used.

Among the nations with students in the United States, rates of non-return calculated from the Institute of International Education Census of Foreign Students are relatively high for Cuba, the Netherlands, West Germany, Ireland, Italy, Haiti, Austria and the United Kingdom, among others (see Table 1, col. 9). Iran just falls in the top one-third of the list when countries are ranked according to non-return. India and Taiwan, frequently cited as nations experiencing large losses, are in the bottom one-half of the ranking.

It is not uncommon to hear that losses through non-return

are 'greater' among students in the United States from developing than from developed nations. However, when rates of intended non-return are correlated with *per capita* income levels, the moderate correlation is direct, not inverse: in general, rates of non-return are higher among students in the United States from more developed nations.[14]

But even if we accept the rate of non-return as an appropriate base for comparison, qualifications are needed. For each country, the rate of non-return varies by field of study, level of study, type of sponsorship and student background characteristics.[15] Considerable variation in non-return is covered up by summary non-return figures at the national level. Among foreign students in the United States, non-return is relatively higher among foreign students who are under 25, self-sponsored, student (F.) visas holders, studying at the under-graduate or Ph.D. levels; non-return is relatively lower among students over 25, sponsored by governments or foundations, holding exchange (J.) visas and studying at the M.A. level.[16] Thus it is possible to operate a programme of training abroad with a low rate of non-return by carefully selecting individuals and conditions of study and by making employment opportunities available upon completion of the programme at the same time that non-return is relatively high among other individuals from the same country.

Another twist involved in interpreting rates of foreign student non-return is illustrated by country A in Fig. 2. In the case of country A, the rate of emigration following study *at home* (category II divided by I plus II) is higher than the rate of emigration following study *abroad* (category IV divided by III plus IV). Under such circumstances, admittedly unlikely, the loss from study abroad could be proportionally less than the loss associated with study at home.

4   A fourth perspective on non-return might be obtained by relating non-return to the total manpower being trained by a nation at home and abroad (category IV divided by I + II + III + IV).[17] In Fig. 2 countries A, B and C have the same proportion of total enrolment in category IV; they appear to be equal on what could be termed an index of 'manpower loss' (see Table 1, col. 8).

When *per capita* income is related to non-return using the

index of 'manpower loss', the moderate correlation found when a rate of non-return was used disappears.[18] Rank order changes drastically from what it was with the rate of non-return. Generally, the position of nations in the ranking of manpower loss accords more directly with frequently voiced impressions about relative losses through non-return. For instance, Iran and Taiwan move well up in the rankings. On the other hand, India remains in a low position.[19] The Netherlands and Germany, which ranked high when the rate of non-return was used, move down on the index of manpower loss.

From the above exploration of non-return, it should be clear that interpreting what constitutes a gain or loss is not straightforward. So far consideration has only been given to numbers of migrants and numbers of individuals being trained. The complexities of interpretation are no less present when we move from numbers to a weighting by 'value', as will be done in the following section. A large absolute number of migrants or a large human capital value associated with migration may not appear so large when placed in proper perspective.

In the cross-national comparisons, no attempt was made to adjust for differences in national ability to absorb educated manpower. The naïve assumption was made that individuals who return home would be able to use their training, hence anyone not returning represented a loss. Where unemployment or under-employment among the educated exists, the assumption must be questioned. Rates of unemployment are frequently used as migration predictors and, where the analysis is internal, not international, movement from areas of unemployment to areas of employment is deemed desirable—migration operates to allocate manpower where needed. On an international plane the same reasoning meets resistance.

A simple but insightful means of approximating national absorptive capacity and relating it to foreign student non-return cross-nationally has been presented by Michel Hervè.[20] To establish what he calls 'effective demand' for high-level manpower, Hervè determined the question representing the best fit between the number of university students per 100,000 population and per capita income for 102 nations. He then used the equation to predict expected enrolments for each country (i.e. enrolments necessary to satisfy effective demand, given the level of *per capita* income). Finally, expected enrolments were compared with actual enrolments to determine the 'surplus' (actual over expected) or 'deficit' for each nation.

As might be expected, Hervè found that many of the countries showing a large surplus, '. . . were also the countries frequently mentioned in connection with brain drain to the United States'.[21] For instance, countries with large surplus enrolments included the Philippines, Taiwan, Korea, Argentina, India, Lebanon and Syria. To term emigration from these countries in which there is an 'excess' or over-production of high-level manpower as a 'loss' does not seem as appropriate as it might if there was a 'deficit'. Deficit countries that are also countries of substantial migration would appear to be experiencing a *bona fide* loss of talent through non-return. Hervè labels such deficit nations 'crisis' countries; although apparently able to absorb more manpower than is being trained, nationals continue to emigrate. Candidates for crisis countries, using Hervè's definition, include Iran, West Germany, Haiti and Norway.[22]

In his analysis, Hervè utilized a very specific criterion by which the relative 'loss' of nations from student emigration could be judged. He did not attempt to 'value' migrants in terms of the cost of their training or in terms of their potential contribution to the home country. Logically, such valuations and the conditions of excess or surplus identified by Hervè should hang together. However, the existence of such a relationship has not been established, nor does it *necessarily* follow that conditions of supply and demand for high-level manpower will be related to migration decisions or to the 'value' of migrants. They might be more closely related to conditions of supply and demand for higher education.

Before moving ahead, let us recapitulate briefly. Using a migration paradigm, 'losses' through non-return of foreign students were defined in several ways: (1) in absolute numbers, (2) relative to total brain drain, (3) relative to the number of foreign students abroad, and (4) relative to the total manpower supply in training at home and abroad. In addition, non-return was related to (5) the 'effective demand' for high-level manpower in the home country, determined from the relationship between enrolment per 100,000 population and *per capita* income. The last three means of indexing non-return were used in cross-national comparisons.

The interpretation of losses through non-return was shown to be anything but straightforward at the level of counting heads. Different indexes of non-return produced very different country rankings and the nature of the relationship between emigration through non-return and *per capita* income depended on which index of non-return was chosen. In interpreting losses and in explaining emigration, level of development did not seem to be a particularly meaningful basis for classifying nations. It would seem that our tendency to divide the world into developing and developed nations for analytical and/or policy purposes is not particularly useful when dealing with brain drain. Even among 'Asian' nations there are notable differences in relative losses (and, perhaps more importantly, in why students remain).

Reviewing the analyses of relative loss, presented here in skeleton form, one is struck, however, by the recurrent positioning of several countries in the upper one-third of all the rankings. For instance, such seemingly unrelated nations as Haiti, Iran, and Norway appeared to be losing talent, no matter which of the perspectives was adopted. Speculation about the reasons for the apparent losses in three such different countries is left to the reader.

With the above as background, we now turn to identifying economic effects and to specifying gains and losses through emigration in human capital terms. In so doing, we will be, in effect, adding a third dimension 'value' to the paradigm and defining value in one very specific way.

Migration losses and human capital values[23]

It is not our purpose to resolve conflicting economic viewpoints about losses associated with migration. To do so would involve a lengthy debate of the definitions, assumptions and/or philosophical positions underpinning each. Nor do we wish to argue strongly for one *versus* another of the approaches economists have applied to examining migration: more than one method may be equally valid and useful. For the moment, it is enough to mention several choices that must be made when estimating economic gains and losses through migration. The listing alone should serve to alert readers to the dangers inherent in the unqualified summary statistics so frequently seen in popular writings about the brain drain.

Whether a net gain or loss is thought to be associated with migration depends on the unit chosen to whom gains or losses are thought to pertain (individual, enterprise, nation, world), on the definition of the relevant unit (is a 'nation', for example, comprised of all individuals who remain within national borders following emigration, either including or excluding new immigrants; or does it refer to all former citizens or national residents regardless of their current location and without reference to national borders?), and on the criterion for judging gains or losses. The criterion chosen depends upon whether emphasis is placed on economic growth (usually indexed by gross national product); on social welfare (usually inferred from what happens to *per capita* incomes of the 'relevant' population); on income distribution (among individuals within a nation or among nations, and measured either by a narrowing of the income range or by shift from one group to another); or on the loss of the flow of savings and taxes. The utility of one versus another of these measures depends on the purposes behind the measurement. Depending on what criterion is adopted, choices may also have to be made between a static or a dynamic outlook (which may involve a decision to either project an economic system into the future as it is at present or as it probably will be according to the best guesses that can be made).

Whether there is thought to be a gain or loss associated with migration may depend on whether one accepts income as a reasonable measure of productivity (i.e. whether a person is paid his true marginal product); on the degree to which the effect of migrating individuals on the operation of other factors of production is thought to be important (i.e. whether there are 'external' economies or diseconomies associated with migration of talent that are not represented in the gains or losses registered through the market—such as missing 'leadership' or an imbalance between skilled and unskilled workers); on whether those who migrate are thought to have a higher rate of savings than those who remain, in which case the rate of investment would decline; on whether one accepts the position that a migrant takes along not only his education (for which the home country paid), but also his fertility, making it unnecessary for those who remain to provide education for the emigrant's children; on whether emigrants are thought to draw on the public purse for welfare benefits in proportion to, or in excess of, the tax revenue they provide; and on whether one accepts the notion that contribution to national welfare can come from emigrants resident outside the home country. Finally, estimates will differ according to whether one adopts a long-run or a short-run emphasis.

The most controversial and thought-provoking theoretical work on international flows of human capital by economists has been that of Harry Johnson and of Grubel and Scott.[24] Their theoretical base in the economics of international trade and their international perspective leads to an orientation towards free flow of goods and people among nations. From their neoclassical economic assumptions and their emphasis on social welfare indexed by *per capita* income effects they develop a well-reasoned argument that unrestricted flow of men among nations for study and work is in the economic best interests of the world.

Countering Johnson and Grubel and Scott are Brinley Thomas and others.[25] From an essentially nationalistic orientation, these writers note benefits from difficult-to-measure economic 'externalities'. They present their arguments in dynamic terms, criticize the free-market, marginal-analysis assumptions and emphasize the effect of high-level migration upon both gross national product and the redistribution of capital among individuals and nations. They conclude that high-level migration, particularly from low-income nations, leads to wider gaps between rich and poor, to a retarding of economic development and to a worsening of the world economic situation.

Other economists stress the value of more than one approach to estimating gains and losses associated with international migration and emphasize that the balance between gains and losses, as well as the methods used to estimate the gains and losses, should depend on the particular circumstances encountered at migrant origins and destinations. If one accepts the possibility of multiple approaches to gains and losses, it would be easy to agree with the statement that 'economic analysis is unclear whether emigration helps or hurts a country'.[26]

While recognizing that many shifts occur as economies adjust in response to movements of human capital,[27] here we are concerned only with aggregate losses and gains of human capital *per se*. Two main alternatives for calculating estimates of human-capital losses through migration are discussed below.

Cost valuations of international migration

A relatively simple method of valuing migration flows in monetary terms is to estimate the cost of 'producing' (or replacing) those who have emigrated. According to this method, national gains are realized if a nation acquires through migration (and at a saving of cost) human capital formed elsewhere. National losses are incurred when a nation pays for the formation of human capital that others then acquire cost-free.

Usually an average cost figure is calculated for a 'typical' migrant with the average amount of training (and sometimes experience) represented in a particular stream of migrants; the cost figure is then applied to all migrants. As an example, the following has been excerpted from a United States Government report on the brain drain: 'If an average cost figure of $20,000 is used, the 1967 scientific emigration to the United States of 7,915 persons represents an investment loss in one year of more than $150 million by the developing countries.'[28]

In the example elements included in the cost figure of $20,000 were not specified. It is difficult to make a judgment about the statement on that point alone. Assuming the general validity of a cost approach (questioned below), one must examine the method of determining costs before blindly accepting such an estimate. Sometimes costs are thought of only in terms of *direct* educational costs, resulting in a gross under-estimate of human capital value. More frequently, however, cost estimates include the opportunity cost incurred by individuals and societies resulting from the decision to forgo entering the work world and hence to forgo earnings in order to continue the process of education. As has been frequently pointed out, forgone earnings probably account for more than one-half of the cost associated with pursuing higher education. There is an additional cost element that is sometimes incorporated into human capital estimates—what it costs to bring up (maintain) a child in the period before the child could enter the labour force. Whether to include maintenance and how to estimate the cost of upbringing are open questions. One method of dealing with the problem of maintenance is to make one estimate incorporating it and one leaving it out.

A second and perhaps more difficult question that must be raised when making cost assessments of the human capital embodied in migrants is whether the appropriate costs of training and of forgone earnings are based on data from the area of origin or of destination. In the example the cost figure of $20,000 apparently represents the cost in the United States of bringing an individual to the educational level of the migrant on arrival. If one is speaking in terms of gains to the United States, that procedure seems appropriate. If, however, one is speaking of the loss to countries of origin, as is the case in the example, the use of United States cost figures can be questioned. Indeed, in the latter situation, estimating what is *embodied* in individuals as measured by the cost of their training may be irrelevant; the United States market may be able to absorb and utilize the embodied skills, but the home country may not be able to, regardless of the cost involved. That possibility brings us to a second approach to estimating human capital values.

Present value estimates and international migration

To measure the human capital value of a migrating individual in present value terms is to ask what he can be expected (or could have been expected) to contribute to society during the remainder of his lifetime as indexed by what society will pay (would have paid) for his services, i.e. by his earnings. The emphasis of a present value approach is on the flow of services in the *utilization* of human capital rather than on the cost of *producing* human capital.

Once appropriate estimates for expected future earnings are determined, year by year, the procedure for calculating present values is relatively simple. The projected earnings expected each year until death (or retirement) can be discounted back to the present and the discounted values for each year can be summed. Thus the earnings stream is represented as a single dollar figure and allowance is made for the fact that a dollar available today is worth more over one's lifetime than a dollar acquired later in life.[29]

If present values are accepted as useful human capital measures for valuing migrants, it remains to define the conceptually appropriate lifetime-earnings streams from which present values can be calculated. Unfortunately, choosing the appropriate estimating procedure for determining future earnings and determining the appropriate discount rate are not as easy as the calculation. Estimates are sensitive to both choices. Typically, the figures for expected future earnings are derived from census data indicating what an 'average' individual at each age with a certain amount of educational attainment earns currently. In effect, a cross-section of the present is projected into the future.

The accuracy of earnings estimates will depend on the choice of characteristics defining each set of 'average' individuals for whom earnings are known. Here we run headlong into a problem of disaggregation. Suppose, as seems to be the case, that age-earnings profiles differ systematically within sex–race–educational attainment–occupation categories. Would it be enough to work with 'average' individuals within each category? Elsewhere, Bowman and I have argued that it is not enough—that differences in expected earnings (i.e. of present values) will remain, related to differences in quality of education and experience.[30] And we have argued that disaggregation by locus of education and employment will pick up at least part of such differences, because quality of schooling and experience can be systematically related to location. For instance, medical training and experience is in general of a higher quality in the United States than in the Philippines. It is quite possible, therefore, that two doctors of the same age, sex and race will expect (and deserve) different earnings because one was born, educated and employed in early years in the Philippines while the other was born in the Philippines, but was educated and first employed in the United States. In valuing losses and gains, then, locus of education and employment should be considered, bringing us back to the paradigm for classifying migrants presented in Fig. 1.

Replacement cost versus present values

If the market equilibrium conditions of theoretical economics existed, valuing human capital at replacement cost or discounted present values would give the same result. However, to make the assumption of equilibrium conditions evades the question; using one or the other method does make a difference.

Measurement of human capital in cost terms as a way of assessing the resources that have gone into the making of a man is quite different from using cost valuations to assess gains and losses through migration. The most serious distortions are likely to occur when replacement-cost estimates exceed present value. For instance, the cost of educating a doctor who is emigrating from the capital city of a Latin American country to the United States (or of educating his replacement) may be much higher than the value his services actually bring in the Latin market. Indeed, this may be one factor which led him to migrate.

If a trained individual emigrates, he takes with him his productivity (and his earnings) from the moment he migrates. If there is a lag between the time of his leaving and the time a trained replacement becomes available, the interim loss of productivity should be considered as part of the loss attending the emigration.[31] Using replacement cost would not pick up this human-capital loss. Where lead-times for training are long, this difference can be substantial, unless a process of continuous replacement is figured into the training system.[32]

On the other hand, if present-value calculations depend on cross-sectional data, and if the cross-sectional cut is made at a point of boom or bust, the profile of the relative earnings across occupations (or across countries) will not be representative and will certainly change; demands for particular levels of skill (and specializations within levels of skill) do differ through time and between localities. In that case, cost may be a more accurate proxy for some 'true' present value than the present value determined from a distorted pattern of relative earnings. Indeed, 'variations from year to year in demands for people with varying amounts and types of schooling would alter present and future occupational groups and hence individual and total discounted values'.[33] The importance of demand differentials will depend on whether occupational categories are broadly or finely defined and whether analysis emphasizes occupations particularly subject to cyclical fluctuations. For broad categorizations there is little problem.

The meaning of earnings profiles in the United States is somewhat clearer than in, for instance, Ecuador. Where a market is characterized by monopsony or where inflexible civil service scales unrelated to relative productivity of individuals dominate, or where earnings in a particular occupation have a bimodal distribution, it may be necessary to use a method of 'shadow pricing' to set earnings streams from which present values can be calculated.[34] And although the desired multiple cross-tabulations by sex, age, school attainment, occupation, locus of schooling and employment, and by earnings are not out of the question for regional analyses using United States census data, it will be many years before similar data are available for most countries.[35]

In general, present values have much to recommend from a conceptual viewpoint as the more appropriate measure of human capital gains and losses through migration, but the availability of educational cost figures combined with the practical difficulties associated with deriving earnings profiles often lead to the choice of cost over present values for attaching a human capital value to migrants. Whichever method is used, the reader should be alert to assumptions and sources from which measures have been derived.

Human capital values and foreign student non-return

The choices that must be made when determining losses of human capital may be illustrated by asking a series of questions about one hypothetical Taiwanese student, and then by presenting a set of estimates for losses associated with non-return of Indian students in the United States.

Suppose a Taiwanese student graduates from a Taiwanese university. He has difficulty getting a job; the supply of highly educated individuals in Taiwan apparently exceeds the demand. The Taiwanese graduate decides to migrate to the United States, but finds he cannot come as an immigrant. He therefore decides to come for advanced study (perhaps with intent to remain permanently in the United States, perhaps with intent to return home). He obtains a Ph.D. after six years, during which he was partially sponsored by a United States university fellowship and was employed part-time at the university as a research assistant. Shortly after receiving his Ph.D. he is granted a visa change from student to permanent resident, having qualified under the preference category reserved for professionals. We would like to know what human capital loss *to Taiwan* and gain to the United States is associated with his act of migration.[36]

A number of questions must be answered: Do we place a human capital value on the student at the time he arrived in the United States or at the time he received his degree? Do we use a Taiwanese or United States base for calculations? If we agree to use the Taiwanese base and value him at the time he left Taiwan, do we use the cost of his education in Taiwan? Or do we also add in a 'maintenance cost'? Or do we look at what the student might have contributed as indicated by expected earnings discounted to the present, assuming he had not come to the United States? How do we estimate the earnings? If we value at the time of completing the United States degree and look at what the student might earn in Taiwan on return and with his new skills, do we net out the cost of his United States education? If so, how do we compare Taiwanese earnings projections and United States educational costs, i.e. how do we make international monetary comparisons? Should we try to incorporate 'external' effects the non-returnee might have produced had he returned home? How?

In aggregating human capital losses and gains, how would we balance our estimate for the case in question with that of a similar student who, instead of remaining in the United States, decided to return to Taiwan at the end of his six years in the United States? Would the base for estimating his human capital switch to that of the United States dollar cost of education in the United States or to what he might have earned if he had entered the labour market in the United States rather than pursuing his advanced studies?

In a somewhat more concrete vein, consider the human capital loss *to India* associated with foreign student non-return among Indians in the United States as estimated in present value terms by Gopal Dorai.[37] From advertisements by the Union Public Service Commission announcing employment opportunities and salaries in India, he calculated present values of expected earnings streams for United States-trained Indians employed in India. Separate calculations were made, using discount rates

of 5, 10 and 15 per cent. Dorai adjusted the totals for unemployment among foreign-educated Indians, and he separated, where
possible, undergraduates from postgraduates.

For the overseas undergraduate, Dorai calculated present
values of \$43,427, \$33,324 and \$14,200 respectively at the 5,10
and 15 per cent discount rates. For a postgraduate the amounts
were \$55,819, \$30,410 and \$20,307 respectively. To estimate the
capital value of non-returning foreign students, i.e. the social loss
to India for the period 1950–66, Dorai multiplied each present
value estimate by the number of non-returnees in each year,
assuming first that all students were undergraduates and then
that all were postgraduates. The results for the 5 and 15 per cent
discount rates are shown in the column of Table 2 labelled
'Total capital values'.

From the Dorai example it is evident that the rate of discount
used makes a significant difference in the total loss estimated.
The amounts involved may seem large, particularly in 1966 value
reflecting a large jump in non-return following the new immigration legislation of 1965. However, it should be pointed out
that in 1967 the total number of scientific, engineering and
medical manpower emigrating from India has been estimated
at only 2 per cent of the total output of scientists, engineers, and
physicians in India in that year and that unemployment among
the educated in India is not a myth.[38]

The absolute values of estimated human capital gain or loss
must be put in perspective in much the way that absolute numbers of migrants must be, as discussed above (see p. 164), before
the values acquire meaning. In the Indian example we have only
calculated the value of category IV of the migration paradigm
by calculating the human capital value of non-returnees. In
effect, the calculation tells us little about the effects of non-return
and provides no particular insight into whether or not study
abroad is a wise policy for India to encourage. And, it would not
be very comforting to adopt Dorai's figures as a basis for determining what compensating payments the United States should
make to India for her losses, even if costs of education were
subtracted out. In short, the interpretation of migration behaviour in economic terms and the analysis of potential strategies in social policy require something more than aggrega-
tive estimates of losses and gains. And popular estimates

Table 2 Estimated capital values at age 20, non-returning Indian students who have studied in the United States, 1958–66 in dollars[a]

Year	Number of non-returning foreign students[b]	Total capital values[c]			
		Undergraduates		Graduates	
		At 5%	At 15%	At 5%	At 15%
1958	96	4,163,992	1,363,200	5,358,624	589,449
1959	74	3,213,598	1,050,800	4,130,606	454,366
1960	69	2,996,463	979,800	3,851,511	423,666
1961	86	3,734,722	1,221,200	4,808,434	528,048
1962	114	4,950,678	1,618,800	6,362,366	699,970
1963	434	18,847,318	6,162,800	24,225,446	2,664,799
1964	158	6,861,466	2,243,600	8,819,402	970,134
1965	140	6,079,780	1,988,000	7,814,660	859,613
1966	1,015	44,078,405	14,413,000	56,656,285	6,232,191
1958–66	2,186	94,931,422	31,041,200	122,028,334	13,422,236

[a] Taken from Dorai, Gopal, 'Economics of the International Flow of Students: a Cost-benefit Analysis', Wayne State University, Department of Economics, 1967 (mimeographed).

[b] For the years 1962–6 the number of non-returning Indian students was taken as the number of students who adjusted their status from student to immigrant in each year. For the remaining years, 1958–61, student non-return was calculated by applying the ratio, student-to-immigrant-visa-adjustment/total immigrants, determined for years 1962–6, to the figure for total immigrants in the earlier years, 1958–61. This procedure was necessary because information on student visa adjustments was not available for years before 1962.

[c] The present values used to obtain the total capital value estimates are:

Undergraduates: $43,427 (at a 5% discount rate)
$14,200 (at a 15% discount rate)
Graduates: $55,893 (at a 5% discount rate)
$20,307 (at a 15% discount rate)

It should be noted that Dorai took his estimating procedure one step further. Assuming that what is lost to India is only that part of future earnings that would have been saved and invested, he multiplied all human capital values by 0·11, a figure representing the rate of saving among Indians. This gave him his final such as that quoted on p. 170 must be viewed with extreme scepticism.

A concluding note

Within the space limitations of this chapter focus has been placed on questions and complexities associated with evaluating emigration as it is linked to education and development, rather than to emphasize tidy answers of questionable validity. It is probably too soon to accept, without reservation, any of the many 'solutions' to the brain drain 'problem'. Most are based on simplistic misconceptions. Our first task, then, is to break the problem down and to look at it from many perspectives, some of which have been discussed in this chapter. The result appears to be negative, but it is preliminary to more constructive research to reintegration of our knowledge and to enlightened policy formulation.

From the foregoing discussion, it should be evident that emigration, even in relatively large numbers, does not necessarily mean that a nation is suffering a debilitating brain drain. And it should be evident that brain drain is not easily related to level of national development. Because each nation is characterized by a unique set of circumstances, questions of gains and losses through emigration, whether 'trained' or 'untrained' emigration, should begin with a country-by-country examination. Grouping nations into developed and developing nations is not sufficient.

Furthermore, the simple fact that many students (or even a large percentage of students) studying abroad will remain abroad to work does not automatically mean that programmes of study abroad should be cut back. We must first sort out programmes, consider differences between non-returnees and returnees, determine causes of non-return, and estimate potential contributions of returnees versus non-returnees. In such an evaluation, human capital concepts are useful, facilitating benefit–cost comparisons among alternative training programmes and among different types of trainees. The human capital approach also aids formulation and testing of hypotheses about the response of migrants to monetary incentives. In this essay these more positive uses of human capital concepts applied to migration have

M

not been explored. One reason for the emphasis on qualifications and cautions is that, although human capital concepts as used in benefit–cost analysis may be extremely useful, there is a danger that they will be misused as they acquire the status of a fad and/or are accepted 'on authority'. Blind acceptance will undercut usefulness, much as it has for manpower planning.

As a footnote to the critical examination of several methods for interpreting losses through migration, a word or two should be included about proposals that have been made to minimize losses through emigration. Proposals take several forms: compensation of losers by gainers; restrictive legislation to prevent emigration; making study at home and abroad more 'relevant' to home-country needs; and reducing differentials between areas of origin and destination that act as incentives to migrate.

The notion of compensating losing nations is a critical feature of arguments offered by 'cosmopolitans', who suggest that something akin to a Pareto optimum is needed for judging migration whereby movement, whether for education or work or both, should not only be tolerated but also encouraged *if* world welfare is thereby increased *and if* no uncompensated losses occur as a result. The first part of the statement is not difficult to accept; the second is. Problems associated with calculating absolute losses and gains have been outlined earlier. But assume we have the necessary statistics and a method for calculating human capital gains and losses. Should we then use the calculations as a basis for formal compensatory payments in much the same manner nations now handle their balance of payments? The answer is that at best such a policy would be premature and at worst unwise. We do not yet know to what extent other compensatory mechanisms (such as remittances or the transfer of 'know-how' or increased communication in the international scientific community) already offset the losses. It is doubtful whether such counterflows totally offset losses, but here is an area for inventive research to be done. Nor do we know what effect compensatory payment schemes would have in allowing countries to export their discontented intellectuals, their Young Turks, their surplus doctors or whatever, thus retarding the real reforms that should be made. Whether or not the payments would be more than a placebo is open to question.

Personal research has convinced the author that legal restrictions at origin or destination have only a marginal impact on losses through non-return and probably on the migration of high-level talent in general. What might have been appropriate and useful for moderating mass migration is not as effective for select migration of the highly educated. Also, costs involved in establishing and enforcing restrictions are hidden; they are seldom taken into account.

In a more positive vein, making study at home and abroad more 'relevant' to home-country needs may cut losses. However, there is a danger here in linking programmes too closely to manpower projections that turn out to be incorrect (and which have not incorporated available manpower being educated abroad). If 'relevant' means linking study to specific jobs, then the amount of emigration that might be drastically reduced for guaranteed employment, in these analyses and others, turns out to be among the most important correlates of return home. On a large scale, however, it is difficult to link study to specific jobs. And, in those cases where unemployment of the educated exists, finding reasonable positions for educated individuals is not easy.[39]

Reducing the differential incentives between origin and destination is much more easily advocated than achieved. However, it is in this area that major efforts should be made. We are beginning to identify the most important incentives to emigration. In some cases a device as simple as granting tariff exemptions on household items accumulated abroad may have an effect. Usually, however, the incentive to emigrate is much closely related to more fundamental inequities in the existing economic, social and political fabric of the nation. To reduce differentials, it may be necessary to restructure institutions, a feat that cannot be accomplished piecemeal.

A variety of monetary incentive schemes might be incorporated under the heading of reducing differentials, including a kind of National Defence Act loan (this Act provides assistance for selected programmes of university study in the United States) for study abroad, with partial forgiveness if, and when, an individual returned following study abroad or remained in the country following study at home to practise his skill. Tax exemptions might be utilized. And the most obvious suggestions involve establishing differential salary scales, breaking the strong influence of standardized civil service schedules on professional remuneration.

Each of the suggestions mentioned above should be carefully examined. Each carries with it various costs which may outweigh the potential benefits. Human capital calculations should be useful in assessing which policies have the most potential for overcoming emigration as an intervening force in linking education to development.

When we go behind the simple statistics describing the magnitude and correlates of foreign student non-return and when we view non-return in the larger contexts of international migration and of educational investment, it seems that we cannot help but be impressed by the positive role of migration for study and the minor place of emigration through non-return in the total picture. The conclusion reached after puzzling through a bewildering array of policy suggestions is that the constructive efforts at present being made are as impressive as the newer measures being proposed for assuring that study abroad contributes to economic and social development at home and that the negative effects of non-return are kept at a moderate level. While there is room for improvement, there is no necessity to indict as irresponsible lost nations or the many countries which send students abroad. In official programmes generally attention has been given to questions of utilization and of return or nonreturn. And when talent losses are real and felt, the losing nations have reacted, not without results. While the United States can more fully support the sending nations in efforts to improve the effects of study abroad, support through additional restrictive immigration measures do not seem particularly appropriate or useful. Positive actions initiated in the areas of origin should receive the greatest attention and support. Investments in people and institutions should be preferred to legal sanctions.

Notes

1 The author is grateful to the Carnegie Corporation of New York for sponsoring the research from which this chapter springs. I am also indebted to Mary Jean Bowman for her part in the development of

ideas presented here. See Bowman, Mary Jean, and Myers, Robert G., 'Schooling, Experience, and Gains and Losses in Human Capital through Migration', *Journal of the American Statistical Association*, lxii, No. 319 (September 1967), 875–98. A more detailed treatment of most topics covered here can be found in Myers, Robert G., 'Study Abroad and the Migration of Human Resources', unpublished Ph.D. dissertation, University of Chicago, Department of Education, 1967.

2 The diversity of treatment can be seen in bibliographies dealing with the brain drain. See Dedijer, S., and Svenningson, L., *Brain Drain and Brain Gain: a Bibliography on Migration of Scientists, Engineers, Doctors and Students*, Lund, Sweden: Research Policy Programme, 1967.

3 See, for instance, Adams, Walter (ed.), *The Brain Drain*, New York: Macmillan, 1968.

4 The names 'trained' and 'untrained' and the paradigm, as presented here, must be credited to Alan Bayer. However, essentially the same classification was developed by the author and Mary Jean Bowman for the purpose of incorporating locus of education and employment into a decision model for evaluating education–employment alternatives. Bowman and Myers, 890.

5 Classification by locus of education and employment is not simply a device to link migration, education and employment. It is predicated on the assumption that there are areal differences in the quality of schooling and experience and in employment opportunity that should be taken into consideration when valuing migrating individuals and/or explaining their behaviour.

6 Disaggregation could also take place within each of the categories, as, for instance, by sex, age, and occupation. Or the paradigm might be applied to a sub-group, such as male engineers over age 25.

7 The calculation is based on UNESCO figures taken from *The Statistical Yearbook, 1966*, Paris: UNESCO, 1967.

8 For one of the best compilations of flows to various developed nations, see Brinley Thomas, 'The International Circulation of Human Capital', *Minerva*, v, No. 4 (Summer 1967), 479–506.

9 United Nations General Assembly, 23rd Session, 5 November 1968, 'Outflow of Trained Personnel from Developing Countries, Report of the Secretary General', A17294, New York: The United Nations, 1968, 5. Mimeograph.

10 Institute of International Education (I.I.E.), *Open Doors*, New York: I.I.E., 1969.

11 'Scientists' usually refer to natural or physical scientists as distinguished from social scientists.

12 Reluctantly, I will omit a discussion of the various bases that might be used to define non-return, such as intent to remain abroad permanently, visa change, length of time in residence abroad, or change of citizenship. Needless to say, the analysis of non-return depends heavily on the definition chosen. Non-return rates calculated for foreign students in the United States range from 5 to 50 per cent. In large part, the con-

flicting calculations can be accounted for in terms of the definition used. In the following paragraphs, non-return is defined in terms of the intent to remain permanently in the United States. The statistics presented in this essay are tied to that definition. Using the I.I.E. Census of Foreign Students, 1964–5, I calculated an overall rate of 16 per cent for that year. It is probably an underestimate. However, the overall rate has little meaning. For greater detail, including a discussion of biases, see Myers, chs. 1–3.

13 United States, Congress, House, Subcommittee on Government Operations, *Hearings on the Brain Drain of Scientists, Engineers, and Physicians from the Developing Countries into the United States*, 90th Cong., 2nd Sess., 23 January 1968, Washington: U.S.G.P.O., 1968, 3.

14 Using the log of income and a rate of return based on intent to remain permanently in the United States, $R^2 = 0.36$ for ninety-six countries. The association does not imply causality.

15 The importance of taking differences in conditions of study into account when making cross-national comparisons of non-return is illustrated by the fact that when a set of regressions was run with the rate of non-return as the dependent variable and with conditions of study among students from the respective countries (sponsorship, visa, level of study) as independent variables, the conditions of study predicted national non-return rates quite well ($R^2 = 0.67$). Adding country characteristics (such as *per capita* income) to the regression had little effect (raising the R^2 to 0.75). There are undoubtedly strong interaction effects between country characteristics and conditions of study that should be sorted out before drawing conclusions.

16 Elsewhere I have pointed out how associations between non-return and other variables are not necessarily causal. In fact, such common 'causes' of non-return as marriage to a United States girl or holding a student visa rather than an exchangee *visa* turn out to be relatively unimportant when other factors, such as availability of employment, are taken into account. See Myers, Robert, 'Education and Emigration', Chicago: University of Chicago, 1969, ch. 7, 46, 47, unpublished manuscript, mimeographed. Also Ritterband, Paul, 'The Non-returning Foreign Student: the Israeli Case', Unpublished Ph.D. dissertation, Columbia University, 1968.

17 Sometimes non-return is related to the total *enrolment*; other times to the total number of *graduates*. Neither practice is entirely satisfactory.

18 For seventy-eight countries, $R^2 = 0.00$ using log of *per capita* income.

19 Even if we assume a much higher rate of non-return among Indian students in the United States than that derived from the I.I.E. data, the manpower loss index number for India would remain relatively low.

20 Hervè, Michel E. A., 'International Migration of Physicians and Students; a Regression Analysis', Washington, D.C., United States Agency for International Development, Office of Programme and Policy Co-ordination, April 1968, mimeographed.

21 *Ibid.*, iv–2.

22 According to Hervè's figures, all sub-Saharan nations for which an

estimate of income and enrolment was available are deficit countries with a deficit that is at least as large as the actual enrolment figure in the home country. Hervè does not take into account the fact that a large percentage of the actual enrolment of students from the sub-Saharan nations is overseas enrolment. He agrees that the deficits computed for these nations would be cut considerably if study abroad could have been taken into consideration when setting the original equation relating *per capita* income and total enrolments.

23 Other means of 'valuing' migrants might be used. For instance, Alan Bayer has valued United States doctorate recipients according to the 'quality' of the institution where they received their degree. When comparing mobility with educational quality of migrants, he found that the highest quality graduates were the most mobile. He also found that several areas of the country which seemed to be net losers of talent when only numbers were compared became net gainers when quality was introduced. Bayer, Alan, 'The Interregional Migration and the Education of American Scientists', *Sociology of Education*, xli, No. 1 (Winter 1968), 88–102.

24 See, for instance, Johnson, Harry, 'An "Internationalist" Model', in Adams, 69–91, and Grubel, Herbert G., and Scott, Anthony, 'The International Flow of Human Capital, the Brain Drain', *American Economic Review*, lvi, No. 2 (May 1966), 268–74 (together with the 'discussion' by Burton Weisbrod, pp. 277–80 of the same volume).

25 Thomas, 479–506, Patinkin, Don, 'A "Nationalist" Model', in Adams, 92–108, and Shearer, John, 'In Defence of Traditional Views of the "Brain Drain" Problem', *Exchange*, Fall 1966, 17–25.

26 Kindleberger, Charles P., 'Emigration and Economic Growth', Banca Nazionale del Lavoro, *Quarterly Review*, September 1965, 235.

27 Such as associated with changes in patterns of consumption and investment, by demographic effects, and by remittances.

28 United States Congress, House, Committee on Government Operations, *Scientific Brain Drain from the Developing Countries*, 90th Cong., 2nd Sess., 1968, Report No. 23, 5.

29 To discount the earnings for year *n*, one simply divides the anticipated earnings (Y) by the value $(1 + r)^t$ where r equals the discount rate—usually the rate of interest one might expect to get on an alternative investment. The present value of a future income stream can be represented, then, by $\sum_{t=1}^{n} Y/(1 + r)^t$. The intricacies of choosing an appropriate discount rate will not be discussed here.

30 Bowman and Myers, 879–84.

31 This loss is apart from the loss that might occur as a result of his making other factors of production temporarily unusable.

32 However, if human capital is being produced in over-supply in order to allow continuous replacement, there is a built-in cost—the cost that society is willing to pay to avoid disruptions.

33 Wilkinson, Bruce W., *Studies in the Economics of Education*, Occasional

Paper No. 4, Ottawa: Canada Department of Labour, Economics and Research Branch, 1965, 19.

34 A number of methods other than use of census data have been employed to collect earnings information from which profiles can be constructed: tax files, job advertisements, labour market surveys, organization records and special questionnaires.

35 One of the most promising United States sources for applying the above is the recent National Science Foundation publication, *Characteristics of Foreign-born and Educated Scientists in the United States*, prepared for the National Science Foundation, University of Pennsylvania, 1968.

36 Several individuals have used human capital values to approximate gains to the United States associated with educating foreign students, taking non-return into account. See Grubel, H. G., 'The Cost of U.S. College Exchange Programmes', *The Journal of Human Resources*, i, No. 2, Fall 1966, 81–98; DeVine, Bruce F., 'The United States Student Exchange Programme: Reverse Foreign Aid?', Claremont, California: Pomona College, Department of Economics, 1969, mimeographed; Levich, Richard, 'An Analysis of Expected Loss from Foreign Student Non-return', Chicago: University of Chicago, Department of Economics, 1969, mimeographed.

37 Dorai, Gopal, 'Economics of the International Flow of Students: a Cost-benefit Analysis, unpublished Ph.D. dissertation, Department of Economics, Wayne State University, 1968. In fairness to Dorai, I should point out that his main purpose in calculating the present values was to examine the private decision to migrate; his estimate of aggregate loss to India was secondary.

38 Blaug, M., Layard, P. R. G., and Woodhall, M., *The Causes of Educated Unemployment: the Indian Case*, London: Allen Lane, The Penguin Press, 1969, ch. 6.

39 This point is underscored by the questionable success of the Indian Manpower Pool. Individuals were brought back to India and placed in the Pool while seeking employment. Time-to-placement has been much longer than anticipated. If recruitment of nationals to jobs at home is to be undertaken abroad, experience indicates that recruiters must have specific opportunities to offer and must have authority to make commitments on the spot. Vague promises are not well received.

ten

Types of schooling for developing nations

LAWRENCE G. THOMAS

In the last two decades, formal education has become a topic of intense international concern, not only to professional educators, but also to anthropologists, sociologists, economists and political scientists. No longer is education seen as merely an individual consumer good for vocational preparation, informed citizenship and personal cultivation. It is now also recognized as an important kind of capital investment in a nation's future and as an instrument for national development, especially in the less industrialized countries of the world. The urgent demand from the developing countries is for sound, expert judgment concerning the strategies each nation should employ in expanding and utilizing its school systems.

To back up the judgments on strategy, there is a critical need for empirical evidence and tested generalizations on the relations of various educational arrangements to the culture, social structure, politics and economy of each country concerned. In collecting such information, the social scientists have differed significantly from the professional educators in the conceptualization of education. In general, the social scientists have tended to be too global in their treatment of the concept, while professional educators have usually been too specific. This criticism can be made clearer with a few illustrations.

Some social scientists appear to assume that formal education is a kind of homogeneous quality, varying only quantitatively in number of years. If this assumption were actually the case, such questions as these would be meaningful to investigate:

1   What is the relation of national productivity to the number of years of required attendance in school?
2   What is the relation of the percentage of 'educated unemployed' to the proportion of youth graduating from senior high school?
3   What is the relation of the percentage of registered voters participating in a national election to the average grade achievement of the adults 25 years of age or older?

Each of these questions assumes the homogeneity of education, i.e. that the education given in one elementary school is equivalent to that given in another, and that ten years of schooling taken here is equivalent to ten years taken there. This assumption is precarious even for schools in the same locality, and becomes extremely dubious for comparisons between different regions. For international comparisons, it becomes grotesque.

Professional educators, on the other hand, have tended to limit their quantitative comparisons to specific aspects of educational programmes, e.g. the effects of different kinds of teaching techniques, the effects of different types of subject-matter, or the effects of different teacher personalities. Comparisons between schools have been largely limited to differences in pupil scores on standardized achievement tests. Comparisons between nations have been restricted for the most part to contrasting descriptions of how various aspects of formal education developed in a number of countries. From these descriptions we know something about the types of schools, the kinds of curricula and the numbers of students enrolled, but we are comparatively ignorant of what goes on in these schools, how the subject-matter is selected, how the students are taught, and what immediate outcomes are sought in the examinations. Professional educators are well aware of the importance of comparing the effects of these differences and have conducted local experiments between different classrooms and between different schools, but they have only started to attack the problem on an interregional or international scale.

A possible first step in a systematic response to this problem is to identify major kinds of schooling according to the educational theories that determine their distinguishing characteristics. The rationale of this tactic is twofold. When an educational theory is used to select the salient features of a type of instruction, these features will be significant, first of all, in making up a coherent pattern of educational effort. Hence, they will have intrinsic significance within the type. For comparative purposes, however, the features of one type of instruction will also be selected for clearest distinction from those of another type. Thus they will have extrinsic significance for distinguishing among types. The educational features which satisfy these two criteria may or may not prove to possess significant relationships to social, economic and political factors, but at least they possess an important kind of educational significance.

Four theories of instruction are briefly described in the following pages as types of schooling—memorizing, training, developing intellect and problem solving. Even a hasty reading should be convincing that these are significantly different kinds of education. For ease of comparison, the descriptions of the types are classified under the same seven headings, but no claim is made that any of the headings is a significant educational variable by itself. Only the composite type is claimed to be an important meaning of formal education, not only because each of the four differs significantly from the others, but also because each type has its own integrity, distinctive emphases, and logical coherence. Readers are invited to judge whether the classrooms, schools and school systems they have known tend to fit one rather than another of these schooling types.

Type M—Memorizing

Suggestive illustrations

(*a*) Grammar schools of colonial New England.
(*b*) Academic schools of Korea, Thailand, Taiwan, etc.
(*c*) The Koran schools in Moslem countries.
(*d*) The Yobiko 'cram schools' in Japan preparing for admission examinations to high school and college.

Identifying principles

1. Sources of the curriculum (when all subjects are to be memorized):
   1.1. The best of the past.

2. Character of the goals:
   2.1. Values claimed.
   2.11. The best of the past is inherently worth learning.
   2.12. The fewer immediate uses a study has, the higher its intellectual value.
   2.2. Breadth of development sought.
   2.21. Efficient memorizing of the best in the cultural heritage is facilitated by the cultivation of certain character traits—persistence, obedience, respectful silence, deference to elders, etc.
   2.3. Goal definition.
   2.31. Traditional examinations define the relevant material to study.

3. Curriculum content (when the entire school is committed to this type of instruction):
   3.1. General organization.
   3.11. Curriculum often consists of classical literature, ancient philosophy, authoritative history, mathematical computation, descriptive science, principles of moral conduct.
   3.111. Could consist of recent conclusions in natural science, social science and humanities if appropriate to memorizing.
   3.12. A variety of subjects is commonly offered, but one principal skill is demanded—precise recall.
   3.2. Study materials.
   3.21. Consists chiefly of classical writings, models to imitate, lecture notes and textbooks of long-established worth.
   3.22. Seldom more than one textbook in a subject is studied at a time.

4. Learning activities:
   4.1. Basic method.
   4.11. R ote memorizing.

4.2. Student activities.
  4.21. Chiefly listening, observing, reading, reciting and writing.
  4.22. Class discussions rarely occur, and questions from students are discouraged.
4.3. Locus of student activities.
  4.31. Generally confined to the classroom and the library. The instructor has no concern nor responsibility for student activities that may go on outside these formal settings.

5. Teaching methods:
  5.1. Teacher activities.
    5.11. To lecture, conduct recitations, give assignments and examine.
      5.111. Lectures are often a substitute for unavailable textbooks. When used, lectures are didactic and are to be copied verbatim in students' notes.
  5.2. Motivation of students:
    5.21. Becoming educated is an austere and exacting process; interest in it is an obligation of educable students.
    5.22. In practice, however, the threat of failure is the chief source of motivation.
  5.3. Control of student conduct:
    5.31. Student habits of obedience, deference and undivided attention are essential and must be strictly enforced by the teacher.
  5.4. Provision for individual differences.
    5.41. Students in the classroom customarily engage in the same learning activities at the same time.

6. Tests of success:
  6.1. Chief expectation.
    6.11. Precise reproduction of facts and principles when specifically demanded.
  6.2. Relation to practice.
    6.21. Intellectual knowledge is simple possession of correct ideas; no relation to action or practice, except in taking examinations.

6.3. Sources of evidence.
 6.31. Extensive use of oral recitations and written examinations.

7. Anticipated outcomes:
 7.1. An accurate and precise memory; disciplined obedience.
 7.2. A well-stocked mind; intellectual conformance.
 7.3. Reverence of the past; resistance to change.
 7.4. Satisfaction of possessing classical learning for its own sake.

Type T—Training

Suggestive illustrations

(*a*) Most secondary-level vocational schools (agricultural, industrial, commercial) in most countries.
(*b*) Normal schools for teachers (U.S. type in 1900).
(*c*) Speech institutes, barber school, stenographic school.
(*d*) Foreign language instruction, especially when focused on oral fluency.

Identifying principles

1. Sources of the curriculum:
 1.1. The current (and sometimes anticipated) tasks or needs in some adult activity in the present society (or the immediate future).
  1.11. For moral training the sources are usually Scriptural and traditional.

2. Character of the goals:
 2.1. Values claimed.
  2.11. In general education, enabling children to learn to do better what they will have to do (or ought to do) anyway.
   2.111. In this instance it is appropriate to analyse adult activities for needed skills and attitudes to be learned by the students, thus producing competence in certain responsibilities (health habits, morality and ethics, political behaviour, family

roles, etc.) rather than developing a marketable skill.

2.12. In vocational education for a particular set of skills, the general goal is the achievement of employable competence at the time of graduation.

2.2. Breadth of development sought.

2.21. The focus is on developing a specific set of skills accompanied by appropriate attitudes, but typically without intellectual depth.

2.3. Goal definition.

2.31. The requirements for developing the skill, instead of the interests of the learners, determine the curriculum content. Hence, the specific goals within this framework are set by the instructor and prescribed for the students.

3. Curriculum content:

3.1. General organization.

3.11. Usually each set of skills is broken into its elemental components for separate treatment. Often each component is further analysed to facilitate drill on particular parts.

3.2. Study materials.

3.21. Extensive use is made of (a) manuals of directions, blueprints, recipes; (b) models, miniature job situations and modern equipment appropriate to the skill.

4. Learning activities:

4.1. Basic method.

4.11. Habituating specific skills and attitudes in action.

4.111. The theory of 'why' of the skill may be ignored or studied in a separate 'theory class'.

4.2. Student activities.

4.21. Much use is made of observation, imitation, drill and supervised practice.

4.3. Locus of student activities.

4.31. Formal class activities are usually subordinate to shop work, laboratory work, miniature demonstrations and on-the-job training.

5. Teaching methods:
  5.1. Teacher activities.
    5.11. To serve as model, make assignments, conduct drill, supervise practice, suggest improvements, locate on-the-job opportunities, recommend students to prospective employers.
  5.2. Motivation of students.
    5.21. Since emphasis is placed on performance rather than study and since the choice of training programmes is usually voluntary, the motivation is often intrinsic (enjoyment of the work itself) and/or extrinsic (the paid job it leads to). However, differences in student interests are seldom allowed to influence the nature of the skills to be acquired nor the standards to be met.
    5.22. For training in unpaid activities (e.g. morals, health habits, political behaviour), the motivation varies from artificial rewards (gold stars, special privileges) through group pressures for conformance (expectations of the family, exciting political rallies) to actual punishment (physical abuse, isolation).
  5.3. Control of student conduct.
    5.31. The teacher sets the rules for proper conduct (and proper use of equipment), and enforces the penalties for any violations.
  5.4. Provision for individual differences.
    5.41. Every student is expected to master the same required competences up to a prescribed level of proficiency.

6. Tests of success:
  6.1. Chief expectation.
    6.11. Sufficient competence in a skill for immediate employment (or, as in the case of unpaid skills, to satisfy the standards of performance set by the teacher or higher authority).
  6.2. Relation to practice.
    6.21. Knowledge is proved by performance; no separation of knowing and doing.
  6.3. Sources of evidence.
    6.31. Demonstrated performance in trial situations at a

specified level of competence is much preferred over written tests.

7. Anticipated outcomes:
   7.1. Automatic habits and well-conditioned attitudes.
   7.2. Precision in execution, fidelity to the model.
   7.3. Freedom from deviation, innovation and inquisitiveness.
   7.4. A high quality product from the skill.

Type D-I—Developing intellect

Suggestive illustrations

   (*a*) Most U.S. high schools and colleges (academic programmes).
   (*b*) The French *lycée*.
   (*c*) The German gymnasium.
   (*d*) British academic secondary schools.

Identifying principles

1. Sources of the curriculum:
   1.1. The range of subjects is largely limited to the contemporary conception of the liberal arts, because they are believed to be generative of lifelong learning and to discipline the mind.

2. Character of the goals:
   2.1. Values claimed.
      2.11. The immediate values of the study of these subjects are intrinsic (developing the intellect), preparatory (the foundation for competent living), and individualized (each student is left free to make whatever application of his learning he chooses).
      2.12. The value of a subject for intellectual development is inherent and is not found in its possible applications or possible uses.
   2.2. Breadth of development sought.
      2.21. Within each subject, the intent is to develop in each

N

student the basic equipment and subject familiarity
needed by a prospective specialist in that field.

2.22. Some attention is often given to character development, but this is usually promoted through such
environmental arrangements as competition for
awards, patriotic rituals, and strictly enforced regulations.

2.3. Goal definition.

2.31. The specific goals within this framework are set by
the instructor (or higher authority) and prescribed
for the students.

3. Curriculum content:

3.1. General organization.

3.11. The content consists of selections from the standard
arts and sciences, i.e. the natural sciences, the social
sciences, the humanities and the formal disciplines
(mathematics, grammar, logic).

3.111. Some adaptation may be made at the primary
grades, where children are just acquiring their
verbal and computational skills, but in all higher
grades these subjects are to be studied systematically according to the internal order scheme of
each field (e.g. chronology for history, simple to
complex for grammar).

3.112. The performing arts (music, painting, drama,
athletics, etc.) are often encouraged (to develop
character and a balanced personality), but they
stand on the periphery of the curriculum (i.e.
they seldom receive any academic credit or marks).
They can become part of the D-I academic
programme only as history, or as musicology,
aesthetics, kinesiology, etc.

3.2. Study materials.

3.21. Consist chiefly of textbooks, which are modern, and
often additional reference books.

3.211. A classically-oriented version is the 100 Great
Books recommended by Mortimer Alder.

3.22. Study resources may also include audio-visual equipment and field trips into the community, but *only*

when these aids are more efficient in promoting a knowledge of the subject than the usual classwork and homework.

4. Learning activities:
  4.1. Basic method.
    4.11. Reflective study of essential ideas to achieve some command of an organized discipline.
      4.111. The essential ideas are memorized, organized systematically, and then used in further analyses, interpretations and syntheses of the relevant subject-matter.
      4.112. In some subjects a type of problem solving is used: the teacher locates and defines the problem, and then assigns it to the students to solve.
  4.2. Student activities.
    4.21. Most frequently they are listening, observing, reading, and writing, but they may include reciting, discussing, questioning, solving predefined problems and doing laboratory work according to a manual.
  4.3. Locus of student activities.
    4.31. The above activities may occur just as appropriately outside of class as in, but the greatest educational value is realized when these activities focus on questions within the structure and content of the subject being studied instead of on practical applications or current social problems.
    4.32. Extra-class activities expressing the social and recreational interests of students are usually permitted, but are seldom regarded as making a serious contribution to the academic curriculum.

5. Teaching methods:
  5.1. Teacher activities.
    5.11. Major features of the teacher's role include lecturing to supplement the textbook, presenting demonstrations, questioning students' ideas, inviting questions of interpretation, composing assignments and examinations.
  5.2. Motivation of students

5.21. If the student finds enjoyment in his studies, this is a fortunate by-product to be welcomed, but not to be made a central intent in curriculum selection.

5.22. Most students require extraneous motivation (marks, honours, privileges, threats) to study what they should and to do their best. The teacher may use rewards as freely as punishment.

    5.221. The motivation is considered an aid to learning, but not a part of the knowledge acquired.

5.3. Control of student conduct.

5.31. The teacher usually sets the standards for proper conduct and enforces the penalties. In some situations, however (such as during examinations), the students may be permitted to administer the established rules and to report violations, sometimes even recommending the proper punishment to the teacher. The classroom atmosphere should be quiet, orderly and attentive to work.

5.4. Provision for individual differences.

5.41. The curriculum content may be varied in quantity for fast, medium, and slow learners, but the students in each group customarily study the same materials at the same time.

6. Tests of success:

  6.1. Chief expectation.

    6.11. Being able to cite and think like a beginning specialist in each subject studied.

  6.2. Relation to practice.

    6.21. Knowing precedes doing; the school is responsible for only the intellectual activities of knowing (except when skill training is combined with knowing, as in mathematics, science laboratories and written composition).

      6.211. Learning to know is conceived as education; learning to do is conceived as training.

  6.3. Sources of evidence.

    6.31. Examinations, term papers, oral quizzes, etc., on the concepts, inner relationships and methodology of the discipline.

7. Anticipated outcomes:
   7.1. Disciplined habits of thinking and mental acuity.
   7.2. Intellectual curiosity and inquisitiveness; devotion to lifelong learning.
   7.3. Readiness to attack adult problems (later) with understanding and insight.
   7.4. Systematic understanding of the good, true, and beautiful in the cultural heritage; reverence for scholarship.

Type P-S—Problem solving

Suggestive illustrations

(*a*) Some elementary classrooms in the United States (a minority).
(*b*) A few progressive private schools in the United States.
(*c*) Experimental programmes in science teaching, selected elementary schools in the Philippines (Orata).
(*d*) Small Industry Extension Training, Hyderabad, India.
(*e*) The advanced proposals of most curriculum theorists in the United States.

Identifying principles

1. Sources of the curriculum:
   1.1. Representative selection from the range of public and personal problems of current concern to adults and to children.

2. Character of the goals:
   2.1. Values claimed.
      2.11. The general goals of schooling are set by the core values of a society and the nature of the problem-solving process. For example, the major responsibilities of teaching include:
      2.111. Developing problem-solving competence through experiences in seeking solutions to personal and community problems.
      2.112. Promoting intellectual interests and competence

through encouraging the 'why' spirit in all learning activities (not just through special subjects).

2.2. Breadth of development sought.

2.21. Promoting the discovery of cultivated enjoyments (which are both the justification for and the consummation points of all problem solving).

2.22. Developing democratic self-concepts and socialized personalities (an essential condition for continued problem solving).

2.3. Goal definition.

2.31. The specific goals within this framework are determined co-operatively and critically by the students and teacher in interaction (instead of given by higher authority).

3. Curriculum content:

3.1. General organization.

3.11. Large blocks of time devoted to major areas of problems—family, civic, recreation, vocation, consumership, health, etc. These areas enter the curriculum, not as content to be studied, but as 'arranged environments' to provoke serious interests and to serve as possible resources as students pursue such interests.

3.12. Learning an organized discipline is seldom a starting point (except for precocious youngsters who see such study as *their* problem to solve). However, after extensive problem solving experiences using materials from a standard discipline (historical materials, for instance, or chemical materials or grammatical materials), the majority of students, it is believed, will eventually seek a systematic command of the discipline itself.

3.2. Study materials.

3.21. The study resources used are distinguished by (*a*) a large number of reference materials, (*b*) extensive use of the out-of-class environment, (*c*) large amounts of subject-matter held in reserve as 'resource units' for possible use whenever the course of student problem solving demands them.

4. Learning activities:
  4.1. Basic method.
    4.11. Problem solving conceived as involving all the following steps:
      4.111. Direct experiencing of an indeterminate situation (puzzling, intriguing).
      4.112. Defining the problem (setting the goal).
      4.113. Collecting relevant data (from books, lectures, observations, interviews, field trips, etc.) and generalizations from past experience.
      4.114. Organizing the data in promising ways (e.g. as hypotheses for testing).
      4.115. Trying out hypothetical solutions to the problem (i.e. actual ways to reach the goal).
      4.116. Drawing conclusions and generalizations (in the light of the satisfactions and disappointments experienced).
  4.2. Student activities.
    4.21. In addition to listening, observing, reading, writing and generalizing, the problem-solving process calls for such distinctive student activities as locating problems, defining problems, committee work and group projects, systematic activities in the community and trying out ideas in action.
  4.3. Locus of student activities.
    4.31. In a problem-solving context, understanding arises from experiencing the 'what', 'how' and 'why' in functional (active) relationships. This kind of activity cannot and should not be confined to the classroom or even the school grounds, but properly extends to the home and community.
    4.32. Extra-class activities like student government, school clubs, and social affairs are considered to be as educationally significant as in-class activities and also an excellent source of certain kinds of problems to be solved.

5. Teaching methods:
  5.1. Teacher activities.
    5.11. Teaching is conceived as the stimulation and guidance

of student inquiry. Thus, while there are occasions for lectures and teacher-led discussions, most of the teacher's time is spent in the roles of data collector, resource explorer, environment arranger, alternative suggester, procedural assistant, expediter, critic and questioner.

5.111. The students retain the ultimate responsibility for defining the specific problems to be solved, although the teacher stimulates new interests, proposes alternatives, and criticizes student choices.

5.2. Motivation of students.

5.21. In the light of the first two steps in problem solving, the motivation is characteristically intrinsic rather than extraneous. A consummatory enjoyment is the normal purpose and anticipated conclusion of problem solving.

5.22. The students' purposes are believed to become part of the knowledge learned (e.g. the kind of motivation which induces students to learn about nutrition becomes an attitudinal part of what they know about nutrition).

5.3. Control of student conduct.

5.31. Most of the classroom rules are composed cooperatively, in the light of experienced problems, and enforced jointly, often through elected student officers.

5.32. A pragmatic attitude is taken towards student movements and noise, restricting them only to a fair consideration for others.

5.33. Review and revision of regulations occur frequently, being regarded as further opportunities for significant problem solving.

5.4. Provision for individual differences.

5.41. The curriculum content may vary both in kind and in amount according to the interests and talents of different groups of students in the class.

5.42. Since a variety of student goals is encouraged, only occasionally (e.g. utilizing a resource speaker, evaluating progress) are most students in the class doing the same thing at the same time.

6. Tests of success:
  6.1. Chief expectation.
    6.11. Enhanced student competence in identifying, defining, and solving new problems. Also, eventually, an organized understanding of the disciplines from which he has previously drawn the chief means of his problem solving.
  6.2. Relation to practice.
    6.21. Knowledge is proved by performance; no separation of knowing and doing.
    6.22. What a student knows is what he can actually do (including reciting accurately and writing acceptable papers as well as choosing a different diet or petitioning the city council for changes in traffic regulations).
  6.3. Sources of evidence.
    6.31. Minimal use of paper-and-pencil tests; extensive use of actual or miniature problem situations.

7. Anticipated outcomes:
  7.1. Self-discipline learned from overcoming natural obstacles to the satisfying solution of one's own problems.
    7.11. Enhances self-confidence and responsibility for self-direction.
  7.2. Enthusiasm for innovation, creativity and qualitative differences among persons.
  7.3. Readiness and competence to continue investigating the problems of a changing society.
  7.4. A broadly pragmatic attitude towards values, standards, rules and truth.
    7.41. Seeing traditions and the past as chiefly resources for present problem solving and future planning.

Testing the validity and significance of the types

At this point the four types of schooling represent theoretical constructions largely. They are drawn, of course, from the practices as well as the beliefs of many teachers, but none of the types is likely to be found in its pure form in any school system or even in any one classroom. They are intended to serve as standards for identifying significantly different tendencies in educational practice. The validity of the four types is more logical than empirical at this stage of our thinking, but, like all theory, they can guide what we shall look for in subsequent research.

The next step in a systematic research programme would be to test their validity empirically and then to explore whether each type is distinctively related to a variety of external factors which affect both the support and the use of formal education in programmes of national development. The major questions that need to be answered would include the following:

1   How good is the fit of these types of schooling to existing educational programmes in various countries of the world? The answer to this question tests the usefulness of the types. If they could be useful if valid, then the next question becomes appropriate.

2   How valid are the claims of each type for functional connections between its preferred means and its professed ends? Granted that these relationships have a logical coherence and plausibility, do they work out empirically as anticipated? Specifically, do the curriculum content and teaching methods recommended actually produce the anticipated outcomes?

3   Are there a few critical factors within each type that distinguish it from the others at least as clearly as the complete type descriptions do now? If a few factors (e.g. the principal method of learning encouraged, the source of standards for judging success, or the relation of knowledge to practice) can be identified which, when taken together, serve as reliable and unambiguous clues to the entire character of the instructional type, much time can be saved and the procedure for classifying schools in a given region can be greatly simplified.

4   In what ways can the approximation of a region-wide level of schooling to one of the instructional types be indicated? This question asks for the exploration of specific techniques for choosing expert observers, standardizing their observations, and quantifying their judgments.

5   What educational conditions are especially influential in enhancing or diminishing the effective operation of each type of schooling in actual practice? This question invites empirical investigation to locate the essential conditions of teaching and learning, not only within each type, but also to a range of external variables. Within the types, the concern might be with

the effects of different ways of motivation, different styles of classroom discipline or different kinds of teacher personalities. The external factors could include economic, political, and cultural variables that are most often associated with the development and maintenance of each type of schooling.

6 What characteristics of a society appear to be associated, in ways that suggest consequential relationships, with long-established schools of a distinctive type? The direction of inquiry in this question is the reverse of the previous one. Although the causes of a society's characteristics are multiple and complexly related, educational planners need to know whether a distinctive type of schooling operating over a sufficiently long period in a given society is related to social change as a major producer, a catalyst, or an elegant decorator.

Significant dimensions on which national societies differ

While the answers to the above questions must depend on careful empirical studies, we need hypotheses to guide the investigations. One set of hypotheses will concern the social and cultural factors that are most closely related to the uses of education for national development. But before these hypotheses can be formulated we need to identify some significant dimensions on which national societies differ, especially those which are most likely to affect, or be affected by, different types of schooling. Some examples of this important kind of national differences are proposed below:

1 *From* a predominantly rural, manual-labour economy *to* a predominantly urban, techological economy.
2 *From* cultural resistance to technological change *to* cultural eagerness for technological advancement.
3 *From* cultural homogeneity *to* cultural heterogeneity (including racial and ethnic composition as well as plural economic systems, religions, classes, etc.).
4 *From* commitment to cultural conformance *to* commitment to cultural pluralism.
5 *From* rigid social stratification *to* fluid social stratification.
6 *From* highly centralized political power *to* widely decentralized political power.

7 *From* autocratic control of schooling *to* popular control of schooling.

8 *From* concern with educating only an élite *to* concern for mass education.

Hypothetical relations of types of schooling to these dimensions

If the four types of schooling outlined earlier turn out to have a considerable degree of empirical validity in national settings, then studies can be undertaken of their distinctive relationships to social, economic and cultural variables like the eight listed above. The following sets of hypotheses are merely speculative, drawn from unsystematic impressions, but they are plausible and may be suggestive of the rich variety of hypotheses that can guide later research when cogent theories are developed first.

M-type schooling

This type of schooling is not intended to produce competent activitists in the economic and political life of the society. Its major concern is with cultivating the inner life of the mind. Its connection with the world of action is largely to serve as a screen or hurdle to be passed before one is admitted to positions of responsibility. Hence it should not be judged for a possible functional contribution to one's performance in the active world.

Preliminary hypotheses

1 Useful in mass education for preserving the beliefs, history and literature of the nation.

2 Useful in mass education for cultivating traits of obedience, reverence of the past, intellectual conformance, deference to elders.

3 If successful memorizing is more a function of effort and persistence than of native ability, M-type schooling for all appeals to the common people as egalitarian in spirit and offering equal opportunity for advanced schooling. Hence, enhances vertical social mobility when schooling is a major index of employment and social status.

4 If only the élite receive formal education, M-type not only fits the genteel tradition of this class, but lies within the capacity of all élite children to master.

5 No direct contribution to developing either leaders or consumers of technological change. May create resistance to technological advancement.

6 Useful in mass education for making heterogeneous groups more homogeneous ('melting pot' policy); unlikely to promote cultural pluralism.

7 Least demanding of all types on teacher preparation; hence, it is the easiest type for which to supply adequate teachers.

8 Neither the teachers nor the students are likely to become critics of the existing social order as a result of M-type schooling.

9 The least expensive of the four types, because it requires so little in learning materials (and need not require extensive teacher preparation).

10 Accommodates indifferently to highly centralized political power and to widely decentralized political power.

11 Accommodates indifferently to autocratic control of schooling and to popular control of schooling.

12 Adapts readily to quantitative individual differences (slow and fast learners), but tends to ignore or eliminate qualitative individual differences (in interests or special talents). Hence, it is efficient for obtaining standardized outcomes with homogeneous groups of students; it is not efficient for obtaining varied outcomes with heterogeneous groups of students.

T-type schooling

This type of schooling is exclusively intended to equip one for the active world, whether in moral behaviour, civic behaviour or vocational performance. The trained person has some specific understanding of what he is about, but the stress is on skilled performance. He may understand the task, but not the occupation; he may understand the economics of his job, but not the economics of his labour market.

Preliminary hypotheses

1 For élite education, it is efficient in teaching the non-intellectual aspects of schooling, e.g. character training (as in

public schools of England), sports skills, art skills, public speaking, etiquette.

2   At its best, it cultivates attitudes of precision, fidelity to models and high standards of workmanship.

3   When applied to vocational preparation and offered as an alternative to general academic schooling, it has mass appeal for its practical orientation. (This practical appeal, however, may be more than counterbalanced by the prestige appeal of academic schooling and the genteel occupation popularly associated with the latter.)

4   Facilitates vertical social mobility only from the lower class to the middle class, i.e. from employment in unskilled and semi-skilled occupations to employment in skilled and commercial occupations.

5   Often believed to be socially degrading because it involves so much practical use of physical skills and so little use of ideas and abstractions.

6   Commonly associated with vocational programmes that terminate schooling at a young age. Children of the élite customarily avoid such programmes, while children from the working class usually fill them, thus producing in effect a segregated education by economic status.

7   Seldom produces innovating leaders of technological change, but may be used to train followers for fixed types of new roles in the emerging social order. Thus, T-type schooling can promote needed vocational skills and consumer attitudes for technological advances, but without providing understanding and control of the new society by the recipients of this training.

8   Probably the most efficient method for quick results in basic literacy, habits of sanitation, voting procedures, etc., especially in adult education.

9   Useful in mass education for making heterogeneous groups more homogeneous ('melting pot' policy); unlikely to promote cultural pluralism, although it could provide the minimal homogeneity needed for cultural pluralism.

10   Usually demands teachers with practical experience from employment in the fields taught. Hence, teacher recruitment is commonly in direct competition with employment in these other fields.

11   Neither the teachers nor the students are likely to become

critics of the existing social order as a result of T-type schooling (except when unemployment of trained graduates is high).

12 Can be one of the most expensive to operate of the four types, because of the consumable supplies and training equipment required.

13 The easiest type of schooling to justify in terms of measurable results of economic value.

14 The easiest type of schooling to turn over to non-professionals for the selection of curriculum content. Selected adult activities can be analysed for the needed skills and attitudes to be learned by students, and each set of skills can be broken into its elemental components for separate treatment.

15 T-type schooling is one of the two (P-S-type is the other) which are most susceptible to public evaluation and criticism. The public participation can range from co-operation to interference.

16 Probably accommodates somewhat better to autocratic control of schooling than to decentralized, popular control of schooling.

17 Like M-type schooling, T-type adapts readily to *quantitative* individual differences (slow and fast learners), but tends to ignore or eliminate *qualitative* individual differences (in interests or special talents). Hence, it is efficient for obtaining standardized outcomes with homogeneous groups of students; it is not efficient for obtaining varied outcomes with heterogeneous groups of students.

D-I-type schooling

D-I-type schooling stresses the learning of subject-matter organized into disciplines (geography, history, botany) and basic skills (reading, spelling). The curriculum content consists largely of concepts, generalizations, theory and knowledge-about. The students are expected to memorize essential ideas, organize them systematically and use them reflectively in further analyses and interpretations of the subject-matter under study. This schooling is claimed to be good for all educable students because it gives them some acquaintance with the organized subjects underlying all knowledge, and also develops and disciplines their minds.

Preliminary hypotheses

1   The successful graduates of D-I-type schooling are character-ized affectively by (*a*) academically intellectual interests, (*b*) research interests or (*c*) habitual motivation for extraneous rewards.

2   Probably 20–30 per cent of normal children become inter-ested in learning this kind of knowledge for its own sake. The rest of the school-age population commonly see little use in it, and hence require extraneous motivation to do this kind of study.

3   D-I-type schooling can produce an adequate proportion of leaders if the upper strata having access to it contain enough children who can profit from it. This type of schooling is not appropriate for mass education, for it either forces a high drop-out rate if standards are maintained or tends to change into M-type schooling so that larger numbers can succeed.

4   When economic barriers are equalized, this schooling facilitates vertical social mobility for students with any of the three motivations noted in 1.

5   Since the curriculum of D-I-type schooling is usually fixed in advance, equal educational opportunity tends to be expressed as identical educational opportunity.

6   The supply of teachers for this kind of schooling, espec-ially at the secondary and higher levels, is drawn largely from those students who enjoyed mastering a subject for its own sake but who are often not competent nor interested in its practical applications (a characteristic shared with M-type teachers).

7   Since this type of schooling aims at understanding more than the development of practical skills, two hypotheses follow:

   a   The practical effects on the competence of graduates (or school-leavers) in such adult activities as politics, occupations, consumership, family adjustment and recreation are difficult, if not impossible, to identify within the first decade after leaving school. (This is not to deny that many such graduates will be given access to choice occupations and higher earning power for pres-tigious reasons, but these reasons are functionally un-related to their academic studies.)

   b   Since this type of schooling approaches its goals through classroom tasks that require very little direct experience in major activities of adult life, the authorities will recognize that it needs to be followed by considerable practical training before the student is competent for employment or successful performance in the relevant adult activities.

8 D-I-type schooling demands freedom of intellectual inquiry and debate, but is seldom the means for producing activist critics of the existing social order.

9 Shares with M-type schooling the distinction of having scholars (college professors) in predominant control of the curriculum.

10 Is strongly resistant to propagandistic uses of education, even though it can adapt readily to an autocratic form of school organization.

P-S-type schooling

Education through problem solving conceives a problem broadly as any desired satisfaction which cannot be obtained merely by wishing, regards student interests as a necessary though not sufficient guide to curriculum construction, insists that knowledge is obtained only by acting on ideas, and contends that a command of organized subject-matter is the end point rather than the starting point of sound schooling. Hence, the general method of this type of schooling is claimed to be appealing as well as appropriate to all ranges of student ability at all grade levels.

Preliminary hypotheses

1 Learning achieved through the intrinsic motivation of problem solving is more enduring and more widely applied than learning from extraneous motivation.

2 Problem-solving schooling is the most likely type to produce activists and critics of the social order without resort to propaganda.

3 At the same time, because of its practical nature and its

o

appeal to intrinsic interests, this type of schooling is more likely to prepare for continuous change and least likely, in urbanized, industrial society, to produce youth who are alienated from the values and concerns of that society.

4 Encourages uniformity in the *method* of identifying and solving problems, but heterogeneity (cultural pluralism) in tastes, standards and ideals.

5 Encourages, by the nature of the problem solving process, a great degree of innovation and creative variation, not only among students but also among teachers. Hence, this type of schooling is the least predictable regarding the particular knowledge the students will acquire, but the most likely type to cultivate intellectual understanding and critical choice in all aspects of living—occupations, consumership, politics, recreation, family affairs, religion, etc.

6 Has the greatest difficulty of all schooling types in securing competent teachers, since it demands teachers with as much practical experience as those in T-type schooling and with even deeper scholarship than those in D-I-type schooling.

a Since the demands on the teacher become increasingly greater as the level of schooling advances, most examples of competent instruction in P-S-type schooling occur in the elementary grades.

7 Is the most likely type to develop both creators and competent consumers of technological change.

8 Is the most likely type to promote an egalitarian respect for individuals and a fluid social structure.

9 Is the most likely type to promote habits of co-operation in dealing with major social problems and the enjoyment of competition in peripheral matters.

10 The administration of the schools tends strongly to be non-autocratic and to invite considerable consultation and participation from both teachers and students.

11 Is the most likely type to develop multiple channels of leadership and a circulating leadership, all in close conjunction with followership.

12 Invites a high degree of co-operative participation by the public in identifying significant problems for study, providing resource materials, and appraising the results achieved.

Conclusion

This chapter has been an exercise in constructing theories and projecting hypotheses. The purpose of the theory construction was to make the concept of formal education a more meaningful variable in studies of the political, economic and social uses of schooling for national development. The four types of schooling presented need to have their distinctive claims validated empirically, but in the meantime their logical coherence offers better variables for social-science research than the undifferentiated conception of education has. The purpose of projecting hypotheses was not only to demonstrate the fruitfulness of the theories presented, but also to stimulate the composition of alternative hypotheses and systematic efforts to verify or falsify all such hypotheses.

These are tasks that command the teamwork of professional educators and social scientists. Together they can create an applied science in the uses of education for human-resource development and national modernization.

eleven

Models for decision-making in educational planning and administration

HECTOR CORREA

I

In any educational plan, whether for an institution or for a national system, three basic elements must be considered. They are the inputs of education, such as teachers, buildings, financial resources, etc.; the demand for education from the school-age population; and the output of the educational system that determines the educational structure of the population. These elements are shown in Fig. 1, in which the educational system appears as the combination of teachers, buildings, financial and other resources, and students that produces educated people as its output. An important point is that the inputs and the demand for education are determined outside the educational system, and the educational structure of the population must satisfy socio-economic needs. The interaction of these three elements determines the characteristics and the evolution of an educational system. As a simple example, the number of students per teacher is one characteristic of the educational system. This is mainly determined by the supply of teachers available, the financial resources that can be used for teachers, and the number of students demanding education. The number of students per teacher will vary according to changes in its determinants.

The simplest approach to educational planning—discussed in detail in references (6) and (7)—has two characteristics: (a) the

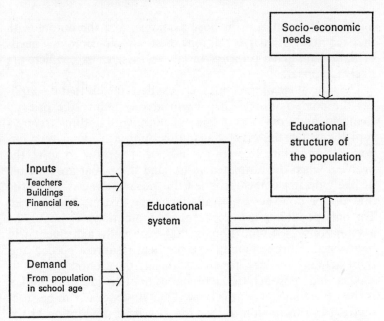

Fig. 1   Basic elements that must be considered in an educational plan

interaction among the three elements in Fig. 1 is partially or totally disregarded and (*b*) the characteristics of the educational system are considered as fixed—for instance, the students–teachers ratio is considered constant.

In this approach one of the three elements mentioned above receives priority, and the others must adapt to it. With the characteristics of the priority element and those of the educational system which are considered fixed, it is possible to estimate what values the other elements must have. For instance, if the number of students and the students–teachers ratio are given, it is possible to compute the number of teachers required.

Naturally, these estimates might not bear any relationship to the inputs that are likely to be available and the educational structure of the population needed for socio-economic development. A symbolic representation of these conditions appears in Fig. 2. It is drawn with the assumption that school-age population receives priority, and is used to estimate the required inputs and the output of the system. The inputs represented might be in conflict with those available, and the output with that required. Similar conditions exist if socio-economic needs or inputs are given priority. In any of these cases conflicts are likely to appear.

The advantage of the approach just described is that it simplifies the computations. They begin at one point—the priority element—and flow in only one direction, with nothing to interrupt them. On the other hand, this approach has a very important limitation. It gives no indication of how to solve the problem when the estimated values and those that are possible or likely do not coincide. When this occurs, there is very little that can be done systematically when the first method is used. The only possibility is to repeat the computations, changing the assumptions used, and hoping that eventually agreement will be reached between human and physical resources needed and those actually available for education and the economy.

A second approach to the preparation of an educational plan is the main concern of this paper. The basic ideas will be summarized in this section. In Section II a brief description of the most important applications is presented, and Sections III and IV include detailed examples.

The second approach to planning is characterized by the consideration given to the interactions among the different elements of the educational system. This does not mean that no one of the elements presented in Fig. 1 has priority, but rather that its value is determined, taking explicitly into consideration the characteristics of the other elements. For instance, the educational structure of the population could have priority. However, in this second approach this only means that the priority element will receive all the attention compatible with the characteristics of the other elements. The educational structure of the population is not used to determine the inputs and demand for education required; rather, these two elements are used to evaluate the educational structure that will be feasible. At this point the difference between the first and second approaches to planning seems to be a question of semantics. In the first approach priority was given, say, to demand for education coming from the school-age population, and it was used to determine the educational structure of the population. In the second approach lip-service is paid to the educational structure

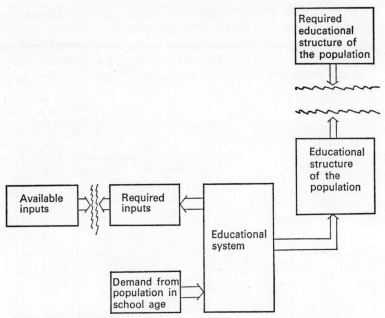

Fig. 2 First approach to planning when the demand from the population in school age has priority

of the population because it is said to have priority, but inputs and demand for education are used to determine the characteristics of the educational structure of the population. This seems to indicate that, despite the priority given to it, the educational structure of the population will actually be determined by the inputs available, and the demand for education from the school-age population. However, this impression is mistaken, because a new element has also been added, as will be seen below.

The substantial improvement provided by the second approach to planning is that the characteristics of the educational system are considered to be variable. In this second approach to planning, the number of students per teacher, students per classroom, etc., are variables. With this approach, each variation in the characteristics of the educational system will give a different value to the priority element. This can be seen in Fig. 3, in which four alternatives for the educational system are considered, and each of them brings about a different educational structure of the population.

Now a new problem appears. Which of the alternatives available should be chosen? The answer to this question is both the basic contribution of the second method to planning, and its weakest point. The answer is that the alternative to be chosen is the one that is optimum from the point of view of the decision-

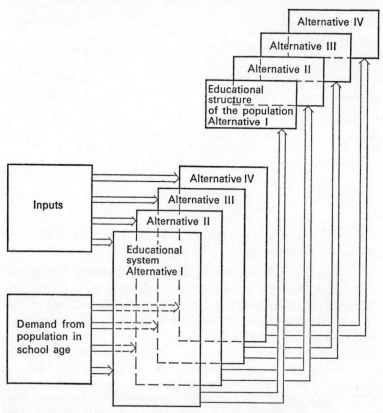

Fig. 3 Second approach to planning when the educational structure of the population has priority, and four alternative characterizations of the educational system are considered

makers, i.e. the one that satisfies their more urgent needs. The answer is the weakest point of the second approach to planning, because it does not explain how these more urgent needs can be determined. Only when they are determined is it possible to proceed with the selection of the best alternative.

In the description made, the basic elements of a decision problem have been introduced—namely, a goal or objective to be achieved, different methods to achieve it, each using different qualities and quantities of resources, and, finally limitation of the resources that can be used. The basic assumption used in the solution of a decision problem is that the objective sought must be maximized within the limits of the human and physical resources available, or a fixed goal has to be reached with a minimum use of resources.

The solution of a decision problem such as this includes:

a The optimum value that can be achieved for the priority element, given the resources available and the methods that can be used.
b The combination of resources that must be used in order to achieve this optimum value. This combination can never exceed the resources available.

The computational techniques used to obtain the solution of a decision problem are far more complicated than those used in the first approach to planning. In these computations each alternative available is tried. In each try a new alternative is compared with the one that has performed best up to that point. If the new alternative is better, the old one is discarded, otherwise it is retained and a new alternative tried. The procedure continues until all the alternatives have been tried. The mathematical technique for this procedure is one of the basic elements of mathematical models for decision-making.

As can be seen, these models, to a large extent, provide only an exact procedure for comparing the alternatives available and choosing which of them fits the criteria that the planner or administrator considers reasonable. They do not replace the planner or administrator in their basic functions, i.e. in the determination of alternatives and basic objectives, but only in the routine comparison of the performance of each alternative.

II

In this section a brief description of some of the possible applications of mathematical models for decision-making will be presented. In this description, emphasis will be placed on the principal alternatives that could be considered. As mentioned before, one of the basic characteristics of the models to be discussed is that they take into consideration the interaction among the different elements of the system studied, i.e. every model includes most if not all of these elements. For this reason the classification below is based on the element which is considered of most importance in the model.

Integration of educational and population planning

In this case it is assumed that a fixed amount of financial resources is available. These resources should be used to optimize the output of education measured, say, in total number of years of education of the population. One alternative way to achieve this end is to use the financial resources to improve the quality of teachers, classrooms and other human and physical inputs of the educational system. In this way the system could accommodate a larger number of students. The quality and quantity of the output would be determined by the combination of good teachers and educational facilities with a large number of students. The second alternative is to use the financial resources available in population planning. In this case teachers and educational facilities of lower quality will accommodate a smaller number of students. The basic assumption is that good teachers teaching a large number of students can obtain results comparable to those obtained by poor teachers with fewer students. However, the costs of these two combinations might not be equal. The combination that should be used is the one that maximizes output by unit of cost. An equivalent statement of the model would be to minimize the cost of achieving a fixed total number of years of education.

A different approach can be taken in the integration of education and population planning. In this approach population planning has priority. The objective could be to approximate as much as possible a desired family size. One way to do this is to use the resources available for the free distribution of the implements required to reduce or increase natality. The other is to educate people with regard to the availability of these implements and their use, and let them obtain the required materials with their own resources. The approach that should be used is the one that minimizes the differences between actual and desired family size per unit of cost.

Integration of educational and health planning

Again, in this case it is assumed that the financial resources available are limited. They can be used to improve the nutrition and health of the students, or the quality and quantity of teachers, buildings and facilities used in education. The alternatives open are healthy students with poor teachers, or less healthy students with good teachers. The combination chosen should be the one that maximizes the educational output.

Also in the case of health and educational planning, it is possible to invert the roles of health and education and consider education as an input for health. In this case, the alternatives are direct applications of preventive or curative techniques, or education of people in the use of these techniques. The objective is to optimize the health of the community.

Integration of educational and economic planning

Both the theory and the application of a mathematical model oriented to the integration of educational and economic planning have received a great deal of attention. Detailed descriptions of these models, when interaction is not considered, appear in references (5), (7), (13) and (14).

The basic characteristics of the models when interaction is considered follow the lines of those already described. Economic goals are usually considered to be the objective of the planning process. The basic alternatives considered are investment in education to improve the quantity and quality of the labour force or investment in physical capital. The type of investment with higher return per unit of cost should receive a higher priority. Detailed descriptions of these models appear in references (1), (2), (3), (7), (14), (15), (17), (20) and (21). Of particular interest are references (1), (3) and (17), where detailed applications to Argentina, Nigeria and Morocco, respectively, are included.

Models dealing with the size and other characteristics of the student body (References (8), (18))

The alternatives considered in this case are a large student body that, due to its own size, would have a large total cost despite low per student cost *v.* a selected student body which in addition receives a better, more expensive education. The number of drop-outs in the first case will be larger than in the second case. However, due to its size, the first combination might produce a larger and/or better output than the second one. The model just described reverses the assumptions used for the integration of educational and population planning. In the present case, sheer size is expected to overcome educational deficiencies. When used together with population planning, a larger size is combined with better education.

Models dealing with the distribution of the flows of students over time (Reference (6))

The simplest type deals with the problem, frequent in developing countries, of opening schools for a back-log of persons who have not enrolled in the educational system, even though they are old enough to do so. If schools are opened for all these persons simultaneously, then when their enrolment is complete there will be an over-supply of educational facilities. This is so because once the back-log is provided for, not all the educational facilities constructed would still be needed. These facilities required for the increase in number of students due to population growth would be used, while the rest would be idle. It is possible to distribute over time the construction of educational facilities needed for a back-log of students, in order to minimize the investment required.

The question considered in this model can be inverted so that the number of persons in the back-log entering the system is maximized with a fixed investment in education.

Models dealing with choice among types of education (Reference (10))

A large number of these models could be considered because there are different ways to classify education by types. As a simple example, the classification between general and vocational education could be considered. The distinction between these two types of education could be made in terms of the probability of its immediate application in a production process. The probability is higher in the case of vocational than in that of general education. This advantage is compensated by the fact that the probability of unemployment for a person with a highly specialized vocational education is also higher, because his specialization might not be demanded. The objective to guide in the choice of these two alternatives could be the total income obtained by educated persons. This income should be maximized with the use of a fixed amount of resources that can be used in education.

Models dealing with choices in adult education (*References* (*4*), (*12*))

The most important forms of adult education are literacy campaigns and on-the-job training. A detailed study of the former will be made in Section IV.

On-the-job training can be seen from the point of view of the trainee, of the institution providing the training, or of the firm where the trainee is working. The trainee exchanges low present income and status for a higher one in the future. For the institution providing the training, all the possible models mentioned before could be considered. For the industry where the trainee works, the main alternatives are workers with low levels of qualification, low salary and perhaps low mobility, and workers with high levels of qualification, high salaries and higher mobility.

It is also possible to combine the models dealing with the education of children considered in the first examples with those dealing with adult education. The problem would be to determine the age-group that should receive more attention.

Models dealing with choice of educational facilities and methods (*References* (*9*), (*11*), (*19*))

The alternatives that could be included in these models range from the choice of school location in a city, state or country as a whole, choice among different types of school constructions, laboratories, teacher aids, etc., and between methods and content of instruction. The main problem in this case is to determine the educational effects of the different alternatives.

III

The characteristics of a model for decision-making will be further explored in this section, using a simple example elaborated from references (8), (14) and (15). An 'educational pyramid' is the aspect of the educational system to be considered. This educational pyramid consists of the students in the different levels of education. It will be assumed here that there are only three educational levels, elementary school, high school and college, and that all students entering a level complete it.

The alternatives to be considered are the different number of students possible in each level. In making this choice, attention will be paid to interaction among the different levels, and also to the interaction between number of students and educational inputs. These inputs could be teachers, buildings, financial resources, or even the time available to the students themselves. In the simple example used here, only financial inputs will be considered. It is necessary to choose among the different numbers of students possible in each level, because of the limited amount of financial resources available. The educational pyramid will be optimal if the number of students in each of these levels is the most adequate one according to the criterion adopted as most appropriate.

For the mathematical presentation, the number of students will be denoted by m_i, $i = 1$ for elementary school, $i = 2$ for high school and $i = 3$ for college. It is possible to express the interaction among these levels in a simple way, if the time dimension is ignored. It can be assumed that the number of students in elementary school must be larger or equal to that for high school, and that the number in high school must be larger or equal to that for college; also that the number in college has a minimum of zero, i.e.

$$(1) \qquad\qquad m_1 \geqslant m_2 \geqslant m_3 \geqslant 0$$

Equation (1) gives a more concrete form to the possible

alternatives. If it is considered advisable to include some students in high school, then there must be some in elementary school; and, if some college students are desired, then there must be some high-school and elementary-school students also. In no case would a negative number of students make sense.

In order to relate the financial resources available to enrolment, the cost per student will be used. Let

c_1 = cost per student in elementary school
$c_1 + c_2$ = cost per student in high school
$c_1 + c_2 + c_3$ = cost per student in college

As an example of numerical values for these parameters, it will be assumed that

$$c_1 = \$2\cdot2 \text{ thousand per student}$$
$$c_2 = \$2\cdot3 \text{ thousand per student}$$
$$c_3 = \$5\cdot4 \text{ thousand per student}$$

With these parameters, the total expenditures are equal to

$$c_1 m_1 + c_2 m_2 + c_3 m_3$$

or

$$2\cdot2 m_1 + 2\cdot3 m_2 + 5\cdot4 m_3$$

The reason why only c_1, c_2 and c_3 appear in equation (2) is that the cost of the m_2 students in high school is included among the m_1 students in elementary school. The same is true for college students.

The fixed amount of financial resources will be denoted by R. For a numerical example, this value of R will be set at $85,817,000, a figure that corresponds roughly to the financial resources available in the United States in 1956. Combining the cost equation with the limitation of financial resources, the following constraint is obtained

(2) $$c_1 m_1 + c_2 m_2 + c_3 m_3 \leqslant R$$

or, in numerical values,

$$2\cdot2 m_1 + 2\cdot3 m_2 + 5\cdot4 m_3 \leqslant 85{,}817{,}000$$

These constraints simply indicate that the financial resources used must be at most equal to those available.

It is clear that there are many combinations of numbers of students that satisfy conditions (1) and (2).

For instance,

$$m_1 = m_2 = m_3 = 100$$

where condition (1) is satisfied because m_1 is equal to m_2 and m_2 is equal to m_3, and condition (2) because the total cost of such an educational pyramid would be

$$220 + 230 + 540 = 990$$

that is, less than R.

Another educational pyramid satisfying (1) and (2) is

$$m_1 = 1000$$
$$m_2 = 500$$
$$m_3 = 0$$

and many more could be found.

The problem now is how to choose among these alternatives. This problem is the most important and difficult one in the decision-making process. A detailed discussion of it appears in references (16) and (18). Several possible criteria for choice will be considered below.

(1) It could be decided that the number of college students (m_3) should be maximized.

(2) Another possibility is to make the number of high-school students (m_2) as large as possible, or

(3) m_1 twice as large as m_2, m_2 twice as large as m_3, and m_3 as large as possible, etc.

In order to choose from among these alternatives, the objective of education should be specified. In the examples above, the objectives chosen were expressed in number of students. This is frequently done, as in the case when 'education for all' or 'elementary education for all' is considered desirable.

A closer look at the examples of educational objectives is worthwhile. To facilitate this observation, they will be expressed in mathematical notation. In this form they are known as the *objective function* of the problem in study. In example 1 above, the problem is to maximize the objective function,

$$Z = m_3$$

subject to the characteristics of the interaction among levels, i.e.

(1) $$m_1 \geqslant m_2 \geqslant m_3 \geqslant 0$$

and to the financial constraints, i.e.

(2) $$2 \cdot 2m_1 + 2 \cdot 3m_2 + 5 \cdot 4m_3 \leqslant 85{,}817{,}000$$

In example (2), the objective is to maximize

$$Z = m_2$$

subject to the same conditions (1) and (2), while in example 3 it is to maximize

$$Z = m_3$$

again subject to (1) and (2).

In each of these examples, the number of students in only one level has been chosen as objective. Why not choose some figures representing the education of all the students in the system? This means to use as objective, say, the total number of years of study for the whole group. For instance, maximize

(3) $$Z = 6m_1 + 6m_2 + 6m_3$$

subject to constraints (1) and (2). Here again it is assumed that the high-school student completes six years in high school, and add only these to those that they completed in elementary school and counted with m_1. The same is valid for college students.

It might be assumed that one year of high school is more or less important than one year of, say, elementary school. In this case, instead of the objective in (3), the following could be used:

(4) $$6m_1 + 5m_2 + 4m_3$$

where six years in high school are considered equivalent to five in elementary school and six years in college are considered equivalent to four in elementary school. Here the unit of measurement adopted in one year in elementary school, and the years in high school and college are valued with respect to it. In this valuation, different criteria could be used. In equation (4) the criterion used is the right to an education. As a consequence, a higher value is placed on providing some education for as many persons as possible, while also paying some attention to the need for educated people at higher levels. If

P

persons having advanced education were considered more important, they would receive a higher value. This might be the case when the needs for educated people in an economy having an advanced state of technology are considered.

Once the question of comparing school years is opened, a large number of possibilities appear. One of them has been used frequently: to weight the years spent in school with the lifetime income of persons having different levels of education. For instance, in the United States, with 1957 data, such an objective function would take the following form:

$$(5) \qquad Z = 108m_1 + 61m_2 + 74m_3$$

where

108 is thousands of dollars of income of a person having elementary education;

$108 + 61$ is that of a person with high-school education;

and

$108 + 61 + 74$ that of a person with college education.

In general, the objective function will take the form:

$$(6) \qquad Z = a_1m_1 + a_2m_2 + a_3m_3$$

where the a's can have any of the interpretations above.

In summary, the problem of an optimal educational pyramid has been reduced to the following: Maximize the objective function

$$(7) \qquad Z = a_1m_1 + a_2m_2 + a_3m_3$$

subject to

$$(1) \quad m_1 \geqslant m_2 \geqslant m_3 \geqslant 0$$

and to

$$(2) \quad c_1m_1 + c_2m_2 + c_3m_3 \leqslant R$$

The precise meaning given here to optimum educational pyramid follows from equations (1), (2) and (7). The educational pyramid, i.e. the number of students by level of education, is characterized in equation (1). According to this equation, an educational pyramid exists if the number of students in elementary school is larger than that in high school, and the number in high school is larger than that in college. According to equation (2), we are interested only in those pyramids that can be paid for with the resources available. Finally, from the many educational pyramids that satisfy conditions (1) and (2), we look for the one that maximizes the objective in equation (7). In this equation, the coefficient a_1, a_2 and a_3 indicates the importance that we give to one graduate from one level, as compared with graduates from the other levels.

No attempt will be made to present here the mathematical method of solving this problem. In any case, the solution will take one of the three following alternatives:

(a) m_1 as large as possible, and $m_2 = m_3 = 0$
(b) $m_1 = m_2$ as large as possible and $m_3 = 0$
(c) $m_1 = m_2 = m_3$ as large as possible

In order to choose among these three alternatives, their impact on the objective function Z should be studied. If alternative (a) is considered, from $m_2 = m_3 = 0$ equation (2) reduces to

$$c_1 m_1 = R$$

or, in numerical values, to

$$2 \cdot 2 m_1 = 85,817,000$$

From this it follows that

$$m_1 = \frac{R}{c_1}$$

or

$$m_1 = \frac{85,817,000}{2 \cdot 2} = 39 \text{ million}$$

Again, using $m_2 = m_3 = 0$, in the objective function (7) one obtains that

$$Z = a_1 m_1$$

or, replacing

(8) $$Z = \frac{a_1}{c_1} R$$

and in numerical values

$$Z = 49{:}09 * 85{,}817{,}000$$

If alternative (b) is considered, a similar analysis leads to the condition that

$$m_2 = \frac{R}{c_1 + c_2}$$

or

$$m_2 = \frac{85{,}817{,}000}{4{\cdot}5}$$

From this it follows that

(9)
$$Z = \frac{a_1 + a_2}{c_1 + c_2} R$$

or

$$Z = 37{\cdot}55 * 85{,}817{,}000$$

Finally, for alternative (c)

$$m_3 = \frac{R}{c_1 + c_2 + c_3} = \frac{85{,}817{,}000}{9{\cdot}9}$$

and

(10)
$$Z = \frac{a_1 + a_2 + a_3}{c_1 + c_2 + c_3} R$$
$$= 24{\cdot}54 * 85{,}817{,}000$$

Comparing the values of Z with these three alternatives, it is clear that the first one should be adopted.

Before proceeding to comment on this result, additional comments on formulae (8) to (10) are required. The meaning of $\frac{a_1}{c_1}$ is return per unit of cost in elementary school. A similar interpretation can be given to the coefficients of R in equations (9) and (10).

The result above is surprising, first because it indicates that enrolment in elementary school should be larger than the

---

* This sign will be used here to denote 'times'.

school-age population in the corresponding year; and, secondly, because it is usually assumed that in a technological society such as that of the United States higher levels of education would pay more.

The model can be corrected in three ways to take care of the first limitation. The easiest one is to consider the school-age population as a maximum limit to the number of students in any one level. The second is to consider the fact that the returns to any level of education would decrease as the number of persons having that level of education increases. Finally, the third approach is to assume that the costs of education would increase after an optimum size is reached. No attempt will be made to put these alternative approaches into mathematical form.

The second limitation can be understood in the light of both the comment that equations (8) to (10) mean that resources should be used where their return is greatest and of the corrections of the first limitations. The result obtained indicates that the average return per unit of cost is highest in elementary school. No consideration is given to the decrease of this return with increasing number of persons having only elementary education, and decreasing numbers with higher levels. Also, no attention is paid to the increase in cost in any one level when less accessible persons have to be reached. When these aspects are considered, more reasonable results are obtained.

The objective functions in equations (3) to (7) show that there is complete flexibility in the specification of the goals of the educational process. The objective function can be adapted to any point of view. In this adaptation it might be necessary to change its mathematical form, but again, within limits, this is not a problem. The real problem is in the precise determination of the goals of education that the objective of a model for decision-making should reflect. In other words, the problem is not in the mathematical formulation of the objective function, but in the clear, unambiguous description of the goal desired for education. However, such a description is extremely difficult to give. First, not all the citizens of a country have a clear idea of the objectives education can have. Second, even if they have some idea of these possible objectives, there would be disagreements as to which goal is the most desirable one. In practice, the function of the political process is to specify the goals of the educational, economic, etc., systems.

IV

In the model to be studied in this section, attention is focused on adult education. The question of optimum distribution of the resources available for a literacy campaign, as presented in reference (4), will be considered. This problem is of particular interest in the developing countries.

It is assumed that two methods can be used in a literacy campaign. Method 1 includes only a teaching programme, while method 2 includes, in addition to the teaching programme, the provision of reading materials on topics of interest to the persons who have just learned to read. The alternatives to be considered are the different numbers of students that could be admitted to programmes based on each of the two methods available. For this, let us denote with

A_j $j = 1, 2$ the number of persons admitted to a literacy campaign with method j

In the present case it is assumed that there is no interaction between enrolment in method 1 and in method 2.

The next problem is to relate enrolment to costs and resources available. For this, let

c_1 be the cost per person admitted when method 1 is used, and
c_2 be the cost per person admitted in addition to c_1 when method 2 is used

For a numerical example, the following values will be used:

$$c_1 = \$1,000$$
$$c_1 + c_2 = \$1,250$$

It is useful here to have notation for expenditures. Let
E_j $j = 1, 2$, expenditures in a programme with method j.

The relationship between persons admitted in the literacy campaign and expenditures is given by

(11) $$E_1 = c_1 A_1$$

and

(12) $$E_2 = (c_1 + c_2)A_2$$

The notation R will be retained for the resources available. In the numerical example, it will be assumed that

$$R = \$150,000$$

The constraint resulting from the limitation of resources is that

(13) $$E_1 + E_2 \leqslant R$$

Again in this case several values of A_1 and A_2 satisfy the constraint in (13): For instance, $A_1 = A_2 = 10$, or $A_1 = A_2 = 20$, and so on. The only way to solve the problem is to decide on the objective desired.

A first possibility is to assume that the output of the educational system can be measured in terms of students enrolled. With this assumption, the objective will be to maximize

(14) $$Z = A_1 + A_2$$

subject to the conditions (11) to (13). In this case the solution of the problem is obvious: use method 1, which has the lowest cost. Such a solution points to the weaknesses in the definition of output of the educational system.

An objective that seems more in agreement with the actual purposes of a literacy campaign is the maximization of the number of persons retaining their literacy skills after a certain period of time. When such an objective is considered, the difference in cost of the two methods might be justified. The point is that, with such an objective, not only the quantity but also the quality of the output is considered. To introduce this aspect, let

S_j $j = 1, 2$, the number of participants in a literacy campaign who retain their skill at a prescribed level

As a consequence, the objective of the campaign will be to maximize the number of persons who retain their skill, i.e. to maximize

$$Z = S_1 + S_2$$

The next step is to relate the number of persons admitted to the literacy campaign to each method, i.e. the A_j $j = 1, 2$, to the output of the campaign, the S_j. For this it will be assumed that the proportions of persons admitted to programme j and who retain their skill are known. This means that

$$S_1 = a_1 A_1$$

and

$$S_2 = (a_1 + a_2) A_2$$

where

a_1 is the known proportion of A_1 who retain their skills; and a_2 is the known addition to a_1 when method 2 is used.

It seems reasonable to assume that the proportion retaining their skill when method 2 is used will be larger than the proportion using method 1—that is, $a_2 > 0$. In the numerical example,

$$a_1 = 0.75$$
$$a_1 + a_2 = 0.85$$

The assumption made that the $a_j, j = 1, 2$, are known will be analysed in more detail. They play a very important role in a decision process because they are the link between the student inputs and the output of educated persons. Without this link, it is impossible to make rational decisions in education. Unfortunately, in most cases, even with lengthy and expensive statistical surveys it is impossible to find accurate values for parameters like the a_j. In these circumstances, rough approximations can be used. However, this reduces the reliability of the final results, and sound judgment should be used when interpreting them. One of the main advantages of mathematical models is that they force the users to give rough approximations for parameters such as the a_j, and then to carefully interpret the results obtained with them.

Once the relationship between A_j and S_j is established, the problem of decision-making in a literacy campaign reduces to:
Maximize

(15) $$Z = S_1 + S_2$$

i.e. the number of persons who retain their literacy skills, subject to

(a) the relationship between persons retaining the literacy skills and persons participating in the campaign, i.e.

$$(16) \qquad \begin{aligned} S_1 &= a_1 A_1 \\ S_2 &= (a_1 + a_2)A_2 \end{aligned}$$

(b) the expenditures required in methods 1 and 2, i.e.

$$(17) \qquad \begin{aligned} E_1 &= c_1 A_1 \\ E_2 &= (c_1 + c_2)A_2 \end{aligned}$$

(c) the constraint that the total expenditures must be at most as large as the resources available, i.e.

$$(18) \qquad R \geqslant E_1 + E_2$$

and

(d) that the number of students with methods 1 and 2 should be larger than zero, i.e.

$$(19) \qquad A_i \geqslant 0 \quad i = 1, 2$$

Using equations (15) and (16), it is possible to express the objective function of the problem as

$$(20) \qquad Z = a_1 A_1 + (a_1 + a_2)A_2$$

and, using equations (17) and (18), the resources constraint becomes

$$(21) \qquad R \geqslant c_1 A_1 + (c_1 + c_2)A_2$$

The problem in equations (19), (20) and (21) is mathematically identical to that in equations (1), (2) and (7).

It is interesting to observe that two superficially different problems can be reduced to logical and operationally equivalent forms.

Without presenting the mathematical steps for the solution of the problems in equations (19) to (21), it can be said that it will take one of the two following forms:

(a) Make A_1 as large as possible and $A_2 = 0$ or
(b) Make A_2 as large as possible and $A_1 = 0$.

To choose between these two solutions, their effect on the objective Z must be considered.

When
$$A_2 = 0$$
$$A_1 = \frac{R}{c_1}$$
$$S_1 = \frac{a_1}{c_1} R$$

and finally

$$Z = \frac{a_1}{c_1} R$$

or, with the numerical values assumed for the parameters,

(22)
$$Z = \frac{0 \cdot 75}{1,000} * 150,000 = 112 \cdot 5$$

When
$$A_1 = 0$$
$$A_2 = \frac{R}{c_1 + c_2},$$
$$S_2 = \frac{a_1 + a_2}{c_1 + c_2} R$$

and

$$Z = \frac{a_1 + a_2}{c_1 + c_2} R$$

i.e.

(23)
$$Z = \frac{0 \cdot 85}{1,250} * 150,000 = 102 \cdot 0$$

The comparison of the results in (22) and (23) makes it clear that method 1 should be used.

The solution of the problem in this section is formally identical to that of the problem in Section II. In both cases, returns per unit of cost are the element used to make the choice. Again, in both cases, the core of the problem is to choose one index of the goal of education to be used as the measure of returns.

V

In conclusion, it should be emphasized that the principal value of scientific models lies in the insight they provide into a problem.

Several examples of applications of mathematical models for decision-making are presented in Section II. Obviously, it is impossible to describe all the possibilities here, because they are as varied as the problems faced by planners and administrators. However, the examples presented do demonstrate the great flexibility of mathematical symbols and techniques. As a final word of caution, it should be noted that the numerical results obtained from such procedures should always be carefully scrutinized, because they reflect many artificial limitations imposed in order to permit the use of mathematical techniques.

References

The main application of decision models of educational planning appear in the following books and journals:

1 Adelman, I., 'A Linear Programming Model of Educational Planning: a Case Study of Argentina', in Adelman, I., and Thorbecke, E., *The Theory and Design of Economic Development*, Baltimore: Johns Hopkins Press, 1966.

2 Benard, J., 'Un Modèle d'affectation optimale des ressources entre l'economie et le système educatif', *Metroeconomica*, xix (January–April 1967), Fasc. I, 1–33.

3 Bowles, S., 'The Efficient Allocation of Resources in Education', *Quarterly Journal of Economics*, lxxxi (May 1967), No. 2, 189–219.

4 Correa, H., and Reimer, E., 'Planning Literacy Campaigns and Other Educational Programmes', *Scientia Paedagogica Experimentalis* (to be published).

5 Correa, H., *Quantitative Methods in Educational Planning*, Scranton: International Textbook Co., 1969.

6 —— 'An Optimum Enrolment Policy for Developing Countries', in Kraft, R. H. P. (ed.), *Education and Economic Growth*, Tallahassee: Educational Systems Development Center, Florida State University, 1968.

7 —— 'A Survey of Mathematical Models in Educational Planning', in *Mathematical Models in Educational Planning*, Paris: O.E.C.D., 1967.

8 —— 'More Schools or Better Schools?', *Scientia Paedagogica Experimentalis*, iii (1966), No. 2.

9 —— 'Optima for Size and Number of Schools', *Scientia Paedagogica Experimentalis*.

10 —— 'Optimum Choice Between General and Vocational Education', *Kyklos*, xviii (1965).

11 —— 'Planning the Educational Curriculum', *Kyklos*, xvii (1964).

12 —— 'Quantity *v.* Quality in Teacher Education', *Comparative Education Review*, viii (1964), No. 2.

13 —— *The Economics of Human Resources*, Amsterdam: North Holland Publishing Co., 1963, 109–112.

14 Davis, R., *Planning Human Resource Development: Models and Schemata*, Chicago: Rand McNally, 1966.

15 —— 'On the Development of Educational Planning Models at Harvard, C.S.E.D.: An Algebraic History of Activity in One Small Place', in Kraft, R. H. P. (ed.), *Education and Economic Growth*, Tallahassee: Educational Systems Development Center, Florida State University, 1968.

16 Froomkin, J., 'Cost/effectiveness and Cost/benefit Analyses of Educational Programmes', *Socio-economic Planning Sciences*, ii (April 1969), Nos. 2, 3, 4.

17 Golladay, F. L., 'A Dynamic Linear Programming Model for Educational Planning with Application to Morocco', Evanston, 1968, mimeograph.
18 Hoenack, S.A., 'Efficient Allocation of Subsidies to College Students', *Socio-economic Planning Sciences*, ii (April 1969), Nos. 2, 3, 4.
19 O'Brien, R. J., 'Model for Planning the Location and Size of Urban Schools', *Socio-economic Planning Sciences*, ii (April 1969), Nos. 2, 3, 4.
20 Tu, N. V. P., 'Optimal Educational Investment Program in an Economic Planning Model', *Canadian Journal of Economics*, February 1969, No. 1.
21 Von Weizsacker, C. C., 'Training Policies Under Conditions of Technical Progress: a Theoretical Treatment', in *Mathematical Models in Educational Planning*, Paris: O.E.C.D., 1967.

Index